The
South
Atlantic
Quarterly
Spring 2008
Volume 107
Number 2

T0311285

Visit Duke University Press Journals at www.dukepress.edu/journals.

Subscriptions. Direct all orders to Duke University Press, Journals Customer Service, 905 W. Main St., Suite 18B, Durham, NC 27701. Annual subscription rates: print-plus-electronic institutions, $178; print-only institutions, $159; e-only institutions, $158; individuals, $35; students, $21. For information on subscriptions to the e-Duke Scholarly Collection through HighWire Press, see www.dukeupress.edu/edukecollection. Print subscriptions: add $13 postage and 5% GST for Canada; add $17 postage outside the U.S. and Canada. Back volumes (institutions): $159. Single issues: institutions, $40; individuals, $14. For more information, contact Duke University Press Journals at 888-651-0122 (toll-free in the U.S. and Canada) or 919-688-5134; subscriptions@dukeupress.edu.

Permissions. Photocopies for course or research use that are supplied to the end user at no cost may be made without explicit permission or fee. Photocopies that are provided to the end user for a fee may not be made without payment of permission fees to Duke University Press. Address requests for permission to republish copyrighted material to Permissions Coordinator, permissions@dukeupress.edu.

Advertisements. Direct inquiries about advertising to Journals Advertising Coordinator, journals_advertising@dukeupress.edu.

Distribution. The journal is distributed by Ubiquity Distributors, 607 DeGraw St., Brooklyn, NY 11217; phone: 718-875-5491; fax: 718-875-8047.

The *South Atlantic Quarterly* is indexed in *Academic Abstracts FullTEXT Elite, Academic Abstracts FullTEXT Ultra, Academic Research Library, Academic Search Elite, Academic Search Premier, America: History and Life, Art Index Retrospective, 1929–1984, Arts and Humanities Citation Index, Corporate ResourceNet, Current Abstracts, Current Contents/ Arts and Humanities, Discovery, Expanded Academic ASAP, Historical Abstracts, Humanities Abstracts, Humanities and Social Sciences Index Retrospective, 1907–1984, Humanities Full Text, Humanities Index, Humanities Index Retrospective, 1907–1984, Humanities International Complete, Humanities International Index, International Bibliography of Periodical Literature (IBZ), Literary Reference Center, MasterFILE Elite, MasterFILE Premier, MasterFILE Select, MLA Bibliography, News and Magazines, OmniFile Full Text V, OmniFile Full Text, Mega Edition, Research Library, Social Sciences Index Retrospective, 1907–1984,* and *Student Resource Center College with Expanded Academic ASAP.*

The *South Atlantic Quarterly* is published, at $178 for (print-plus-electronic) institutions and $35 for individuals, by Duke University Press, 905 W. Main St., Suite 18B, Durham, NC 27701. Periodicals postage paid at Durham, NC, and additional mailing offices. Postmaster: Send address changes to *South Atlantic Quarterly,* Box 90660, Duke University Press, Durham, NC 27708-0660.

ISSN 0038-2876

The Rhetoric of Safety

SPECIAL ISSUE EDITOR: LAWRENCE R. SCHEHR

The
South
Atlantic
Quarterly
Spring 2008
Volume 107
Number 2

David F. Bell

Bunker Busting and Bunker Mentalities, or Is It Safe to Be Underground?

Not long after the invasion of Afghanistan in the wake of the 9/11 attacks in the fall of 2001, a debate about the development of a Robust Nuclear Earth Penetrator (RNEP) weapon, commonly referred to as a nuclear bunker buster, erupted in political and military circles in the United States. It called into question a moratorium on the development of low-yield nuclear weapons that had been in effect since 1994 in the United States. In a brief white paper on the issue of nuclear bunker busters, Global Security.org recalls the essential history of this moratorium: "Shortly after Bill Clinton entered the White House, Representatives John Spratt (D-S.C.) and Elizabeth Furse (D-Ore.) introduced an attachment to the FY 1994 defense authorization bill, prohibiting U.S. weapons labs from conducting any research and development on low-yield nuclear weapons. The measure, which was passed and signed into law by President Clinton, defined low-yield nukes as having a yield of five kilotons or less."[1] The Spratt-Furse amendment to the defense authorization bill was ultimately a response to a report—"Potential Uses for Low-Yield Nuclear Weapons in the New World Order"—issued by a group of Los Alamos

South Atlantic Quarterly 107:2, Spring 2008
DOI 10.1215/00382876-2007-063　© 2008 Duke University Press

nuclear weapons scientists in 1991. The report suggested directions for a post–cold war nuclear strategy, one no longer enmeshed in the logic of mutually assured destruction dominating the post–World War II period of confrontation between the two nuclear superpowers.[2] The hubris of the last years of Ronald Reagan's administration, as the world witnessed the collapse of the Soviet Union, is apparent in the title of the report.

Without delving into the detail of this debate of the early 1990s, suffice it to say that the issue of nuclear bunker-busting weapons came back in spades after the fiasco at Tora Bora, during which U.S.-Afghan forces shelled the mountainous redoubt of Taliban and al-Qaeda forces, cornering Osama bin Laden on the heights of Tora Bora and then allowing him to escape. World attention was briefly focused on the elaborate system of underground caves and passages crisscrossing the peaks and ridges of this extremely rough terrain. Occasional photographs of these passages and bunkers appeared in print and television media, attesting to the human-made reinforcement of the natural caves characteristic of the region. Little was said, of course, about the fact that the United States had furnished some of the funds and materials used to rework the natural hideouts in the Tora Bora region during the Soviet occupation of Afghanistan—in support of the guerilla fighters busily sapping the strength of the Soviet occupiers. The very existence of these bunkers and their effectiveness in countering the surveillance and the bombardment of U.S. forces in the fall of 2001 seemed to be an affront to the supposed overwhelming superiority of American military might. How dare these ragged fighters escape our gaze and the explosive power of our bombs and shells by going underground! Never mind the fact that bunker-busting technology would have had little effect on the deep underground passageways dug into Tora Bora. Never mind as well that the fundamental problem of bunker busters is ultimately not the size and force of the explosive warhead but the penetrating potential of the weapon. No matter how powerful the warhead, if a bomb cannot penetrate more than a few tens of meters into the earth, a deeply buried and reinforced bunker can easily survive the effects of the blast. Moreover, a nuclear bunker buster cannot even penetrate deeply enough in propitious terrain (let alone rough and rocky terrain) to avoid substantial nuclear fallout that jeopardizes the health of thousands of civilians in the immediate area surrounding the bunker under attack.

All of these rational elements of a truly careful debate about the feasibility and strategic implications of developing RNEP weapons could not overcome the veritable fascination—dare one say *fetishism*—that seemed to mark the notion of the bunker for the George W. Bush administration after the Tora Bora events. In the 2003 fiscal year budget for defense, an appropriation for research on RNEP weapons reappeared in the authorization bill (under carefully stipulated conditions), and it was not until fall 2005 (in the 2006 fiscal year appropriations debate) that this yearly appropriation was finally removed: "On October 25, 2005, US Senator Pete Domenici indicated that negotiators working toward an agreement on funding for the Department of Energy for FY2006 had agreed to drop funding for continued research on the Robust Nuclear Earth Penetrator (RNEP) project at the request of the National Nuclear Security Administration."[3] The obsession with attacking and destroying bunkers undoubtedly runs much deeper than military adventures on Afghan terrain, which simply brought it to the fore once again. It certainly ran deep enough, as events demonstrated, to provoke military strategists into acts of research and development that threatened the nuclear equilibrium of the period and had the potential to provoke another arms race, creating a new class of weapons with all the attendant difficulties of monitoring and securing new warheads.[4] In this essay, I would like to explore briefly, from a historical and strategic perspective, the fascination with bunkers and their putative safety in the modern era of warfare, beginning with reflections on texts by W. G. Sebald and Paul Virilio and culminating with a series of unsettling meditations about what many have termed the "bunker mentality" of the Bush administration. I will not be able to present anything like a complete historical argument here and will confine myself instead to highlighting potential directions for such a history.

In the first pages of Sebald's last completed novel, *Austerlitz*, the unnamed narrator speaks of travels to Belgium in the 1960s, during which several chance encounters with Jacques Austerlitz occur.[5] Austerlitz is a researcher whose institutional affiliation is not quite clear at this stage of the narrative. His office near the British Museum soon becomes the narrator's favorite haunt, where he listens to mesmerizing descriptions of Austerlitz's research while trying to decide whether to return to Germany to take up his professional life there. The enigmatic Austerlitz has embarked on a vast study of the rise of capitalism reflected in architectural styles in England and various other European countries, with a special interest in railway stations and in the notion of networks, of which railroads are the physical and architectural symbols.[6] He later admits that he was ill-advised to choose this dissertation topic, because the subject has a tendency to expand infinitely, preventing him from completing the project. It is through reflections on architecture that the two characters first strike up their acquaintance in Belgium.

One of the principal subjects of the conversations between Austerlitz and the narrator in these first days of their friendship is military fortifications. Says Austerlitz tellingly, "It is often our mightiest projects that most obviously betray the degree of our insecurity" (14). An architectural and historical presentation of the fortifications built to protect Antwerp ensues, and the discussion of this sustained construction project is the occasion for Austerlitz to remind the narrator of the extraordinary investment of time and creative thought that has historically gone into building fortifications: "No one today . . . has the faintest idea of the boundless amount of theoretical writings on the building of fortifications, of the fantastic nature of the geometric, trigonometric, and logistical calculations they record" (15). The conversation continues as Austerlitz recounts the history of the fortifications built around Antwerp and then proposes an explanation of their uselessness. Despite the geometric perfection of the architecture of such buildings, laboriously theorized over centuries to resist the force of projectiles and the invasion of foreign armies, they cannot ever fulfill their desired purpose. First, they compel their builders to adopt a defensive military posture, immobilizing large forces and resources, thus leaving the enemy free to maneuver just beyond their reach. They call attention, moreover, to the very geographical and topographical points of weakness they were conceived to protect, thereby informing enemies about where to launch a successful assault and considerably simplifying an opponent's strategic planning. This is clearly the opposite of the desired effect. Finally, as fortifications grew in architectural complexity, the length of time it took to build and secure them made them obsolete even before they could actually serve their imagined purpose (15–18).[7] Austerlitz concludes: "Such complexes of fortifications . . . show us how, unlike birds, for instance, who keep building the same nest over thousands of years, we tend to forge ahead with our projects far beyond any reasonable bounds" (18).

All of this is recounted in a tone of obvious fascination with the thought and endeavor required to build such monuments to futility. The conversation with Austerlitz about these matters draws the narrator's attention to a subsequent newspaper article about the fortress of Breendonk just outside of Antwerp, which he decides to visit. But there is a cruel twist: the article informs him that the fortress, surrendered to the Germans in 1940, had been transformed by them into a penal camp. The foreboding appearance of the structure and its painful past create a sense of dread, and the narrator enters the buildings only reluctantly after he arrives by train. As he penetrates into the bunkers of the fortress, the confusion of the architectural proliferation of passages, chicanes, and geometrical complexities within the walls and eventually in the underground passages leads to an experience of surreal and frightening incomprehension:

> From whatever viewpoint I tried to form a picture of the complex I could make out no architectural plan, for its projections and indentations kept shifting, so far exceeding my comprehension that in the end I found myself unable to connect it with anything shaped by human civilization, or even with the silent relics of our prehistory and early history. And the longer I looked at it, the more often it forced me, as I felt, to lower my eyes, the less comprehensible it seemed to become. (20–21)

The sense of doom only increases as the narrator visits additional narrow underground passages and identifies places where the torture of Nazi prisoners took place. As his meditation continues, the fortification and its attendant underground bunkers are transformed from places of protection and defense into places of death, as if they had never been anything else: "The fort was a monolithic, monstrous incarnation of ugliness and blind violence" (21).

The sadistic cruelty practiced in the depths of the fortified bunkers at Breendonk, remembered by the narrator more as a theater of torture than for any safety it ever afforded to soldiers or civilians, had already found implicit expression in Sebald's extraordinarily graphic, gruesome, and moving "Air War and Literature," the published form of the lectures he delivered in Zurich in 1997. In this essay, Sebald describes the devastation wrought upon German cities by the Allied fire bombing that began in 1942 and his fellow Germans' refusal even to remember these events, much less to think about what they meant.[8] The intensity of the bombing and the technical means adopted to carry it out transformed basements, bunkers, bomb shelters, and cellars—subterranean sanctuaries of all types—into tombs. The safety sought underground by civilians attempting to escape from the destructive fires provoked by the indiscriminant bombing was completely illusory, and their bunkers, makeshift or otherwise, ultimately became killing fields. The stench of the aftermath attested to the presence of the thousands, the tens of thousands, of corpses buried alive beneath the rubble of the Allied onslaught. One could not escape by retreating below ground when the whole point of the bombing tactics was precisely to bring about the utter destruction of the edifices attacked—that is, to cause buildings, no matter what their architectural structure, to collapse upon themselves, completely leveled and returned to the flat barrenness of the surrounding plains, thereby rendering them literally and completely uninhabitable, whether above or below ground.[9]

"Air War and Literature" vividly re-creates events that Germans themselves refused to remember after the war, and there is no small irony in the fact that Sebald, too young to have experienced firsthand the events of which he speaks, is forced to take up the task of recollection. His descriptions in "Air War and Literature" call to mind certain brief autobiographical remarks made by another European thinker, who belongs to the generation immediately preceding Sebald's, the French urbanist, architect, and philosopher Paul Virilio, old enough to have experienced the Allied bombing of Nantes firsthand. As Virilio says in the opening pages of *L'Insécurité du territoire*: "The Second World War was my mother, my father. The extreme nature of the situations I lived through taught me, not simply about complacent violence . . . but about an unalterable vision of the world. The second war is an indispensable source of meaning for the second peace, which is ours."[10] Virilio's experience of the Allied bombings revealed to him the newest frontier of war's vectors, the unlimited expanse of the sky, from which weapons rained down to transform—in a matter of minutes—the cityscapes on which they were dropped. One thing is certain: from the start of the bombings, Virilio rejected the temptation to hide in basements to avoid the destruction: "What taught me my lessons was not the horror of those buried alive in basements, asphyxiated by gas lines that had broken, drowned by leaking water mains, but the sudden transparence, the visible change of urban space, the motility of inanimate objects, of the supposedly immobile buildings (simply put, when I heard the air raid sirens, I refused to go down into shelters, preferring garden courtyards, preferring the risk of shrapnel impacts to the imprisonment of ruins)" (16). To go below ground in order to escape the explosions (and Sebald makes this clear as well) was to discover that the bunker was not a safe haven and that the domestic and public architecture of walls and enclosed spaces was no longer the horizon that spectators and participants in the war were forced to heed. The new horizon was the verticality of the sky, and building architecture would have to be adapted to this new given in order to provide any safety at all.

Virilio's rejection of the illusory protection of the basement bunkers that were used for shelter in Nantes and his fascination with radically refashioned cityscapes after the bombings he witnessed brought him back, more than thirty years later, to reflections on the notion of the bunker, the visible remains of Hitler's attempt to build Fortress Europe. In Bunker Archeology, an exhibit for which he was the curator at the Musée des Arts Décoratifs in Paris at the end of 1975 and the beginning of 1976, Virilio displayed photographs of German bunkers that he had taken between 1958 and 1965.[11] In his hikes along the Atlantic coastline of France, the rediscovery of which was one of the fundamental pleasures afforded by the end of the hostilities of World War II, Virilio realized that one could walk great distances along that coastline without ever losing sight of a German bunker of some shape or form. The immensity of the architectural project of securing the coastline against invasion prompts the same sort of reaction that Sebald's Austerlitz had described: "The immensity of this project is what defies common sense; total war was revealed here in its mythic dimension" (12). Virilio will quickly designate Hitler's fortress composed of bunkers along the coastline as the last gasp in the story of defensive frontiers throughout history: "From the Roman *limes* to the Great Wall of China; the bunkers, as ultimate military surface architecture, had shipwrecked at lands' limits, at the precise moment of the sky's arrival in war; they marked off the horizontal littoral, the continental limit. History had changed course one final time before jumping off into the immensity of aerial space" (12).

Virilio takes two perspectives on the evidence provided by the Atlantic bunkers in the repertoire of photographs he assembles. The first is to see these constructions as evidence of the inevitable defeat of the Nazi armies. As he recalls to his readers, the German military tactics of World War II, as devised by Hitler and his generals, consisted of lightning offensive advances, known otherwise as the blitzkrieg, occupying territory, and moving ever forward. The arrival at the shores of the Atlantic Ocean meant the encounter with the limits of this strategy, since the watery realm left no possibility for occupation or colonization and, moreover, condemned an army built on the principle of movement to the static duty of defense: "With Fortress Europe, failure was inevitable. . . . Lightning war, which allowed the Führer to rapidly acquire all the western European coasts, would later oblige him to adopt a defensive strategy. The continental Finistère was the defeat of the Nazi offensive, and the Allies did not have to fire cannons or land a single soldier; implicitly, the defeat was in the inner logic of the Nazi state" (29). Despite the message suggested by certain popular war movies in the past few decades, which have romanticized U-boat maneuvering in the Atlantic, Hitler ultimately declined to develop the forces necessary to master either the water or the air.[12] Planted solidly on the last remnants of land before the Atlantic, the German bunkers mimicked fortresses and yet could not really function as such. They looked out over the vast expanse of a sea that could not be invaded and that held all the dangers of unlimited and uncontrollable military movements against the Reich. They were "the fantasies of a man fearing to advance over the sea, which gave birth to the last West Wall, the Atlantic Wall, looking out over the void, over this moving and pernicious expanse, alive with menacing presences; faced with the sea, Hitler rediscovered ancient terrors: water, a place of madness, of anarchy, of monsters, and of women, too" (30; translation slightly modified). The bunkers were the cenotaphs of the Reich's ambitions, and their very architecture was a curious mixture of rounded and sculpted lines, designed to resist artillery and bombs in their seamless concrete construction, and of the enclosed memorial space of a burial monument.

The second perspective adopted by Virilio has more to do with an analysis of the modernization of warfare that inevitably produced bunkers. Such constructions were the foreseeable product of a new military vector, aerial space, a space in which the vehicle, the airplane, had become both vehicle and projectile—and whose unimpeded flight over battlefields and enemy concentrations provided an unobstructed view of the sites that were its targets. The walls of ancient fortresses had towered over the surrounding topography, giving the defenders unhindered sightlines to observe the adjacent countryside. With the advent of military aviation, defenders needed to find shelter from the sightlines provided by mastering the empty expanse of the sky. They did so in part by building bunkers, which were characterized by the reduced asperities of their walls (rounded edges whose goal was to disperse the energy of explosions), moving these structures underground whenever possible or, at the very least, designing them to blend in with surrounding topographies in order to camouflage their locations. Warfare was quickly transformed into an escalating race organized around the invention and application of mechanisms of sight and thus of detection of the enemy hidden in bunkers. Virilio argues that the World War II bunker took on its particular characteristics precisely as a result of these developments: "It was no longer in distance but rather in burial that the man of war found the parry to the onslaught of his adversary; retreat was now into the very thickness of the planet and no longer along its surface" (38). Ordinary constructions have roofs and walls that protect against the elements, but bunkers have to protect against elements that go beyond the natural, bombs built to destroy "ordinary" architecture:

> Linked to the ground, to the surrounding earth, the bunker, for camouflage, tends to coalesce with the geological forms whose geometry results from the forces and exterior conditions that for centuries have modeled them. The bunker's form anticipates this erosion by suppressing all superfluous forms; the bunker is prematurely worn and smoothed to avoid all impact. It nestles in the uninterrupted expanse of the landscape and disappears from our perception, used as we are to bearings and markers.
>
> This unusual aspect of bunker forms—absolutely different from the forms of ordinary construction, scandalous on a snapshot—paradoxically is able to go unnoticed in a natural environment. (44)

Virilio's insistence on the unnatural naturalness of the bunker, its capacity to mimic forms created by erosion, its refusal to function as a landmark, encapsulates the necessities of defensive strategies in an era of air warfare and ultimately of stealth bombing. If the airplane/projectile can see all, and if it can descend on top of its objective to destroy it from just about any direction, then the target must transform itself into a structure that both resists the force of explosions and makes it difficult for the pilot to pick out a human-made structure from the natural background in which it nestles.

The strategic trends toward concealment and burial represented by bunker construction during World War II were reinforced by the dawn of the nuclear era. If the destruction of Dresden and other German cities was striking to the eye of the observer contemplating the flattened rubble of these sites, one can only imagine how much more arresting the iconic photographs of the utterly destroyed landscapes of Hiroshima and Nagasaki must have seemed at the time.[13] The bunker, as it was conceived and built in all of its varieties by the German Reich along the Atlantic wall, would no longer suffice, but its general architectural principles still retained a certain familiarity, even for the modern observer, despite the fact that it was suddenly outmoded because of the destructive force of nuclear bombs: "The blockhouse is still familiar, it coexists, it comes from the era that put an end to the strategic notion of 'forward' and 'rear' (vanguard and rearguard) and began the new one of 'above' and 'below,' in which burial would be accomplished definitively, and the earth nothing more than an immense glacis exposed to nuclear fire" (46). As the U.S. government reflected on the consequences of the impending nuclear arming of the Soviet Union, the immediate impulse was to prepare a protected underground space where war operations centered in the Pentagon could be moved in case of a nuclear attack. As one historian of the conception and construction of cold war command and control bunkers puts it, "By 1948 however, as a consequence of President Truman's declaration that the USSR was 'a clear and present threat to the USA,' worries grew regarding the vulnerability of the Pentagon to aerial attack from Russian bombers due to its enormous size and highly conspicuous signature from the air."[14] The largest building in the world at the time of its construction in 1941–42, the Pentagon had become a strategic liability within a decade of its completion. Aerial war with the threat of nuclear weapons had changed the architectural necessities of bunker construction—nothing above ground could be counted on to survive a nuclear blast.

Nick McCamley chronicles the construction of the bunker at Raven Rock, in eastern Pennsylvania, conceived as a command and control facility manned by a limited number of military personnel and completed in 1953. It was soon followed by the building of Mount Weather in northern Virginia, which was envisaged as a veritable alternate seat of government in the event of a nuclear war and was completed in 1958. These two underground facilities were among the first in the United States to take into account what might be needed to protect basic governmental infrastructure from the devastation of a nuclear conflagration. But the fear that provoked the building of these command bunkers and gave rise to a desire to place the U.S. government and war machine in the safety of a deep burial site was not limited to government alone. Scarcely more than a decade after the USSR demonstrated that it possessed the nuclear bomb, the Berlin crisis in 1961 significantly increased the chances of a nuclear confrontation between the United States and the USSR. It was the occasion for a speech by John F. Kennedy, pronounced on July 25, 1961, in which he evoked in direct and explicit terms the possibility of nuclear war and the potential necessity for the American population to take cover in fallout shelters. It had become important, he suggested, for civil defense authorities to "identify and mark space in existing structures—public and private—that could be used for fall-out shelters in case of attack."[15] Kennedy had finally put into words what everyone had implicitly understood since the early 1950s: "The American home had been put on the front lines of the Cold War."[16] If Europeans in France, Belgium, Holland, and Germany had in some sense absorbed the meaning of "bunker culture" as a result of having been targets of intense bombing campaigns during World War II, now it was the Americans' turn to experience this threat—one that was not actualized in the 1960s, however, as it had been for Europeans in the 1940s.[17]

In any case, Kennedy's speech touched off an intense debate within both government and the wider civilian community in the United States about whether to build fallout shelters and whether this was the responsibility of the federal government or of individual citizens. In *One Nation Underground*, Kenneth Rose describes the avatars of this national discussion, rendered explicit by Kennedy's rash brinksmanship (the Cuban missile crisis would soon follow the Berlin crisis). Strategists of all stripes eventually came to the same understanding: safety underground during a nuclear attack was an elusive concept at best. How deep to dig? How long would people need to remain underground? And what to do with less-prepared fellow citizens, who might fight to get into the bunker space of their neighbors? As Rose concludes, "The evidence indicates that very few Americans took any steps toward preparing their homes against nuclear attack. . . . After 1963, the public's involvement with the issues of fallout shelters and nuclear arms rapidly fell off."[18] Faced with the questionable efficacy of such shelters and the costs of building them, the Kennedy administration quickly backed off its calls for an ambitious national program of shelter building. Characteristically, Europeans were never swept up in the nuclear shelter hysteria of 1961–63. Paul Virilio explains why: "During this period, the myth of the anti-atomic-bomb shelter spreading like wildfire in the United States had no hold in Europe, where the memory of strategic bombing in 1943–44 removed all credence to a policy of 'passive defense.' Everyone realized from experience that populations would not have enough time to get to the shelters in case of a nuclear attack" (200). Those who had experienced the effects of intense bombing campaigns knew full well that not only was it difficult to survive such an experience in an underground shelter of any sort, but that life after the conflagration would be tenuous at best, as it had been for tens of thousands of Europeans for nearly a decade after the cessation of hostilities in Europe at the end of World War II.[19]

The era of aerial warfare and soon afterward of space warfare—when countries began to place satellites in geospatial orbits, the better to detect enemies' movements—meant quite simply that conventional warfare was no longer strategically viable. An adversary who moved across the surface of the earth was henceforth exposed to immediate attack. "The strategy of deception (or, to put it differently, the strategy of making use of decoy devices and disinformation) has won out over classical attack and defense strategies, to the point that 'offensive' and 'defensive' stages in strategy have almost totally coalesced" (201), as Virilio puts it so aptly. The only way an enemy can maneuver without detection is to use subterfuge and whatever technologies are available to mask his or her whereabouts and thus to trick the observer, who is glued to the video screen as instantaneous satellite or drone images of the surveillance target appear in ghostlike form. Virilio closes his catalog text on the Bunker Archeology exhibit with a final striking remark: "The *war of real time* has clearly supplanted the war in real space of geographical territories that long ago conditioned the history of nations and people" (206).

The frustration of Tora Bora, which I described at the beginning of this analysis, must be seen in light of a broader perspective on the role the bunker has played in the imagination of both military and civilian populations in the modern era. The obsession with the bunker/bomb shelter, which was so much a part of European culture during World War II and of American culture during an intense period of the cold war, surfaced characteristically in the sequence of events at Tora Bora and in the subsequent plan to develop a nuclear weapon that would, once and for all, do away with enemies who would dare hide out of sight of the American juggernaut. In an era of warfare where surveillance reveals any targets that stand out on the earth's surface (and thus any enemy forces that dare to move), the victor is theoretically the one whose technologies of vision are the most precise and whose satellite coverage blankets the globe in real time. But the well-constructed and well-concealed bunker calls into question that vision: it can be deep enough and hardened enough to defy surveillance and attack. Small wonder that in the course of the Afghanistan and Iraq invasions, orchestrated more than a decade after the Gulf War had demonstrated the parameters of a new type of warfare based on speed and on real-time surveillance, the bunker reappeared as a challenge to the potentially overwhelming advantage of the American war machine.[20] The dream of a nuclear bunker buster to end all bunker busters is an avatar of the fantasy of total military dominance. In answer to the question posed in my title, then, one would have to say that faced with an adversary possessing satellite surveillance technology of the sort deployed by the United States, it is safer to be underground (preferably very deeply) than to be on the surface of the earth. And this fact is at the origin of all contemporary strategies employing the concept of "sleeper cells," that is, potential enemies hiding attack preparations by blending into civilian populations until the right moment. Sleeper cells are nothing but the manifestation in a sociological mode of the architectural concepts behind the notion of the bunker.

But if bunker busters are the dream of an American military that wishes to suppress all opposition to its force, better bunkers at home are always the flip side of the coin. We develop a technology to destroy their bunkers, but ours have to be impervious to attack. The back-and-forth between these two perspectives can well be seen to have given rise to a "bunker mentality," a metaphor that emerged as journalists encountered the secretive nature of the Bush regime in the wake of 9/11. The isolation of the administration from the normal reality check of confrontation with ideological adversaries in the field of public discourse has only reinforced this impression. Indeed, it is all but certain that when Vice President Dick Cheney disappeared from public view for long stretches of time after the 9/11 attacks, he was staying at Raven Rock or Mount Weather. The repeated refusal of the Bush administration to reveal how policies are debated and created within its inner circles inevitably leads to the conclusion that the Bush presidency exists in a "bubble." But that bubble is in no way transparent (and thus the metaphor of the bubble is misleading): it more likely takes the form of the hardened underground control room. Well before the invasion of Afghanistan and the failed encircling of Tora Bora, the administration had activated a strategy of shadow governance directly linked to government bunkers. In the March 1, 2002, *Washington Post*, Barton Gellman and Susan Schmidt broke the story of contingency plans, put into effect after the 9/11 attacks, to move top-level government bureaucrats to bunkers in order to manage the federal government in the event of a nuclear or biological attack on Washington: "President Bush has dispatched a shadow government of about 100 senior civilian managers to live and work secretly outside Washington, activating for the first time long-standing plans to ensure survival of federal rule after catastrophic attack on the nation's capital."[21] This decision was based on a presidential directive—never before actually applied—concerning contingency plans in the event of a nuclear attack and dating back to Harry Truman's presidency, when the threat of nuclear war had first reared its ugly head. The application of the directive in the aftermath of 9/11 began a rotation of high-ranking federal managers in and out of government bunkers: "Officials who are activated for what some of them call 'bunker duty' live and work underground 24 hours a day, away from their families. As it settles in for the long haul, the shadow government has sent home most of the first wave of deployed personnel, replacing them most commonly at 90-day intervals."[22]

A veritable obsession with governmental continuity was at the heart of the application of this directive—yet another avatar of 9/11. Moreover, whereas the first version of the contingency plans included only about a hundred important federal managers, they quickly evolved into a broad series of measures designed to insure that an increasingly large number of federal agencies would remain intact and operable in the aftermath of a disastrous attack. In June 2006, William Arkin of the *Washington Post* wrote about a massive federal drill designed to test the plans that had been mandated and created:

> On Monday, June 19 [2006], about 4,000 government workers representing more than 50 federal agencies from the State Department to the Commodity Futures Trading Commission will say goodbye to their families and set off for dozens of classified emergency facilities stretching from the Maryland and Virginia suburbs to the foothills of the Alleghenies. They will take to the bunkers in an "evacuation" that my sources describe as the largest "continuity of government" exercise ever conducted, a drill intended to prepare the U.S. government for an event even more catastrophic than the Sept. 11, 2001, attacks.[23]

The correlation between "continuity of government" and the survival mentality characteristic of the first wave of fear of nuclear attack in the 1950s is not difficult to imagine. Nor is it farfetched to see in these contingency plans the worst of the excesses of the bomb shelter movement of the Kennedy presidency. As Arkin puts it, the June 2006 exercise was "a focus of enormous and often absurd time, money and effort that has come to echo the worst follies of the Cold War."[24] What had intervened between the first invoking of the contingency plans for governmental continuity after 9/11 and the practice exercise carried out in June 2006 was an inclusion of ever more government services in the plans—to the point that the number of officials designated for protection promised to clog the exit routes from the capital and to render any evacuation impossible: "The main defect—a bunker mentality that considers too many people and too many jobs 'essential'—will remain unchallenged."[25]

There is more at stake here than the logistical impracticality of accomplishing the transfer of large segments of the government to bunkers in order to avoid the disorder occasioned by a nuclear or biological attack.[26] Historian Thomas A. Spencer casts the problem in broader and more troubling terms:

> I would argue that one should stop and consider this "shadow government" proposal in a more philosophical way. What does it mean to serve in a public office? Are those who serve the public allowed to do so in private? Shouldn't public officials do their duties in public? Isn't it wrong for the Vice President to spend half his time out of the public's view in a bunker? By doing this, isn't he working as a federal employee rather than a public official? Part of the role of those who serve the public is to be visible to the public, accessible to the public and, at the very least, to BE public.[27]

Exactly what is the status and—the crucial related question—the *accountability* of a large group of government officials hidden away in bunkers? It is striking, for example, that the mainstream media articles devoted to reporting about the activation of the contingency plan for establishing a shadow government studiously avoided naming the bunkers or providing any information about their whereabouts. Homeland security trumps representative democracy: the very basis of democracy ought to be that officials designated by elections to carry out the business of the country— and those to whom elected officials delegate managerial tasks—actually accomplish their work within view of the citizens who elected them in the first place. The figurative expression "bunker mentality," what Spencer calls a "delicious metaphor,"[28] applied with delight and rhetorical flourish by so many journalists since the Bush administration began reacting to the 9/11 attacks, turns out not to be so figurative after all. The obsession with governmental continuity, taken to the extreme in an era of defensive warfare as Virilio has described it, means that the hidden space of the bunker becomes the actual space of power, and the metaphor, now taken literally, becomes reality.

Notes

1   GlobalSecurity.org, "Weapons of Mass Destruction (WMD): Robust Nuclear Earth Penetrator," www.globalsecurity.org/wmd/systems/rnep.htm (accessed November 14, 2006).

2   Ibid. For a discussion of the implications of this report and the strategies it advocates,

see Greg Mello, "The Birth of a New Bomb: Shades of Dr. Strangelove" *Washington Post,* June 1, 1997, consulted online at Los Alamos Study Group, www.lasg.org/archive/1997/birth-bomb.htm (accessed November 10, 2006).

3   GlobalSecurity.org, "Weapons of Mass Destruction."

4   I shall not address in detail here the strategic gamesmanship with nuclear moratoriums on testing and weapon building that the RNEP weapon represented. It may be the case, in fact, that the goal of the RNEP—namely, to destroy deeply entrenched bunkers—was secondary to the goal of loosening the boundaries of the nuclear equilibrium.

5   W. G. Sebald, *Austerlitz*, trans. Anthea Bell (New York: Modern Library, 2001). Hereafter cited parenthetically by page number. *Campo Santo*, an incomplete novel, was published posthumously in 2003. Sebald, *Campo Santo*, trans. Anthea Bell (New York: Random House, 2005).

6   The fascination with the railroad later finds its logic in Austerlitz's personal story, in which the reader discovers that as a very young child Austerlitz was put on a train by his parents in order to be carried away from Czechoslovakia and therefore away from almost inevitable death at the hands of the Nazis, as the ethnic cleansing of Czechoslovakia gained momentum.

7   The French Maginot Line comes inevitably to mind here.

8   W. G. Sebald, "Air War and Literature," in *On the Natural History of Destruction*, trans. Anthea Bell (New York: Random House, 2003), 1–104.

9   The fate of the World Trade Center had already begun to be prepared by the tactics used in the Allied bombing campaign.

10 Paul Virilio, *L'Insécurité du territoire* (Paris: Galilée, 1993), 15. Unless otherwise indicated, all translations are my own.

11 Paul Virilio, *Bunker Archeology*, trans. George Collins (Princeton, NJ: Princeton Architectural Press, 1994). Hereafter cited parenthetically by page number. This is a translation of the catalog/book produced by Virilio for the exhibit of the same name and published originally as *Bunker Archéologie* (Paris: Centre Georges Pompidou, 1975).

12 Wolfgang Petersen's film *Das Boot* (1985) is, in fact, the perfect antidote for such romanticizing. The second half of the film is centered on an extended sequence during which the German submarine, badly damaged by an encounter with Allied warships at Gibraltar, sits precariously on the bottom of the ocean in a grotesque rendition of the bunker/cenotaph. The crew members miraculously repair the vessel and limp back to base. The muted triumph of their return, however, is immediately and tragically interrupted by a random Allied aerial bombing and strafing attack that kills a number of them, including their profoundly humanitarian captain, and summarily sinks the submarine at its mooring. The aerial vector of the modern warplane definitively trumps even the vaunted submarine.

13 I have in mind, for example, the photographs of bombed-out Hiroshima, containing the grotesque skeleton of Genbaku Dome standing out against the utter destruction of the leveled city surrounding it. In fact, the shock of contemplating such photographs has diminished little over the past few decades. See, for example, the following: www.mctv.ne.jp/~bigapple/dome.gif (accessed January 10, 2007), or for an aerial photograph of the devastation, www.moonofalabama.org/images/Hiroshima-big.jpg (accessed January 10, 2007).

14 Nick McCamley, *Cold War Secret Nuclear Bunkers: The Passive Defence of the Western World*

during the Cold War (Barnsley, UK: Leo Cooper, 2002), 15. The 9/11 hijackers of American Airlines flight 77 had no trouble, of course, recognizing the Pentagon's "conspicuous signature" when they arrived in the airspace over Washington, D.C.

15 Quoted in Kenneth D. Rose, *One Nation Underground: The Fallout Shelter in American Culture* (New York: New York University Press, 2001), 2.

16 Ibid., 4.

17 The ultimate actualization of the threat of an air attack when the 9/11 events occurred provoked a veritable public psychosis, which Americans have yet to overcome. Understanding European sympathy for the United States immediately after the 9/11 attacks surely requires remembering that the form the attacks took was closely related to the experience of being bombed that characterized World War II in Europe.

18 Rose, *One Nation Underground*, 10–11. There are many similarities between the short-lived public interest in personal protection in the event of a nuclear war and the public interest in personal protection against biological terrorism in the wake of the anthrax scare of September 2001. All sorts of advice was dispensed about making one's home safe from such an attack, but the public's interest in actually carrying out the necessary measures (whose effectiveness was suspect from the beginning anyway) quickly waned.

19 See Tony Judt's extremely sobering historical description of that decade in *Postwar: A History of Europe since 1945* (New York: Penguin Books, 2005).

20 The elaborate shell game played by Saddam Hussein as he dodged American forces and bombings in the first weeks of the U.S. invasion (only to be found later in a provincial bunker) is another case in point. See Michael R. Gordon and Bernard E. Trainor, "Iraqi Leader, in Frantic Flight, Eluded U.S. Strikes," *New York Times*, March 12, 2006. The second attempt to kill Hussein, on April 7, 2003, using two 2,000-pound conventional bunker-busting bombs, demonstrated that bunker-busting and precision weaponry, supposedly limiting civilian collateral casualties, were largely incompatible. Eighteen Iraqi civilians paid with their lives for being in the neighborhood of the tremendous percussion wave generated by these two huge bombs.

21 Barton Gellman and Susan Schmidt, "Shadow Government Is at Work in Secret," *Washington Post*, March 1, 2002.

22 Ibid.

23 William A. Arkin, "Back to the Bunker," *Washington Post*, June 4, 2006.

24 Ibid.

25 Ibid.

26 Let us not forget that the bumbling federal "inexperts" of Hurricane Katrina fame are the very ones outlining contingency plans for the evacuation of designated federal officials from Washington. Not particularly promising for the officials involved, one might suggest . . .

27 Thomas M. Spencer, "Bush in the Bunker," History News Network, George Mason University, March 11, 2002, http://hnn.us/articles/614.html (accessed January 15, 2006).

28 Ibid.

Elspeth Probyn

Troubling Safe Choices:
Girls, Friendship, Constraint, and Freedom

It was never an issue except among feminists who felt
we were telling women to stay at home. We're saying
that's okay. But that's not all we're saying. We're saying
they have a choice. It's a tough world out there.
—Leslie Savan, *Village Voice*, March 7, 1989

Mr Howard said women today had greater awareness
of the disadvantages of leaving childbearing too late
and are more confident about their choices.
—Australian Associated Press, December 30, 2006

Does anything ever change? In the late 1980s,
I recall a *Good Housekeeping* campaign perfectly
in tune with the time. Depicting happy white
middle-class women with their children in front
of beautiful homes, the magazine reassured
women that the home was a safe choice. With
Ronald Reagan and George H. W. Bush in the
White House, the push was to get women back
in the home. Two decades on, Australian Prime
Minister John Howard expressed confidence
that women were making the right choice by
returning to the home to have babies. This was
accentuated by Treasurer Peter Costello, who
implemented tax incentives to exhort women to
choose to have more children to boost the falling
birth rate in Australia. His catchy phrase echoes

South Atlantic Quarterly 107:2, Spring 2008
DOI 10.1215/00382876-2007-064 © 2008 Duke University Press

the image of a game show in which one has to choose door number one, two, or three. In Costello's terms, it's "One for Mum, one for Dad, and one for the nation."[1]

In this essay I want to chart some of the ways in which choice has been articulated around women. In the West, choice is the benign bedrock of our society. Be that in regard to the consumer imperative of choice to the all-pervasive political philosophy of self-fashioning, it is not possible not to choose (pace Jean-Paul Sartre). But while choice is everywhere, it becomes visible and malignant as a problem only when attached to women and increasingly, it seems, to young women. I want to begin by remarking on the recurring image of the home, which as the advertisers for *Good House-keeping* tell us is the safe haven against a tough world.[2] Whether the world has become tougher in the intervening years since that remark was made is questionable. What is certain is that more and more attention is focused on women and girls who are labeled "at risk." A Google search, for instance, turns up some twenty million sites on the topic. Beyond the tragedy of the risks women face in situations of war and conflict, most of the risks they face are posed as the consequences of their choices. Against this panoply of risk, it's no wonder that the home can be easily portrayed as safe. But can something defined as "safe" really constitute a choice? Choosing is tough, and it is inherently risky.

At one level the representation of the home as safe haven can be quickly disrupted by drawing attention to the obvious risks that women face in the home. Women are overwhelmingly more at risk of violence in their homes than they are on the streets. While Howard may think that it is advantageous for women to have children early, the question is for whom? The disadvantages to women, and perhaps even to their children, are many. It is difficult to stay calm in the face of such statements and the blithe indifference that so many politicians demonstrate toward women's well-being and development. Why should women accept that their natural lot is to be several steps behind men in terms of career choice and fulfillment? Why should women put up with government indifference and failure to provide material support in concrete terms such as maternity benefits and child care provisions that might mean that they could actually make a realistic and logical choice to have children? What about the women rendered invisible as such by their lack of childbearing capacities or desires? Excluded from the national reproductive discourse, what safe choices do they have?

These concerns may be dismissed as the unfashionable rantings of feminists. However, if choice was once a central tenet within feminism, it seems that it now haunts feminism for its supposed failure. The undertow of much public commentary is that feminism is to blame for the increased range of choices available. Equally the argument seems to be that feminism has somehow allowed the rise of sexualized culture, which encourages young women to make bad and unsafe choices. If this were not confusing enough, in the last several years there has been the clamor of betrayal voiced by mainly middle-class professional women that feminism duped them into thinking they had a choice. As one Australian feminist characterizes the situation, "She had failed to become a satisfied human being because of the manner in which feminism had created a dichotomy between the downtrodden role of the housewife and the exciting self-actualisation that awaited the successful career woman."[3] In an amazing feat of non-sense, women who by their own accounts may have felt empowered to rise in the corporate world are now bitter in their resentment and blame feminism for having missed out on babies, marriage, and a good man. The younger siblings of this generation, widely known as Gen Y, are then vilified for being incapable of making the right choices—such as getting married and settling into a mortgage. The accepted line is that they would rather save the world than provide for their own "safe" futures.

At the younger end of all this, girls constitute the locus of moral panic about having too much choice. It is especially in the realm of consumer culture that girls are seen to be at risk. Binge drinking, oral sex, midriff tops, cosmetic surgery, pro-anorexia sites, online porn—newspaper headlines regularly scream about how girls are being forced into bad choices. The tone oscillates between trying to find someone or something to blame, thus rendering girls as the duped and unwilling half-subjects of their imposed choices. Alternatively, it focuses on girls as the demonic product of popular culture—the mean girls, the princess bitches, and the mindless Britney wannabes. Girls are blamed for following fashion and equally are construed as helpless in the face of consumer choice.[4]

In the early and mid-1990s, I attempted to analyze discourses of choice, or what I called—following Savan—choiceosie.[5] It was motivated by the emerging television and popular representations of choice, particularly regarding sexuality and sexual choice. I drew on the work of Michèle Le Dœuff and her use of the trope of the chiasmas.[6] Analyzing what was vaunted as the first "lesbian kiss" on television (between C. J. and Abby on *L.A. Law*), I argued that the movement caused by that image disturbs the logic whereby one is already straight or gay. As choice builds on choice, the question of sexual choice is only a wink away.[7]

While a wider presentation of sexuality in popular culture has indeed become much more prevalent, choice seems to be as thorny as ever. The issue I failed to raise is that choice is always sexualized when it comes to women. My analysis left untouched the very ground upon which choice is articulated, which is to say the status of women as subjects—capable of agency without which no choice is possible. What defines the conditions of possibility in which women come to make sense of their subjecthood and thus the ground from and in which to make choices?

With these questions in mind, I now return to the question of choice with a more critical frame of analysis. The theoretical questions concern the conflicting cultural modes that on the one hand privilege genealogical subjects and on the other autological or self-fashioning discourses. There has been a gradual historical shift in the West from a genealogical base in which subjects were formed within the dictates of kin and tradition to the emergent formation of a system promulgating self-fashioning subjects. The latter was of course aided by the Enlightenment and liberalism; however, deep traces adhere to genealogy as a sense-making mechanism in governance and especially in everyday life. In broad terms, genealogical forms operate on various modalities of constraint, operated by community. The promise of liberalism was and is that of freedom, of subjects released unto their own making. Choice, I want to argue, operates within this frame to demarcate cultures of constraint versus those of freedom.

This, then, rearticulates safety and risk in interesting ways. In a genealogical culture, where the constraints come from tradition, heritage, kinship, and relatedness, there is very little choice, understood as an individual and free act. But equally if one remains, as Louis Althusser would say,[8] comfortably interpellated within these structures, one is safe.[9] If we recall his discussion of religion, whereby the subject is interpellated by the Subject (God, the Law, the Name of the Father), the subject's submission is mutually recognized, and her existence is guaranteed. In the language of Christianity, "Ainsi soit-il" ("So be it"). Conversely, within cultures of self-fashioning, the onus is on the individual to make the right choices. Here choice is inherently risky, and scary. Choice is painful. I know that whenever I have had to make an important choice, my body feels ripped apart. Choice by definition refuses the comfort of stasis and always occurs in change.

There are several different factors and technologies, including those of the self, at work in the formation of subjects within a genealogical complex. And there are a number of different theoretical languages and descriptors that all flag the constraints that limit subjects just as they hold them in relative safety—from their selves as much as from others. But unlike, say, Althusser's description—where we move seemingly abruptly from regimes of repressive apparatuses to those that inculcate obedience through ideology—the reality is that we live viscerally between interpellation and freedom. This epitomizes the situation of women and choice, where to choose is to put oneself at risk, be it only the risk of social opprobrium—which still overwhelmingly penalizes women.

Starkly put, individual choice operates along with dictates to pull oneself up by one's bootstraps, where a safety net has long been ripped down. If these terms readily summon a certain view of the United States or of Howard's Australia in which industrial relations have been completely and utterly evacuated of any collective form of safety, it also depicts non-Western countries. I think we can usefully gain from reviewing how choice is framed outside of the West. One of the most compelling social experiments precisely along the lines of freedom and choice within a genealogical society is that of the People's Republic of China. As I will describe later in more detail, the twinned mechanism of social change inaugurated some twenty years ago—the one child policy and economic reform—has produced a set of conflicting discourses. For the first time in Chinese history, daughters are regarded on equal terms as sons, if only because there is one child. This has huge ramifications for their education as well as for a profound disruption of familial lines of constraint as girls and women experiment with new freedoms. The situation in China and other Asian states may illuminate the painful move from a genealogical society to one in which individuals may be free to take on their own risky ventures.[10] As we will see, the research emerging from China and Hong Kong dramatically challenges and reworks what we think we know about choice, intimacy, constraint, and freedom.

The Trouble with Choice

From the second wave on, feminism became wedded in the public mind with the question of choice. In micropractices such as consciousness raising and in larger ways such as legal reform, feminism posed choice as a way out of heteronormativity, with its all-pervasive constraints on women's bodies and sexualities. It beckoned a brave and quite frightening world of responsibility, of risk taking and radical experimentation with life. Choice came to be understood as freedom—and it promised for some, for many, a leap of freedom into an unknown world. At a fundamental level, this was the freedom to escape women's traditional roles in upholding gene-alogical society, their enforced positions as caretakers, mothers, daughters, and so on. The choices were hard ones—pro-choice and "our bodies, our selves" implied something far more frightening than is now credited. Lest we forget, adequate child care and equal pay for equal work were framed as human rights, not individual choices. Notwithstanding this distinction, it is important to remember just how breathtaking these choices were for individual women: imagine being the first woman in your family and com-munity to not get married, to have an abortion, to go to university, and to have a career often far from your community. In short, this was to break with genealogical destiny.

It's hard to believe that we would move so quickly from this basis where women painfully or joyously ripped themselves out of the genealogical fab-ric. In three decades women have moved from being the guardians of the home to being the flag wavers of consumer culture. If in the 1950s deciding on the color of consumer goods constituted the extent of women's choices, now advertisers and celebrity entrepreneurs such as the Olsen twins greedily eye the female market as they invent new consumer types such as tweens (preteen girls).[11] In her recent work on postfeminism, Angela McRobbie focuses on the media's role in using girls as a metaphor for social change and how the media via the representation of girls determine appro-priate codes of sexual conduct.[12] One could say that the media continu-ally appropriate girls' diverse experiences and render them into condensed moral stories. The main thrust is to demonstrate the unsafe effects of cul-ture on girls or, conversely, the deleterious choices girls make and how this then influences popular culture. In this way, consumer culture is portrayed in the popular media as out of control through the figure of the out-of-control girl. The tone is chiding. On her blog, one journalist describes the Olsen twins' image as "their pre-pubescent paedophile bait clothes, which promote . . . apprentice prostitutes."[13] It soon becomes apparent that femi-nism—under the guise of "sexual liberation"—has promoted this wayward and sexualized culture. Britney Spears and Paris Hilton sans underwear or Kate Moss snorting cocaine become synecdoche for what's wrong with popular culture and what's wrong with girls. The underlying blame is rationalized by the fact that these figures would not exist if it were not for the consumer choices of young women and that it is young women who consume these images.

Of course it is one thing to read about the antics of rich princesses and quite a leap to consider that young women will emulate them or are to blame for them. However, the issue is complex and is not helped by the comments of previous feminist figures. For instance, Fay Weldon, the well-known and formerly self-identified feminist novelist, has this to say to young women: "Just fake. Happy generous-minded women not too hung up about emotional honesty fake. . . . Faking is kind to male partners . . . Otherwise they too may become anxious and so less able to perform. Do yourself and him a favour, sister: fake it."[14] While Weldon's so-called advice may be made for shock value, her comments are radically shocking. If women are not to expect any sexual pleasure, what are their chances that sex will be consensual and safe? As we know, there is a worldwide epidemic among young people of easily preventable sexually transmitted diseases, but in Weldon's depiction and recommendation that we go back to the Dark Ages, there's little hope that men will be encouraged to have protected intercourse. Even if HIV has diminished as a perceived threat to young women in the developed world, in the West there is an epidemic of STDs, including chlamydia, among the sixteen-to-twenty-six-year-old demographic; chlamydia is now on the WHO's list of top morbidities due to the risk of death from ectopic (entopic) pregnancies.[15]

Weldon exemplifies McRobbie's comment that the media "pass judgment and establish the rules of play" ("Notes," 13). But in this instance it is a new twist on an old ploy. As Charlotte Brunsdon argues, "the censorious feminist" has been a constant figure in the last thirty years of popular culture. Now we have former feminists evoking and "remak[ing] the cultural memory of the censorious feminist."[16]

Blame Games

The reality (of publishing) seems to be that attacks on "the censorious feminist" are the big winners. As mentioned earlier, the tone of many polemics, often written by women, is that of complaint and betrayal. Feminism is portrayed as preventing women from having babies.[17] Feminism is to blame for sexualized fashion or conversely for producing a generation of prudish young women.[18] Feminism is responsible for raunch culture[19] as well as for what Maureen Dowd refers to as "yummy mummies," young women who squander their high-priced education to bring up children instead of leading the revolution.[20] In her book on young adults and the diatribes against them, Kate Crawford sums up the tone: "The argument persists that somehow, somewhere, feminism has led women away from the altar and children and feminists are to blame for robbing women of the hope that life will be . . . good."[21]

However illogical it is to make feminism the scapegoat for whatever particular anxiety passes through culture (economics, fashion, fertility, and so on), there is no doubt that feminist arguments have been used to frame a discursive perimeter around girls. Education scholars Victoria Jane Ward and Beth Cooper Benjamin argue that resilience and risk and their accompanying emotive charges of alarm and celebration continue to limit how we can think about girl culture.[22] While some feminist arguments have promoted this simplistic framing, Ward and Benjamin also add that "risk and resilience, alarm and celebration persist as themes in popular girls' studies because they are real cultural contradictions in the lives of all girls and women."[23]

Freedom, Constraint, and Intimacy

I queried at the outset whether anything ever changes. McRobbie argues that there is something new going on: "Young women have come to the fore as the pre-eminent subjects of this new ethic [of freedom]" ("Notes," 12). Following the theses about self-reflexive modernity advanced by Ulrich Beck, Anthony Giddens, and Scott Lash, and Nikolas Rose's analysis of the encroachment of governmentality as a defining feature of neoliberal life,[24] McRobbie notes how girls are placed as the embodiment of freedom: "Through the trope of freedom, enacting generational differences and thus bringing them into being, these forms successfully drive a wedge between women, which sets off the mother, the teacher, and the feminist into the realms of a bygone age" ("Notes," 13). The dominant framing of the context in which young women may or may not be able to make choices is severely limited. As McRobbie points out, it is difficult for any communication between and among women. Why would young women turn to feminism when older and successful women like Weldon make outrageous and unsafe claims to devalue it? On the other hand, we have a highly sexualized popular imaginary in which the only choices around sexuality are equally outrageous and unsafe. Within this climate McRobbie questions whether "female individualisation can indeed be regarded as both one outcome of feminism and a reward for its abandonment?" ("Notes," 11). She points to the ways in which New Labour in Britain has successfully integrated choices for women into its profile. Equally she describes "female consent and participation [and] the idea that these are all personal choices" ("Notes," 13). All of this is, of course, quite true. But I think we need to extend McRobbie's insights in order to investigate how the figures of women and choice complicate the intersection between constraint and freedom. The tension between self-fashioning freedom and genealogical constraint is much thicker than McRobbie allows.

We can see this encapsulated in how young women understand and enact intimacy today. As we have seen, there is no lack of denunciation about young women's sexuality within an overly sexualized culture. But as Deborah Tolman and others have pointed out, there is still little academic discussion, let alone popular questioning, of "how girls enter into their sexual lives and learn to negotiate or respond to their sexuality."[25] There is even less consideration of the distinctions they enact between sexuality and intimacy. Sexuality is seen as either consumer choice or an object loaded with risk. But if we consider sex as an ensemble of activities, practices, and discourses, it is obvious that at times intimacy enters into the equation and at other times it is something quite differently experienced.

In her inspiring book *The Empire of Love*, which investigates the dilemmas of living between genealogical and autological cultures, Elizabeth Povinelli asks: "Which forms of intimate dependency count as freedom and which count as undue social restraint; which forms of intimacy involve moral judgment rather than mere choice; and which forms of intimate sociality distribute life and material goods and evoke moral certainty, if not moral sanctimoniousness."[26] To reframe her argument in the terms discussed here, one can begin to ask which aspects of this equation allow young women to envision intimacy as freedom outside of the moral sanctimoniousness of popular media representations. How do the various forms of culture and consumption as well as their representations limit freedom? How do choice, sexuality, and intimacy play out for young women today?

Freedom in Povinelli's formulation is produced within the wider arrangements of what she calls autological society. These arrangements consist of "discourses, practices, and fantasies about self-making, self-sovereignty, and the value of individual freedom associated with the Enlightenment project of contractual democracy and capitalism" (*Empire*, 4). Obviously in the West and under late capitalism, it is the self-fashioning subject who rules. However, the foundation on which the conditions of possibility for current forms of autology are constructed is deep. As Povinelli states, "Many names have been given to this form of subjectivity across many languages: the autological subject, the *parvenu*, the self-made man, *die Autonomie*. Each of these terms signals at once the dissemination of this form across liberal diaspora—across, for instance, French republicanism, American pluralism, Australian multiculturalism, and Turkish secularism—and at the same time the reunification of this dissembled form into a coherent singularity called Enlightenment freedom" (*Empire*, 183–84). In this way, Povinelli gives depth to self-making, an ensemble of practices that are often conceived of as immediate, without history, and requiring endless repetition. In distinction to liberal Anglo-European discourses of self-making, Povinelli draws on her extensive fieldwork and relationships with Aboriginal people to explore what she sees as "maximally embodied social relations" or "thick life" (*Empire*, 45).[27]

Constraint is not only enforced from on high; different forms of constraint (as to how you can marry and the distinct and guarded spaces for different ceremonies) are essential. This is to say that constraint here should be thought of not only as a form of subjection to power. It is also constraint that demarcates different forms of power as generative of deep meanings. In comparison, self-fashioning subjects are proud of being just that—individuals who make themselves, be it through commands to pull oneself up by one's bootstraps (the mantra of the American society) or through intricate dictates to fashion a better self, a less dependent one, and so on.

Chinese Choices

In contrast to the Western context, Chinese cultures are more evidently imbued with genealogical constraints. The expectation of an heir—a male child to look after the parents—and familial obligations are all being profoundly disrupted by the twin phenomena of the one child policy and Deng Xiaoping's call in 1986 for economic opening. These two occurrences engineered spectacular social changes, which are embodied by a new generation of young educated women with access to comparatively high levels of disposable income. While many writers caution against too rapidly assuming that the Chinese are undergoing sexual as well as economic liberation, one of the most striking reactions to this is the way young people are now taking up a discourse on romantic love.[28] As James Farrer writes in his fascinating book on sex and youth culture in the context of market reform in Shanghai, this is producing some very interesting mixtures: "Dating has become part of a consumer culture that values choice, pleasure, play, and the pursuit of fashion. Youth must balance these individualistic consumer expectations with relational codes of romanticism, face preservation, respect, domesticity, and loyalty."[29] While the looming potential disaster of the urban-rural split—70 percent of the population still lives in the countryside—dwarfs the "merely cultural" phenomenon of youth culture in urban, newly middle-class China, youth are living nonetheless on a shaky experimental ground. As Farrer remarks: "In societies characterized by rigid and strategic family relations, romance is only possible outside of marriage. . . . On the other hand, in a society characterized by atomistic relations of mobility, competition, and individuality, the 'couple' becomes a refuge against the hostile world of strategic market relations, and romance is sought in courtship and marriage" (*Opening*, 192). Here we clearly see the difficulties that arise in the tension between genealogical and autological cultures. The relationship to the family, which is so important in Chinese society despite the years of communal work-unit-based relations, is but the most obvious way in which genealogical subjects are marked by constraint. More generally, *guanxi*—the wide-ranging notion of connectiveness, relatedness, and mutual obligation—is all pervasive in Chinese culture. *Guanxi* could be said to perfectly incorporate mutual recognition, which was for Althusser at the core of interpellation. As I discussed earlier, there is safety in being sutured into a web of interconnected relatedness and mutual obligation, but obviously it allows for very little freedom or Western notions of free choice.

In any case, there is no easy demarcation between the constraint of rigid family and the constraint of the pursuit of an ideal of romantic love. Indeed, as Farrer writes elsewhere, there is already a backlash against the romantic ideal.[30] Farrer recounts the example of well-known Web columnist Mu Zimei and her radical attack on the emergent discourses about romance and love among young Chinese people. Mu—a prolific and very popular public persona in China—opposes an emergent trend toward romantic love. As she told a *New York Times* reporter, "I do not oppose love, but I oppose loyalty; if love has to be based on loyalty, I oppose love."[31]

For young people like Mu, there seems to be little choice between the traditional Chinese emphasis on familial relationships over Western "free" love. One should be hesitant before claiming Mu's opposition to romantic love as a Chinese version of queer transgression. Equally, as Farrer argues, Giddens's model of plastic love and his celebration of sexual modernity cannot simply be applied. Farrer critiques "Giddens' approach as missing the social context of this intensified rhetoric of 'romance' and 'intimacy,' specifically young people's cultural accommodations to labor, marriage, and consumer markets" (*Opening*, 11). There is no clear dividing line that would make one side of the coin "purer" or more progressive. As reported in a Shanghai newspaper, "Love has become a kind of consumption" (*Opening*, 152).

In our Hallmark society where every aspect of human existence can be turned into a cute card, it is hardly shocking to think of love as a commodity. For our purposes, this becomes more fascinating in the realm of friendship, love, sex, and intimacy. In her discussion of Aboriginal society, Povinelli observes, "Friendship opens kinship into a relation between individuals, into a variant of intimate love" (*Empire*, 23). This understanding of intimacy troubles Western notions of who belongs where and to whom. As Foucault famously declared, it was "friendship as a way of life" among gays, not sex, that posed the greatest challenge to dominant Western society.[32]

Foucault's interview on friendship raises several points, which if anything have become more widely salient. His oft-cited main thesis is that "the problem is not to discover in oneself the truth of sex but rather to use sexuality henceforth to arrive at a multiplicity of relationships" ("Friendship," 204). These relationships are enabled by and produce "affection, tenderness, friendship, fidelity, camaraderie and companionship" ("Friendship," 205). At the time of the interview in the mid-1980s and compared to the freedom and radical experimentation he found within gay culture in the United States, Foucault could conclude only that this mode of relating was in stark contrast to the heterosexual norm: "between a man and a younger woman the marriage institution makes it easier" ("Friendship," 204). Here again we can hear traces of the ways in which genealogical institutions may produce through their restraint a kind of ease and pleasure compared to the turbulence and sheer risky hard work of self-fashioning.

Twenty years later, it's clear that dramatic changes to the structure of marriage and the increased visibility in cultural representations of alternative modes of being have deeply changed the conditions of relationships.

Over the last decades, television has served to portray a much wider view of different modes of relationships. From the "bad mother" example of Roseanne Barr to the bad girls of New York, the boys of *Queer as Folk*, and the camp consumer advice of *Queer Eye*, a shift can be seen in how relationships can and might be understood. A notable change has been the incorporation of what was previously seen as a gay mode of life into straight and middle-class society. As Ethan Watters notes of "urban tribes"—his term of new ways of relating and types of attachments—regardless of their sexual orientation young people are taking from queer culture "to create loose, flexible networks connected through weak ties to other networks."[33] In her analysis of *Sex and the City*, Crawford cuts through the dominant view that the last season in which the women all settle down with partners returns us to a traditional heteronormative view of the world. As Crawford notes, friendship was at the heart of the entire series.

This is not to say that there is a happy and continuous movement toward a greater acceptance of other intimate ways of being together. But what it does demonstrate is that there is a growing gulf between neoconservative attempts to socially engineer the nuclear family through tax breaks and other fiscal arrangements, as well as outright banning of gay marriage and civil unions, and the reality of the world. That reality includes the ways in which young people are actively enacting friendship, thereby refusing the choice between kin and friend, sexual object and intimate. As Foucault might have put it, they are "refusing the choice" between love, friendship, and intimacy (*Empire*, 233).

This is a gradual shift in the making. Many years ago Marilyn Friedman noted a philosophical trend to understand the self as "a being constituted and defined by its attachments, including the particularities of its social relationships, community ties, and historical context."[34] This is an early acknowledgment of the ways in which "chosen" or autological identities mingle with genealogical ones. "Social relationships and attachments are . . . sought out, rather than merely found, created as well as discovered" ("Feminism," 285). Long before the occurrence of the Internet with its dizzying array of modalities of finding, seeking, and discovering different forms of relationships (from those centered on sex to sites such as Friendster or MySpace), sociologists such as Melvin Webber were arguing for recognition of "community without propinquity" ("Feminism," 288). Of course we now know that virtual communities and networks of relationships generate proximity in different ways. It is nonetheless astonishing to consider how many choices of different kinds of relationships are offered to anyone with Internet access.

The "Thick Lives" of Young People

Perhaps what is new are the more widespread ways in which young people are actively enacting intimacy, choice, and discovery. John Erni and Anthony Fung's project on youth culture in Hong Kong found that this is a defining characteristic of life for young Chinese ("Dislocated"). Their study investigated how youth in Hong Kong navigate the Western discourses of choice and sexual freedom with their long Confucian history of familial obligation: "'Sexing friendship,' as it were, becomes the means for opening up the many scenarios of sexual possibilities available to young people, who are caught in the paradox between sexual curiosity and sexual self-restraint, in a society in which an autonomous, auto-referencing, open, or socially affirming discourse about youth sex is largely absent" ("Dislocated," 33–34). Their argument is that only within "a socially oriented consumption environment" ("Dislocated," 33) can codes of friendship be found and chosen. In other words, there is no simple choice between the self-fashioning world of consumption and the genealogical one of depth and putative authenticity. As we've seen in the examples of Western Gen Y, this is not confined to, although it is differently articulated within, Chinese societies.

This is where the challenge lies: young people, for numerous reasons, are refusing the either/or terms of choice and are instead fashioning forms of relationships, of socialities, that also refuse to choose among love, friendship, and intimacy. As I've tried to demonstrate, there has for some time been an emerging ensemble of discourses, a heterogeneous collection of statements about choice, family, friends, and consumption, and a fluidity of understandings about what can constitute relationships of intimacy. It is not surprising that young people are now enacting some of these discourses in their everyday practices, but it should be taken seriously.

Catharine Lumby and I interviewed and held focus groups with girls in a project called Girl Cultures.[35] We noticed a continual blurring of sex, friendship, and connection in the girls' talk. Listen, for instance, to this fifteen-year-old girl from an inner-city private girls' school:

> Um, if my best friend was a slut, um, I'd probably just try and help her through whatever she was going through because, um, in my experience, I mean I've been in situations like that . . . and I've had

friends that have been in situations like that . . . and it's usually, it's not because you're just a slut . . . and it's going to be with you for the rest of your life, it's caused by something, it's usually caused by loneliness or some sort of thing, so I'd just try and support her, like whatever, if she was you know, if she felt that she was actually damaging herself or if she was feeling like she was changing into something that she didn't want to be, I'd try and just support her and help her through it. . . .

I think a lot of the girls who might be sluts are girls who are really insecure and aren't just doing it for fun, and you've just got to really look after those girls because those girls often really need you to help, and you know that you've got to realize that you're not the counsellor, and you can only be a friend to her.[36]

It's clear that a physical and emotional connection becomes the setting in which to discover and find ways of being together. A sixteen-year-old girl remarks:

Madeleine and I are also quite close physical people in that we like physical contact in general; you know, I like hugs and closeness physically and that doesn't change when it comes to confrontation. It's like sort of, I enjoy but would like to have that physical closeness and confrontation just like you do with friends in some situations.

It's really weird, we all, because this is the first single-sex school that I've been to . . . and it's weird, because all the girls, like they're all beautiful . . . like they're beautiful girls, and like they've all got these different bodies, but it doesn't really matter, they sort of just take you, you know, everyone loves each other in that, you know, sort of, whatever, and we're all really close.[37]

Sociologists Barrie Thorne and Zella Luria have noted that "girls become mutually vulnerable through self-disclosure."[38] From my research and that of others, what is interesting is how relations of friendship straddle a number of divisions and form the basis from which choices can be discussed and made. As I mentioned previously, it is not in itself surprising that young people have a wide repertoire of discourses to draw on. However, I want to conclude by noting that a subtle but seismic shift is underway within youth cultures. The tension I've described as that of genealogical constraint and the freedom of self-fashioning no longer seems to map out a demarcation between safety and discovery. While mainstream society still figures the family and genealogical embeddedness as the site of safety, girls seem to be remaking friendship—that most chosen of relational forms—as their safety network in which to reflect and to actively engage in a totally other way of negotiating the risks and the joys of different intimacies. I stress risks because the trust they seem to give each other makes them extraordinarily vulnerable. As anyone who has been let down or betrayed by a best friend knows, the pain of ruptured intimacy can be devastating. This is a form of relatedness for which the West has few rules. By contrast in Chinese society, young people are learning how to transpose the long lessons of *guanxi*, understood as mutual obligation, into the new site of freedom offered via the choices of consumer society.

It is of course far from evident how or whether younger generations will continue to try to forge friendships and ways of relating that do not obey sanctioned cultural choices. But given the continuing governmental and public discourses that dismiss their choices, it is clear that it will not be easy. However, as Foucault once remarked, when the ground under one's feet is being moved, it's best to laugh.

> A passage in Borges [where he quotes a "certain Chinese encyclopaedia"], out of the laughter that shattered, as I read the passage, all the familiar landmarks of my thought—our thought, the thought that bears the stamp of our age and our geography—breaking up all the ordered surfaces and all the planes with which we are accustomed to tame the wild profusion of existing things, and continuing long afterwards to disturb and threaten with collapse our age-old distinction between the Same and the Other.[39]

Notes

My thanks especially to Jennifer Germon and to Clifton Evers, Grant Farred, and Larry Schehr for their comments.

1 Michael McKinnon and Clara Pirani, "Baby Bonus Boosts Birthrate by 10,000," *Australian* (Sydney), September 16, 2006, www.theaustralian.news.com.au/story/0,20867,20420 374-601,00.html.

2 As cited by Leslie Savan in "Op Ad: The Trad Trade," *Village Voice*, March 7, 1989.

3 This is a comment in the *New Humanist* referring to the Australian journalist Virginia Haussegger's complaint that feminism "stole" her babies. Lesley Johnson, "Domestic Bliss!" *New Humanist* 119.6 (2004), http://newhumanist.org.uk/804 (accessed January 24, 2007).

4 The panic around pro-ana sites, Web sites that actively promote an anorexic "lifestyle," is particularly interesting in this regard. Against decades of medical and feminist discourse about how powerless anorexics are and, indeed, a framing of anorexia as a causal result of

media images, these sites constitute a strong backlash in terms of staking out a full and forceful subjectivity on the part of anorexics. It is hard to "make sense" of these sites, in part because they are such strong statements of a collective sense making and, indeed, of a community. The challenge they offer is at least twofold: to the medical community, they constitute a threat to the medicalization of anorexia, which has increased significantly and yet still has little in the way of a cure for anorexia; to feminists and others, they seem to say "stop using us as a metaphor." See Hailey Baldwin, "Understanding Pro-Anorexic Identities: Self-Expression, Tribal Thinking, and the Internet" (honors diss., University of Sydney, 2006), for an interesting initial attempt to map out the voices and different subject positions offered by these sites. Desiree Boughton conducted ethnographic research within anorexia treatment programs and offers a definitive challenge to the medical establishment. Boughton, "Anorexia in the Clinic" (PhD diss., University of Western Sydney, 2005).

5 See Savan, "Op Ad," 49; and Elspeth Probyn, "Perverts by Choice: Towards an Ethics of Choosing," in *Feminism Beside Itself*, ed. Diane Elam and Robyn Wiegman (New York: Routledge, 1995), 261–82.

6 Michèle Le Dœuff, "Pierre Roussel's Chiasmas," *I and C* 9 (1981–82): 39–70.

7 Probyn, "Perverts by Choice."

8 Louis Althusser, "Ideology and Ideological State Apparatuses," in *Lenin and Philosophy, and Other Essays*, trans. Ben Brewster (New York: Monthly Review Press, 1972), 86–129. For the best feminist use and critique of Althusser, see Teresa de Lauretis, *Technologies of Gender* (Bloomington: Indiana University Press, 1986).

9 One could also think here in the terms delivered by the economic historian Harold A. Innis and his distinction of societies based in time versus those of space. Little happens in the former, which are stable and rooted in spatially limited forms of communication. The latter, exemplified for Innis in space-embracing forms of communication, are inherently unstable but more open to change and individual innovation. H. A. Innis, *The Bias of Communication* (Toronto: University of Toronto Press, 1964). For one of the best explanations and extensions of Innis, see Arthur Kroker, *Technology and the Canadian Mind: Innis/McLuhan/Grant* (Montreal: New World Perspectives, 1984).

10 In this I am indebted to John Nguyet Erni's research with Anthony Fung on youth cultures of consumption and friendship in Hong Kong. Erni and Fung, "Dislocated Intimacies: A Social Relational Perspective on Youth, Sex, and the Popular Media" (paper presented at the "Communicating Sexual Health" workshop, Department of Gender and Cultural Studies, University of Sydney, August 2006), also published in *Perspectives: Working Papers in English and Communication* 15.1 (2003): 30–51; hereafter cited parenthetically by page number as "Dislocated." Erni and I are at the early stages of a comparative project on youth, and we are both fascinated by youth culture in mainland China. The insights of Australian researchers—such as Chris Berry, Fran Martin, and Audrey Yue, eds., *Mobile Cultures: New Media in Queer Asia* (Durham, NC: Duke University Press, 2003), and Elaine Jeffreys, ed., *Sexuality and Sex in China* (London: Routledge, 2006)—about Chinese sexual cultures have been central to reorienting my thinking. While I make no pretense to being an expert on Chinese culture, my discussions with fellow researchers and the experience of teaching gender and consumption to young people from the People's Republic of China have reignited my interest in how young people

navigate cultural consumption and changing patterns of intimacy in ways that seemingly disrupt the ontological status of choice.

11   To quote from CNN, "Mary-Kate and Ashley Olsen, who entered celebritydom when they first starred as infants on the TV show *Full House,* successfully transformed their star appeal into an entertainment and consumer products empire through their company Dualstar Entertainment. The twins now have a slew of licensed products, such as books, video movies and dolls." In addition to sexualizing "tweens," Mary-Kate was a pinup girl on pro-anorexia sites because of her defiant and starving body. Parija Bhatnagar, "Olsen Twins Pitch New Clothing Line to Wal-Mart," CNN, March 29, 2006, http://money.cnn .com/2006/03/28/news/companies/walmart_twins.

12   Angela McRobbie, "Notes on Postfeminism and Popular Culture: Bridget Jones and the New Gender Regime," in *All About the Girl: Culture, Power, and Identity,* ed. Anita Harris (London: Routledge, 2004), 3–14. Hereafter cited parenthetically by page number as "Notes."

13   Margo Kingston, blog, http://webdiary.smh.com.au (accessed January 24, 2007; site now discontinued). Kingston is an independent Australian journalist.

14   Fay Weldon, *What Makes Women Happy* (London: Fourth Estate, 2006), 47–48.

15   WHO, *The World Health Report 2005 — Make Every Mother and Child Count,* www.who.int/ whr/2005/en/index.html (accessed September 10, 2006).

16   Charlotte Brunsdon, "Feminism, Postfeminism, Martha, Martha, and Nigella," *Cinema Journal* 44.2 (2005): 110–116, 113.

17   See Leslie Cannold, *What, No Baby?* (Fremantle, Austr.: Curtin University Press, 2005); Virginia Haussegger, *Wonder Woman: The Myth of "Having It All"* (Sydney: Allen and Unwin, 2005); and Virginia Haussegger, "The Sins of Our Feminist Mothers," *Age* (Melbourne), July 23, 2002, 7.

18   Helen Garner, *The First Stone: Some Questions about Sex and Power* (Sydney: Pan Macmillan, 1995).

19   Ariel Levy, *Female Chauvinist Pigs: Women and the Use of Raunch Culture* (Melbourne: Schwartz Publishing, 2005).

20   Maureen Dowd, *Are Men Necessary? When the Sexes Collide* (New York: Putnam, 2005).

21   Kate Crawford, *Adult Themes: Rewriting the Rules of Adulthood* (Sydney: Pan Macmillan, 2006), 91.

22   Victoria Jane Ward and Beth Cooper Benjamin, "Women, Girls, and the Unfinished Work of Connection: A Critical Review of Girls' Studies," in *All About the Girl,* 15–28.

23   Ibid., 25.

24   Ulrich Beck, Anthony Giddens, and Scott Lash, *Reflexive Modernization: Political Tradition and Aesthetics in the Modern Social Order* (Stanford, CA: Stanford University Press, 1994); and Nikolas Rose, *Inventing Ourselves: Psychology, Power, and Personhood* (Cambridge: Cambridge University Press, 1996).

25   Deborah Tolman, "Doing Desire: Adolescent Girls' Struggles for/with Sexuality," in *Sexualities: Identities, Behaviors, and Society,* ed. Michael S. Kimmel and Rebecca F. Plante (New York: Oxford University Press, 1994), 87–98.

26   Elizabeth A. Povinelli, *The Empire of Love: Toward a Theory of Intimacy, Genealogy, and Carnality* (Durham, NC: Duke University Press, 2006), 3. Hereafter cited parenthetically by page number as *Empire.*

27 I can flag here only the ways in which connection to country and a complex kinship network function within Aboriginal society. They are also the grounds on which any request for reparation of land can be effected. In Australia, Aboriginal groups need to demonstrate their continuous affiliation to the land (since the time of British sovereignty) in order to attempt a Native Title Claim under the Native Title Act 1993. In addition, claimants need to be recognized by other Indigenous Australians as having that connection. The Native Title Act was established to provide legal mechanisms for land claims by traditional owners after a significant High Court decision in 1992, known as the Mabo decision, recognized that indigenous rights to land had survived British occupation.

28 Suiming Pan, "Transformations in the Primary Life Cycle: The Origins and Nature of China's Sexual Revolution," in *Sexuality and Sex in China*, 21–42; and Elaine Jeffreys, introduction to *Sexuality and Sex in China*, 1–20.

29 James Farrer, *Opening Up: Youth Sex Culture and Market Reform in Shanghai* (Chicago: University of Chicago Press, 2002), 179. Hereafter cited parenthetically by page number as *Opening*.

30 James Farrer, "Sexual Citizenship and the Politics of Sexual Storytelling among Chinese Youth," in *Sexuality and Sex in China*, 102–23.

31 Ibid., 113.

32 Michel Foucault, "Friendship as a Way of Life," in *Foucault Live Interviews, 1966–84*, ed. Sylvère Lotringer, trans. John Johnston (New York: Semiotext(e), 1989), 203–9. Hereafter cited parenthetically by page number as "Friendship."

33 Ethan Watters, *Urban Tribes: Are Friends the New Family?* (London: Bloomsbury, 2004), 117.

34 Marilyn Friedman, "Feminism and Modern Friendship: Dislocating the Community," *Ethics* 99 (1989): 275–90. Hereafter cited parenthetically by page number as "Feminism."

35 Catharine Lumby and I conducted Girl Cultures, a three-year project that was funded by the Australian Research Council between 1999 and 2004. The project's aims were to ascertain how girls understood the media directed at them.

36 "Amy," interviewed by author, Sydney, November 10, 2005.

37 "Meg," interviewed by author, Sydney, November 10, 2005.

38 Barrie Thorne and Zella Luria, "Sexuality and Gender in Children's Daily Worlds," in *Sexualities*, 74–86.

39 Michel Foucault, *The Order of Things* (New York: Vintage, 1973), xv.

David Thomson

Jump City: Parkour and the Traces

> Thus, one of my plebeian philosopher's essential budget headings was "shoes," for the emancipated man is a man who walks and walks, moving around and conversing, putting meaning into circulation and promoting the movement of emancipation.
> —Jacques Rancière, *On the Shores of Politics*

Introduction

What could be more unsafe than moving across, over, between, or under the city's structures with what seems to be a joyous and blatant disregard for their intended use? *Parkour*, an urban practice of rapid on-foot movement that follows the maxim "keep moving forward," seems, with its spectacular running and jumping, disconcertingly unsafe. It is, in fact, dangerous, both for the practitioner, who risks being hit by cars, breaking bones, and irritating security guards, and for the logic of the city itself. Downtown cores are arranged so as to assist flows of transaction and consumption, and local ordinances seek to restrict tangential activities that could disrupt that flow. Parkour is not so much a manifesto as an instance of the unruly intersection between capital flow and the flow of human

South Atlantic Quarterly 107:2, Spring 2008
DOI 10.1215/00382876-2007-065 © 2008 Duke University Press

bodies; instead of coinciding, they may intersect at angles of varying and appositional intensities.[1]

This essay engages the figure of the wanderer (in parkour terms, the *traceur*) in the urban landscape. I want to call this space "capital city": the urban concentration of transnational capital flow and consumption. As Guy Debord has argued, the city is a spectacle, and it is a physical manifestation of a hankering for democracy. In its public spaces and its government buildings, it suggests a history of a dream of collective consciousness fully present to itself. Civic and commercial structures are the two sorts of buildings that traceurs are most likely to push off from and move across.

Parkour traceurs move against the backdrop of capital city, putting into relief what is there. Glimpsed against the rectangles of the buildings of the business sector, parkour is art set in its frame. This contemplation is as much about the city as about parkour and unruly wandering.

The quirky, *off-piste* body involved in capers and high jinks downtown—often in privileged, relatively safe Western cities—might seem ephemeral. Depending on the definition of *urban*, in 2007, about half of the world's people lived in cities. Worldwide, capital city is at the tipping point and about to become slum city, as Mike Davis continues to warn us.[2] But that is my point—capital city seems so solid and present that people can literally climb on it, yet the city is absent in the sense that it ceaselessly refers elsewhere. Parkour is an aesthetic that, though lacking any particular politics of dissent, helps the viewer see a significant feature of the city, its tendency to allude.

Arcade City

"Dream City" (Walter Benjamin), "Situationist City" (Anthony Vidler): Paris has been called various names, as writers and artists have sought to depict its modernity and the movement of people on foot.[3] Benjamin's 1935 and 1939 exposés, both titled "Paris, the Capital of the Nineteenth Century" (*Arcades*, 3, 14), demarcate the ways in which capital city was clearly going to be a time as well as a space. Benjamin's particular interest was in the juxtaposition of two emergent technologies: ironwork, and *magasins* clustered into arrangements that were effectively department stores. The significant thing about the ironwork was its ability to suspend glass and to form arcades. The specular economy was born. "These arcades, a recent invention of industrial luxury, are glass-roofed, marble-paneled corridors extending through whole blocks of buildings, whose owners have joined together for such enterprises. Lining both sides of these corridors, which get their light from above, are the most elegant shops, so that the *passage* is a city, a world in miniature" (*Arcades*, 2). Benjamin was interested in the figure of the stroller, the flaneur, in these arcades (and by extension in the European city). He quotes Balzac on the "perfect flaneur" for whom "it is an immense joy to set up house in the heart of the multitude" (*Arcades*, 436). But the flaneur cannot be neatly set in artistic opposition to capital, for in one of his personae he is "the observer of the marketplace. His knowledge is akin to the science of industrial fluctuations. He is a spy for the capitalists, on assignment in the realm of consumers" (*Arcades*, 427). And although the tempo of the flaneur can be judged, Benjamin tells us, by the fact that "in 1839 it was considered elegant to take a tortoise out walking" (*Arcades*, 422), the flaneur is certainly not a dandy, or a traveler, or a tourist for that matter, and even the stroll has a certain vertigo. For the flaneur, "every street is precipitous" (*Arcades*, 416).

In Situationism, a version of the stroll with a good deal more explicit antagonism to capital than that evinced by the flaneur is called the *dérive* or drift. Debord defined the *dérive* as "a mode of experimental behaviour linked to the conditions of urban society: a technique of rapid passage through varied ambiances."[4] If we draw a line from the flaneur to the *dériveur* and then to the traceur, clearly there will be many exclusions, most notably that of the surrealists. The city today includes flash mobbers, sewerers, and other hipsters together with old-fashioned skateboarders (including the more prosaic longboarders), mobile petty criminals, grocery cart pushers, streakers, hitchhikers, car fighters, unemployed messengers, lowbaggers, in-line skaters, builderers, culvert kayakers, through-bikers, and their ilk. So the filiation of flaneur to traceur may not be a direct one, fraught as it is with detours, but clearly the stroll in capital city has gained some momentum from Debord's "rapid passage."

Parkour was formalized as a discipline by David Belle: "[It] is a natural method to train the human body to move forward quickly, making use of the environment that's around us at any given time."[5] This movement is the "art of displacement," by which one site refers and links to the next across the city. The corrupted French spelling is a hint that deviation is likely. Parkour (or PK) is an excellent training regimen for outrunning the police, and it functions potentially as a low-tech answer in a world of helicopters and gadgets to the perennial question for bad boys, "What you gonna do when they come for you?" That its roots lie in the imaginary space of outrunning Vietcong soldiers in Indochina should give pause to anyone who wishes to link the movement in any simple fashion with protests against capital. The most direct trace (or genealogy) from Belle to Vietnam is through his father, a Vietnam veteran and an adept at obstacle courses. That ability, in its turn, can be traced to Georges Hébert, the twentieth-century physical fitness guru. Hébert had been stationed in St. Pierre in Martinique in 1902 when the town was subject to a volcanic eruption. In accounts of the event, Hébert features as a sort of antithesis of George W. Bush in the latter's response to disasters in Manhattan and New Orleans. Hébert heroically organized the city and, more important, developed a lasting impression that the physical fitness of the citizenry is crucial.

Parkour's enlistment in politics recalls Slavoj Žižek: "One should radically reject the notion that discipline (from self-control to bodily training) is a 'proto-Fascist' feature."[6] Of kung fu gangs who watched Bruce Lee movies three decades ago, Žižek asks, "Was it not obvious that we were dealing with a genuine working class ideology of youngsters whose only means of success was the disciplinary training of their only possession, their bodies?"[7]

There is a lot of talk in parkour about seeing the city in new ways. Toronto traceur Graham, for example, did an ad hoc reading of a glass bus stop that had an advertisement for a backpack on one side. "The bus stop is considered for its physical properties, and the product is ignored," he said. "You don't want to make a mistake and crash through all that glass."[8] Flaneurs in arcade Paris might well have had similar thoughts about the fragility of glass.

On the other hand, traceurs and traceuses, even when spurning products, are likely to become products themselves. Despite recent "gains" in miniaturization, cameras bearing heavy wide-angle lenses are the best for making athletes look like they're flying. And they are flying. Where there's parkour, there's usually a camera not far behind. In addition to YouTube and documentaries with a fairly wide international distribution such as *Jump London* and *Jump Britain*, parkour dominates the opening sequence of *Casino Royale*, the 007 movie, and appears in *Live Free or Die Hard* and other feature films.[9] A new generation of photographers is learning to shoot the city with traceurs in the foreground.

Capital City

From the roofs of tall buildings, cities resemble motherboards, the insides of computers. Seen thus, urban physical movement can be said to be conducted and semiconducted in rectilinear fashion (in computers, even circuits tend to be rectangular), variously without impedance, with partial impedance, or with full stops. In fact, the display is probably less a symbol of computation than an instance of it, since the city is quite literally, day and night, in the midst of an infinity of local tallies, reckoning its total share of global capital. Angel Rama has written concerning the cities of the Americas in their historical situation, arguing that they exist on both a physical plane and a symbolic one, though his book *The Lettered City* suggests that the features arise together as one.[10]

The symbolic order acts not so much in superimposition as a key that can deconstruct the meaning of the city. Rather, the city comes into being as a symbolic order. It is not as if the city has been an organic formation that is later subjected to the protocols of reading, though to be sure the city has a grammar. Instead, the city is formed as an embodiment of an originary rhetoric, even without direct machinations such as Le Corbusier drawing plans for Rio from an airplane. The computer analogy could be extended to make anyone on foot that moves against the grain of the city into a sort of bug in the machine. But there is not a single aerial vantage point for consolidating this perspective, since the city is a cluster of superimposed grammars, discursive overlays, and intertwined systems and sets of systems, such as electrical grids funneled through subway tunnels. The individual in such a milieu has access to so many perspectives that these tend to be bundled, just like systems of systems.[11] Simply going for a walk can be a challenge.

In his reading of Plato and the modernists, part of his larger project of assigning values to the aesthetic and the political, Jacques Rancière seems to have convened the elements for an elegant model of the footloose within an urban context. Modernist discourse, he says, bestowed on itself the discovery that pictorial abstraction could come home to two dimensions: "By revoking the perspectivist illusion of the third dimension, painting was to regain the mastery of its own proper surface."[12] The modernist claim is understandable, given that perspective thus rendered is a fiction that hints at the third dimension. If you are going to refer to it, why not just produce it? Conversely, there does seem to be a certain honesty about producing nonillusory art as paintings simply in two dimensions on a flat surface. It is not hard to imagine an ascending series of accommodations in this direction, from painting to statuary to theater. Such an ascent can be an increase in verisimilitude, but it also begins to look rather like a parable about presence: "For Plato, writing and painting were equivalent surfaces of mute signs, deprived of the breath that animates and transports living speech" (*Aesthetics*, 15). Any time a theorist writes "living speech," a warning flag is clearly going to be raised about false claims to presence. Without considering Rancière's critique, however, there is still the endpoint of this progression. If two dimensions can be the backdrop for a perspectivist illusion, three dimensions might be the backdrop for a temporalist illusion, which would make available that fourth dimension, time. Can we posit parkour tracings as inhabiting the authentic end of a continuum with abstraction at one end and authenticity at the other? It certainly works schematically, with the artists leaping out from the urban concrete planes, away from "the 'planarity' of the surface of depicted signs" (*Aesthetics*, 17). And the unpredictability and danger of street theater seem to correspond with the vitality of Plato's tragic theater, over against the uninspired letter of flat depiction. What Rancière calls "optical depth" plays a large part in the story (*Aesthetics*, 16), and depth perception is what keeps traceurs alive. The question about visual art that parkour seems to ask implicitly is one the psychogeographer is likely to pose as well: If you're going to depict it, why not act it, live it? Only those who truly see the city can truly render it. Does this not make parkour the supreme urban visual art form? Do we not have all the transcendence we need from the moment the feet of the traceur "loose the surly bonds of earth"?[13]

An obvious problem with this is that as a YouTube phenomenon, not to mention an opener for a 007 film, parkour reinscribes the old illusion of a plane referring beyond itself. Even out there in the city of the real, there isn't much time. Is there any? The traceur working a wall several stories above street level is not in any useful sense progressing through time. Time collapses in a measure corresponding to the effort of concentration. In fact, mortality hectoring time into an ever-smaller pinprick might serve as a definitive measure of parkour *event*, a sort of distillation of the psychological part of a jump sequence. By contrast, one might say that to the extent the traceur (or traceuse) experiences time, he has been outside the moment and thus outside the trace.[14] With no time in which to exist, the traceur as traceur does not exist, and it will be difficult to deploy the traceur politically. Yet the dream of a city of jumpers working outside the flow surely persists as an evocation of political possibility. *It's a bird. It's a plane.* No, it's the traceur, able to leap tall buildings in a single bound. As urban dwellers that are likely to catch glimpses of the traceur in his or her "transports," we shall have more leisure eventually to consider where this figure coincides with, or diverges from, the police and with the social structure of the city.

The polis is the center of economy and democracy and is thus the nexus of an extreme ambivalence about abstraction and presence. If we were to define economy as a cluster of moving abstractions that stand in for our varied desires, we could find a counterpart in democracy as the dream of ourselves being subjects present to ourselves. Economy as absence and democracy as presence. The couplet is a little too neat, but perhaps at the least we should have a provisional sense of the urban medium—just what is it that the traceurs are leaping through, on top of, around? When people are jumping on and off buildings in the city, they are trafficking in an evocative set of binarisms: inside/outside, public/private, here/not here. Traceurs need not be clambering onto the roof of the Palais de Justice for us to get the general sense that they are onto something. Whether democracy and economy are in collision or collusion, the architecture of the city has already traced the history of this interaction. This is true not only because of the particulars of urban configuration—arrangements of buildings that serve to manage and control dissent—but for a more formal and no less important reason, what we might call the *hardness* of cities.

Imagine a soft city, one that might conform more readily to the whimsical nature of the psychogeographer's trajectory: buildings with sails so that the structures weathercock into the wind, buildings with permeable sides so that citizens amble through even where there are no product displays, buildings that serve breakfast but are not there at lunch, no buildings at all, save a compensatory city hall in a set of labile see-through bubbles to ensure maximum transparency. This is probably an overly literal version of what Lisa Robertson would call "soft architecture."[15] Hardness, by contrast, denies contingency and suggests that the city we have is the city we were always going to have, that it has been set in stone because it was always going to have been set that way. Cities of steel and mortar may in fact be soft in the sense that there are likely to have been many cycles of decay and renewal, but to the person in the street this truth is dissimulated by the brute fact of the pitiless material of the city. The subject in capital city is thus asked to submit not so much to the police as to submit to time, to a certain version of retrospective temporality. Life is hard.

Absent City

Paper money's slyly allusive rectangles conjure multiple elsewheres, from Fort Knox to the gestural infinities of product lines. Money is a crinkly vicarious atonement for absence. Abstract, it rephrases the concrete. Is there anything money doesn't mean? As a counterfactual, I could tender Robertson's version of John Ruskin, applauding a whitewash that "shows itself for what it is, and asserts nothing of what is beneath it" (*Soft Architecture*, 140).

We might well take Ruskin's architectural plans, like the self-referential art rectangles of the modernists, at their face value. But when cashiers in Calcutta take orders in real time from McDonald's customers in London, there is a sense in which London *means* Calcutta.[16] Town and countryside have always mutually implicated each other like a pair of "I'm with Stupid" T-shirts, and late capital's urban matrix hardly has time to be itself in the haste with which it hums a threnody of global evocations.[17] Is the city even here?

Politically, the traceur works in no time. Spatially, he or she works nowhere, lofted out in the inner space of the city. Keeping in mind that utopia is literally no place, it is tempting to establish a binarism between the grave, crusty persistence of the city and the ephemeral jinks of the traceurs. But if the city itself isn't there, then, Houston, we have a problem.[18] For their part, traceurs have a faithfulness of correspondence with their host buildings, and this trustworthiness can be calibrated on a mortal scale. "Scaffolding is analogy," writes Robertson. "It explains what a wall is without being a wall" (*Soft Architecture*, 163). Of the explanatory value of traceurs, we shall be able to say more once we can assure ourselves of what a city, to use Robertson's word, "is" (*Soft Architecture*, 163).[19]

Cities appear to be geometric shapes that ought to have a center that could serve as a focal point around which the structure could be organized. But we hardly need to appeal to theories of the uncanny to be spooked by the way in which the center of the globally connected city is elsewhere, making of the city the impossible, a structure without a center.[20] Benjamin considers the possibility of "Dream City": "Paris the dream city—as an aggregate of all the building plans, street layouts, park projects, and street-name systems that were never developed" (*Arcades*, 388, 410).

In *The Shores of Politics*, Rancière says pragmatically, "Utopia is not the elsewhere. . . . It is an intellectual construction which brings a place in thought into conjunction with a perceived or perceptible intuitive space."[21]

But intuition frees a lot of space for elsewheres. Parkour inventor Belle's three-story drops seem unbelievable. As a movement, parkour is insistent on being the good face of urban movement, a movement about movement, self-consciously distancing itself from skateboarding, for example, which has been more confrontational with the police, and parkour theorists speak of reimagining the city in terms that are frankly utopian.

The traceur trains in such a way that his or her body becomes an instrument by which many urban constraints can be reconsidered. At such moments, Belle works in a part of the city's space-time that has never been previously visited. Urban theorist Jane Jacobs's interest in "infilling," increasing urban density by revisiting the empty internal spaces of metropolitan areas rather than consuming more space external to the city, seems of a piece with these vibrant once and future activities (especially to the extent that Jacobs's practical utopias do not come without political risks for their adopters). The city ceaselessly refers elsewhere, yet surely one of the most significant elsewheres is, unfailingly, inside city limits.[22]

How is a city absent? Ricardo Piglia misplaces the absence that is crucial to his version of the city even as he seeks to explain it, as if the need to lose the city rehearses something vital to the urban experience. "The central quality of narrative is this flow, this apparent fleeing movement toward another story line. I have tried to narrate this feeling," he claims, reasonably. "I believe it is the origin of *The Absent City*."[23] Yet it is possible to forget in reading Piglia's summary that the essential and dynamic absence in the book is after all that of a woman, a lover. Her absence is forgotten here, absence itself leaching out even from the privileged authorial summary of urban loss. Henri Lefebvre enacts a similar absence of an absence (to the third degree, in fact) in his reading of the Roman architect Vitruvius, who may have been the first to transpose quasi-omniscient perspectives acquired from sea voyages back onto the urban context. Psychogeographers, too, might well be sympathetic to his project. "The work of the Roman architect contains an elaborate attempt to establish term-by-term correspondences between various elements of social life in the context of spatial practice."[24] Yet Lefebvre calls our attention to a prevailing irony of the work, that the elephant in the room of such spatial chronicling is the city itself. "Though he is speaking of nothing else," Lefebvre writes, "he never addresses it directly."[25] For their part, readers who labor diligently through the esoterica of the "Spatial Architectonics" chapter of Lefebvre's *The Production of Space* (169–228), on the body and its capacity for "occupation," might find relief at a sudden extended and very corporeal quotation from Norman Mailer's *Why Are We in Vietnam?* The quotation itself is not relevant here, but the appearance of it in Lefebvre's book confirms a suspicion that his philosophical considerations have been naming a certain political absence in the French/American context of the occupation of Indochina. This is not to say that this is the "real" focus of the book. But absent city might be a useful rubric for a range of urban affects, occupations, international references.

It seems likely that cities are multiply absent from themselves, like parallel universes in a Borgesian library. Money is a "concrete abstraction," says David Harvey, and we could say that cities are "abstract concretions," reference-rich agglomerations that are also capable of, incidentally, keeping the rain off and providing some shelter.[26]

Attuned to the city's cross-referencing potential, the practical psychogeographer might thus find a certain satisfaction in a mildly dangerous practice like attempting to navigate Toronto with a map of Saigon or Baghdad, which would have affinities with the non sequitur use of buildings implicit in parkour. A map of utopia would serve as well but ought to be strictly adhered to. Could there be a map of the city that is the same size as the city, as in Jorge Luis Borges? Maps work not by reproducing the city but by deleting all of it except a trace. The trepid Toronto traveler might take note of the unused subway stops in the phantom subway tunnel of the old Bay Street line and either see it on YouTube or take advantage of the occasional subway rerouting to film his or her own version. Check out *Infiltration*, the Toronto zine "about going places you're not supposed to go," where you can discover how to negotiate subway tunnels and sewers in the spirit of a gambol, and in a hilarious discussion of the semiotics of warning signs find all the license you will need for your adventures. The founder of the zine, incidentally, died from undisclosed causes.[27] Tour guides that conceptually link the sewers of Toronto with those of, say, Canada's trade partners in the developing world are undoubtedly on the Internet or will be shortly.

What isn't the city? Traceurs are even now scaling the walls. Scaling is the mapmaker's prerogative, putting the city at his or her disposal. We will have an information age when we have the means to rid ourselves of most information, and the search for a search engine commensurate to the task is ongoing. The traceur narrows tumultuous plenitude to a single wall, a single moment. The city is everything else.

Notes

1 In *The Arcades Project*, Walter Benjamin quotes Edmond Jaloux:

> A man who goes for a walk ought not to have to concern himself with any hazards he
> may run into or with the regulations of a city. If an amusing idea enters his head, if a
> curious shopfront comes into view, it is natural that he would want to cross the street
> without confronting dangers such as our grandparents could not have imagined. But
> he cannot do this today without taking a hundred precautions, without checking the
> horizon, without asking the advice of the police department, without mixing with
> a dazed and breathless herd, for whom the way is marked out in advance by bits of
> shining metal. If he tries to collect the whimsical thoughts that may have come to
> mind, very possibly occasioned by sights on the street, he is deafened by car horns.

Benjamin, *The Arcades Project*, ed. Roy Tiedemann, trans. Howard Eiland and Kevin McLaughlin (Cambridge, MA: Belknap Press, 1999), 434. Hereafter cited parenthetically by page number as *Arcades*.

2 Mike Davis, *Planet of Slums* (London: Verso, 2006).

3 *Arcades*, 410; and Anthony Vidler, *"Terres Inconnues*: Cartographies of a Landscape to Be Invented," *October* 115 (Winter 2006): 13–30, 30.

4 Situationist International Online, www.cddc.vt.edu/sionline/ (accessed August 3, 2007).

5 PKTO.ca: A Southern Ontario Parkour Community, http://pkto.ca/parkour.php (accessed August 3, 2007).

6 Slavoj Žižek, afterword to Jacques Rancière, *The Politics of Aesthetics: The Distribution of the Sensible*, trans. Gabriel Rockhill (London: Continuum, 2004), 78.

7 Ibid.

8 Graham, interview by author, Toronto, July 29, 2007.

9 *Jump London*, directed by Mike Christie (London: Channel 4 Television Corp., 2003); *Jump Britain*, directed by Mike Christie (London: Carbon Media Ltd., 2005); *Casino Royale*, directed by Martin Campbell (Los Angeles: Sony Pictures, 2006); and *Live Free or Die Hard*, directed by Len Wiseman (Santa Monica, CA: Cheyenne Enterprises, 2007).

10 Angel Rama, *The Lettered City*, trans. John Charles Chasteen (Durham, NC: Duke University Press, 1996), 27. On the significance of aerial views of the city to Situationist rhetoric, see Vidler, *"Terres Inconnues"*; and David Harvey, *The Urban Experience* (Baltimore, MD: Johns Hopkins University Press, 1989), 1. Also see M. Christine Boyer, "Aviation and the Aerial View: Le Corbusier's Spatial Transformation in the 1930s and 1940s," *Diacritics* 33.3 (Fall–Winter 2003): 93–116.

11 Richard Sennet argued for organic cities against utopian planners of the 1960s who imagined renewed urban sectors first, then demolished neighborhoods and installed their "vision." At best, the results are comical. Sennet, *The Conscience of the Eye: The Design and Social Life of Cities* (New York: W. W. Norton, 1992). See also Bill Bryson, *Notes from a Small Island* (New York: Doubleday, 1999), on attempting to walk in the planned city of Milton Keynes, England.

12 Rancière, *The Politics of Aesthetics*, 15. Hereafter cited parenthetically by page number as *Aesthetics*.

13 On two and three dimensions, Harvey paraphrases Stephen Kern (*The Culture of Time and*

Space, 1880–1918 [London: Cambridge University Press, 1983], 144–52), on the cubists, "whose tensions between 'the world of three dimensions that was their inspiration and the two-dimensionality of painting that was their art' generated canvases that were as fragmented and shattered in their appearance as the urban social landscapes that they often sought to depict." Harvey, *The Urban Experience*, 179.

14 "The trace is the appearance of a nearness, however far removed the thing that left it behind may be" (*Arcades*, 447). On the question of tempo, compare the following: "Poetry and art . . . derive from a 'quick inspection of things' . . . velocity is introduced as an essential feature of artistic intuition: 'that "mind's eye" whose rapid perception can engender within the soul, as on a canvas, the most diverse landscapes of the world.'" Ernst Robert Curtius, quoted in *Arcades*, 436.

15 Lisa Robertson, *Occasional Work and Seven Walks from the Office of Soft Architecture* (Toronto: Coach House Books, 2006). Hereafter cited parenthetically by page number as *Soft Architecture*.

16 Globalization is still a rough sketch, however. It takes twenty-one business days for funds to clear from a check cashed in Toronto drawn on a London bank, and this is between countries whose currency is denominated by the blandly reassuring face of the same queen.

17 In 2007, for example, certain strata of the American working class have been off-shored so quickly they have not yet had time to mourn, and only practiced pessimists have been quick enough to chant the loss. See Joe Bageant, *Deer Hunting with Jesus: Dispatches from America's Class War* (New York: Crown, 2007). "The contradiction between town and country" is a phrase from Marx and Engels quoted by Benjamin in "The Flaneur," *Arcades*, 432.

18 Houston is fifty feet above sea level, and New Orleans is ten feet below. New Orleans thus adds the ontological to a long list of ways in which the emerging city of late capital will not be there.

19 Other phrases from Robertson's scaffolding that seem to more or less directly invoke parkour are "directional lability" and "the negative space of the building" (*Soft Architecture*, 165).

20 The notion of a structure without a center comes, at least, from Jacques Derrida, "Structure, Sign, and Play in the Discourse of the Human Sciences," *Writing and Difference*, trans. Alan Bass (London: Routledge, 1978), 278–94.

21 Jacques Rancière, *On the Shores of Politics*, trans. Liz Heron (London: Verso, 1995), 14–15.

22 Jane Jacobs, *Dark Age Ahead* (Toronto: Vintage, 2004), 217.

23 Ricardo Piglia, *The Absent City*, trans. Sergio Waisman (Durham, NC: Duke University Press, 2000), 141.

24 Henri Lefebvre, *The Production of Space*, trans. Donald Nicholson-Smith (Oxford: Blackwell, 1984), 270.

25 Ibid., 271.

26 Harvey, *The Urban Experience*, 167.

27 Infiltration, "Warning Signs," http://infiltration.org/ethics-warning.html (accessed June 17, 2007). On general sewering techniques, see Urban Exploration Resource, "Sanitary

Sewer," www.uer.ca/forum_showthread.asp?fid=1&threadid=5703 (accessed June 17, 2007). On Paris sewers, consult Joe Kissell, "Paris Sewers: Exploring the Dark Underbelly of the City of Light," Interesting Thing of the Day, January 17, 2005, http://itotd .com/articles/432/paris-sewers/. Paris sewers are wide, and the system parallels the city above it, including street signs at intersections. Benjamin's (inevitable) set of quotations on Paris sewers can be found in *Arcades*, 411–12.

Gregory Tomso

Viral Sex and the Politics of Life

Faced with plague, one can no longer simply go on with business as usual. One is forced to call one's habits, values, and pleasures into question, precisely because the world in which they had a place is in the process of slipping away, disrupted in a way that always feels like an imposition, and seems unjustified, senseless.
—Linda Singer, *Erotic Welfare*

Men who intentionally engage in unsafe sex with other men—barebackers, bug chasers, gift givers, tweakers, virus breeders, those living on the "down low"—are commonly regarded today as murderers and suicides.[1] In the scientific and popular media, "barebackers" and "virus breeders" have been singled out as the targets of moral furor or, among the more liberally minded, as targets of state surveillance and scientific management. In the popular press, outright moral condemnation is not uncommon, nor is the sentimental fearmongering of journalistic exposés.[2] Viral sex, intentionally unsafe sex, produces for all these constituencies the question, "What makes them do it?"[3] Finding an answer to this question is the impetus behind an ever-growing number of public health studies that have, for better and for worse, begun to catalog the rea-

South Atlantic Quarterly 107:2, Spring 2008
DOI 10.1215/00382876-2007-066 © 2008 Duke University Press

sons why some men choose not to use prophylactics.[4] In short: blame, fear, and the impetus to produce knowledge about the motivations of particular sexual subjects are all part of the first wave of responses to what seems to be a mind-boggling set of sexual behaviors that fly in the face of scientific orthodoxy and the instinct for self-preservation.

As an alternative to these approaches, this essay isolates viral sex in the field of power relations that makes it seem so dangerous in the first place, before particular individuals and their personal lives are submitted to scrutiny by the moralist or researcher. Viral sex, as a Foucauldian condition, constitutes a historical phenomenon, the product of a disciplinary discourse that brings to light three initial observations that are obscured by psychologism and morality. First, since the availability of protease inhibitors in 1996, viral sex has emerged as an object of disavowal, scorn, investigation, and surveillance. Whatever else it may be, viral sex is distinctly the result of changes to technological innovations in the management of HIV. Its origin is therefore historical and material as much as it may be biological or psychological. Second, viral sex is rendered intelligible to a large degree through discourses predicated on identity as opposed to choices or acts. These identities are the latest disciplinary products of a regime knowledge that goes at least as far back as the appearance in the nineteenth century of "the homosexual" himself. Third, approaches that seek to understand the meanings of viral sex in terms of an individual's psychology or personal "experience" internalize, in the figure of the individual risk taker or of his aggregated "risk group," what are quite often relations of power external to the subject and his or her psychology. As a result, power dynamics that contribute to the formation of the subject remain obscure in the current analysis of viral sex.

This essay focuses on the third aspect, the problem of power, or what might be called the political economy of viral sex. Viral sex is analyzed not as a crisis to be solved by morality or social science but as the latest development in the phenomenology of homosexuality as it continues to evolve in the era of what Michel Foucault calls "biopower" and within the domain of liberal political rationality. Thus, the term *viral sex* refers, in this analysis, primarily to the discourses describing risky sex between men. In reading these discourses collectively, and often at face value, I temporarily set aside important epidemiological questions concerning the frequency of, and distinctions among, the risky sexual behaviors they describe.

Viral sex, as a discursive field, provides a philosophical and historical opportunity for thinking about sexual politics in ways not organized around the traditional liberal subject. Instead, it challenges coercive modes of sexual subjugation through a unique form of biopolitical resistance to state power. Thinking biopolitically provides a way to organize political resistance around a critique of subjugation as opposed to the state-centered notions of citizenship, rights, and sovereignty. As Andrew Barry and others have noted, a move "beyond the state" leads to "a politics of life, of ethics, which emphasizes the crucial political value of the mobilization and shaping of individual capacities and conduct."[5] Viral sex calls into question the political meanings of life that emerge within the liberal discourse of natural rights and state-centered notions of sovereign power. By doing so, it reopens, in a way not subject to liberalism's constraints, the question of sexual freedom.

As gay men near the end of the third decade of the HIV/AIDS epidemic, what, if anything, is left of the liberal notion of sexual freedom? This is a question that queer theory has inherited, in one important way at least, from Foucault, for whom the answer could not have taken into account the longevity and reach of the epidemic to date. At a time when many gay men no longer feel at liberty to pursue their sexual freedom, at least not in the same way Foucault did in the late 1970s and early 1980s, it is soberingly clear that liberalism does not guarantee sexual freedom. Rather, as Foucault himself suggests, freedom is a horizon in which we continuously renegotiate the terms of our own subjugation.[6] In its pursuit of sexual freedom, viral sex suggests new forms of political action distinct from the liberal politics of the "new gay center" in the United States—those of the Human Rights Campaign, for example, which ardently pursues the liberal political "good" of same-sex marriage.

Since the rise of protease inhibitors in the mid-1990s, life with HIV has become, for many people in Western countries, immanently more livable, as the possibility of an extended future with HIV unfolds. The new culture of viral sex is one of the most vital and precious products of this technological achievement. While the possibility of a life, or a future, with HIV was practically unthinkable in the first decade of the epidemic, that state of affairs has changed for many of those with the means to afford the new drugs, for those who cannot sustain the panic mentality of the 1980s and early 1990s, and for those who have come of age after the epidemic's initial years of collective mourning and trauma. While viral sex does not lead to an upbeat, liberal politics organized around the "pursuit of happiness" in the Jeffersonian sense, it does invite a serious reconsideration of what a politics of life might look like. Viral sex points in the illiberal direction of a politics of illness and epidemic, a politics of enduring loss that nevertheless still makes room for the pursuit of pleasure. Its most important political "goods" are the literal and symbolic life of the body and the dominant discourses through which such life becomes politically viable.

The Political Economy of Viral Sex

The political value of viral sex emerges through its conflicted relationship with liberalism and neoliberalism. Particularly in terms of liberal identity politics in the United States, one of the most radical aspects of the culture of viral sex is the unprecedented proliferation of male sexual identities that it has spawned. Defined by the risk of viral transmission and the pleasures of same-sex eroticism, the new identities of risk endemic to the culture of viral sex are commensurate neither with "homosexuality" nor "gayness," nor even, at least not fully, with the academically mandated, antinormative politics of "queerness." Instead of providing the ground for a relatively stable, politically resonant claim to oppositional sexual identity, the new identities of risk serve in many instances to eschew political recognition. As one barebacking Web site puts it, "Our guys f—k and suck without any barriers, lectures or bullshit."[7] Rather than serving as an embarrassment to mainstream gays (as queens and leather men often do), those who practice viral sex often pursue pleasures that fall outside the purview of gay identity as such. Is viral sex the political vanguard of a postgay world?

Historically coincident with the rise of gay centrism and social assimilationism, viral sex functions as a foil to those gays who see themselves as "virtually normal," challenging the rational, ethical, and identitarian norms of liberal gay politics.[8] To make this claim is not to celebrate barebackers and other risk takers as heroes or as stylish "dissenters," but both to limit and to resist the ethical, moral, social-scientific, and psychological habits of thought that reduce viral sex to a crisis of (gay) sexual subjectivity. Can viral sex not be more productively read as a historical shift in dominant modes of sexual representation and constructions of healthy individualism? Those who engage in risky sex refuse not only to be "virtually normal" but also to be safe and even, at times, to be well. The most radical gesture made by discourses about bug chasing, gift giving, and other forms of risk taking may be, then, not their rejection of gay identity, but their symbolic and sometimes literal refusal of rational, state-supported notions of human well-being. In this regard, viral sex poses ethical challenges to progressives and conservatives alike, regardless of their attitude toward "homosexuality." It is precisely at this point of estrangement from mainstream political values that a stringent critique of the politics of the subject, in both its liberal and neoliberal incarnations, becomes crucial.

Neither liberalism nor neoliberalism can respond to viral sex as anything but a major ethical or moral crisis. Viral sex leads, on the one hand, to a crisis in liberal ethics to the extent that liberals must decide between regard for the sexual freedom of the individual or the sacrifice of such freedom for the good of the many. In this view, the mandates of public health, as dictated by the state, compete with individual and collective claims to sexual freedom. "Super confidential" (as opposed to anonymous) HIV testing and mandatory partner reporting for HIV-positive persons are classic liberal examples of the state's encroachment on individual rights to privacy and personal liberty, and one could say the same about the recent emergence of viral sex as a public health crisis. Public health, in this sense, can be understood as a form of state-sponsored violence against the rights of the individual. Neoliberalism, on the other hand, is far less concerned with the ideal of sexual freedom than classic liberalism. Neoliberalism brings notions of economic efficiency, rationality, and risk aversion to the conduct of affairs not traditionally associated with the economy, such as the management of life and health.[9] According to neoliberal rationality, one should confidently stand behind a state- and corporate-sponsored version of "expert" truths on health and safety while developing "compassion" (if not outright moral condemnation) for those whose needs, desires, and behaviors place them outside the norm. The aim is to ensure the sexual health of individuals who, entitled by the state and within the confines of what the state deems morally acceptable, have access to private assets that allow them to protect their own health. "Compassion" for those who fall outside the boundaries of entitlement (such as certain immigrants) and conventional morality (promiscuous "gay" men) allows for an essentially sentimental response—indeed, one that is cherished within the ethos of Protestant piety—that maintains the social, legal, and political invisibility of the marginal. Those who can become increasingly healthy and feel virtuous for doing so and those who lack the necessary economic, cultural, and social capital experience a widening gap between themselves and the entitled while being blamed for their personal shortcomings.

Nowhere is the cultural influence of neoliberalism more apparent than in the field of public health, focused as it is today on health promotion, risk management, and "lifestyle" change. As a form of governmentality, public health alters self-conduct and self-perception, as when people voluntarily change their behaviors—sexual, dietary, and otherwise—in the pursuit of health and become "health consumers" and "health promoters" in the course of their professions or everyday lives. In its specifically neoliberal incarnation, public health suggests efficient ways to preserve and manage the life of a population by making individuals morally responsible for their own health. Perhaps the most striking example of this rationality in the United States to date appears in recent efforts to reform Medicaid. In the state of West Virginia, for instance, patients must sign a pledge "to do my best to stay healthy," as part of new, federally backed efforts to promote "personal responsibility" in health care.[10] Those who refuse to sign the pledge or to attend mandatory antiobesity or antismoking classes can be denied medical benefits available to other, more "responsible" citizens. Thus, to be unhealthy in a neoliberal, biopolitical regime is not only to be sick or suffering but also to be inefficient, selfish, irresponsible, and irrational—and to be an economic burden on the state.

As the HIV/AIDS epidemic has unfolded in the West, safe-sex education campaigns have augmented neoliberalism's links to the biopolitics of AIDS by creating the idea of a rational actor who, taken as the generic subject of public health, is thought to possess a personal responsibility to protect his or her life and health.[11] As a result, protecting oneself and others from HIV infection today is widely regarded as a moral and legal duty in which rational behavior ensures the well-being of individual and society alike. This focus on the rational subject helps to explain how the political aspects of viral sex have become so difficult to pin down, namely because traditional safe-sex discourses remove viral sex from its cultural context, reducing its fundamentally political and historical tensions to intrinsic qualities of the individual. In effect, neoliberalism makes adhering to the biopolitical norm of health seem like a profoundly personal, ethical choice, to the extent that individual subjects internalize the demand to protect and foster life in accordance with state reason. In other words, neoliberalism helps to naturalize biopolitical aims.

By contrast, in terms of political economy, viral sex is a claim to sexual freedom, a problem in the history of liberalism as it is "haunted" by the contemporary biopolitics of HIV and AIDS.[12] The hegemony of biopolitical governance, facilitated by the proliferation of safer sex campaigns and, more generally, by the rise of the "new" public health with its emphasis on risk management,[13] has clouded the issue of liberal freedom, particularly sexual freedom, in ways that Foucault could not have foreseen, given how early his death came in the epidemic. Yet for many gay men, especially those who have been hit disproportionately hard by the AIDS epidemic and who are now faced with a complicated array of choices regarding their sexual lives, questions of sexual freedom are especially difficult. At stake in any act of sex between two men is a complex series of questions about the economy of health and pleasure, about the interrelation of care of the self and care of others, and about the very meaning and value of life itself. While the same might be said of sex between any two people, gay or straight, male or female, these issues are now weighing heavily on gay men in particular because they face the challenge of rebuilding gay culture, and especially gay sexual culture, after the initial (and ongoing, in some parts of the world) devastation of AIDS.[14] As the thirty-year-old epidemic continues and gay men experiment with alternatives to the safe-sex mantras of "abstinence first" or "use a condom every time," the problem of how to conduct oneself in the face of sexual freedom looms large. One of the most urgent questions facing gay men today is about how to practice sexual freedom in the extended shadow of the epidemic, especially now that strict adherence to the orthodoxy of safe sex is no longer the only imaginable option for the ethical conduct of homosexual life.

If there is a nascent sexual politics to be gleaned from viral sex, it is not, liberally speaking, a politics of the subject, nor is it a politics directed at a single political good, such as the right to marry. Instead, viral sex may constitute, as Foucault would say, a "practice of freedom" in response to configurations of power specific to early-twenty-first-century life in the United States.[15] One way viral sex does this is through its connection to HIV itself. The new identities of risk herald a relocation of the symbolic site of sexual identity within the body, a shift from a conceptual model of biological immanence (where sexuality is contained, privately and inviolately, within the body) to one of exchange and supplementarity (where sexual identity is predicated on bodily states or behaviors that result from shared experiences of transmission and outlaw forms of fluid exchange). The language of feeding, seeding, and breeding commonly used today in Internet chat rooms and personal ads exemplifies this difference. As the personal ad for one would-be virus breeder in San Francisco puts it: "Really get into nasty top men breeding my ass . . . walkin [*sic*] and use my holes. drop a load and go, Little or no talking. Just dump a load and go. Have one load [of semen] in me now. Seeking a few more tonight. Front door opens in an hour." Another ad reads, "Looking for a RAW top to take out this aggression on my hole! seed me deep and then leave."[16] The emphasis in these examples on exchanging and collecting semen draws on a different set of representational norms from those involved in experiencing, as Foucault would say, the "truth" of one's homosexuality. The eroticism of male-male sexual contact is predicated not on finding another person who shares one's hidden identity but in experiencing the transfer of a charged "load" from one man to another. The ability of semen to "breed" and "seed" does not result, in this case, from its potential to fertilize an egg inside a woman's body, but instead results from its ability to transmit and replicate HIV inside another man. Especially in the first example, the more "loads" the receptive partner collects—hoards, even—the more thrilling the contact with other men becomes.

In addition to the language of breeding and seeding, the discourses of viral sex have given rise to a complicated system of signs in which the signifiers "bug" and "gift" metonymically substitute for the virus itself, highlighting its ties to a metaphorical economy of excess and exchange. "Bug chasing" and "gift giving" are, at their core, economic metaphors, semiotic indicators of excessive forms of exchange or circulation that run counter to the hyperrational economics of risk society. While bugs and gifts may, at first glance, appear to have little in common, they are both closely related in terms of gift economy.[17] Gifts, like bugs and viruses, circulate in society and in the environment in ways that are not easily subject to regulatory laws or to attempts to curtail or monitor their movements. Bugs are especially powerful metaphors in this regard. Bugs are ubiquitous, stalwart, teeming with life; they find ways of reproducing in vast numbers even in the face of extraordinary deprivation; they resist our real and figural attempts to exterminate them; and despite the ravages of nature and technology, they endure. Bugs disrupt our best-laid plans, block our chosen paths, devalue our property and our investments, and imperil our health. They are intelligible almost exclusively in terms of collectivity, refusing the logic of separateness and rendering individualism absurd. Like gifts, bugs confound the terms of both classic and neoliberal economics and challenge the atomism that they foster. Both gifts and bugs make powerful symbols of outlaw forms of exchange, reproduction, and affiliation. Does it come as any surprise that certain Western men, during this interminable middle phase of the AIDS pandemic, would invent the symbolic practices of gift giving and bug chasing not as a psychologically aberrant means of seeking individual death but as a historically contingent, symbolic means of ensuring collective survival?

The emerging signs of excess in the political economy of viral sex are developments consistent with what cultural theorist Linda Singer has called the production of "erotic surplus" in the time of epidemics.[18] Singer's work analyzes the political economy, especially the sexual economy, of the AIDS epidemic. In *Erotic Welfare*, she shows how "sexuality . . . can be thought of as a political economy, a systemic grid of differences which produce, circulate, and order value" (34). Specifically, Singer argues that epidemics produce both an increase in technologies of population management—"a mobilized effort of control" (27)—and a "proliferative surplus" (121) of new forms of pleasures and new demands on the body. Counting "safe sex" as a primary example of that surplus, Singer distrusts such developments to the extent that they solidify neoliberal safeguards that liken bodily management to portfolio management. Analyzing the surplus sexual economies of pornography, prostitution, and addiction, Singer traces the ways in which these economies, shaped in the era of AIDS by what she calls "epidemic logic," have produced new subjects and pleasures incited by the market imperatives of profit making and workforce management that complement efforts at social-sexual control in times of epidemic disease (39). Yet, as Judith Butler notes, "Hegemonic power tends to produce an *excess of value* that it cannot fully control."[19] Barebacking, bug chasing, and gift giving appear to be part of this unanticipated excess, the erotic surplus of the AIDS pandemic.

The symbolic excesses of viral sex function as a kind of political communication—one not necessarily legible at the level of the individual subject—whose semiotic and economic intelligibility is made ripe through the metonymy of "bugs" and "gifts." As such, viral sex represents an intensification and extension, in specifically economic terms, of the politically resistant, identity- and subjectivity-altering effects and of certain forms of male-male sex celebrated by queer theory. David Halperin explains that sadomasochism, for example, was important to Foucault because it "represents a re-mapping of the body's erotic sites . . . a breakup of the erotic monopoly traditionally held by the genitals," adding that sadomasochism "make[s] possible the creation of a masculine sexual identity that need no longer be centered in the penis."[20] It is precisely through such challenges to identity that seemingly private sexual acts become, in effect, political ones.

There are, however, some important differences in the ways sadomasochism and viral sex disrupt the formation of male sexual subjects. Whereas queer theory has traditionally recognized the temporary dissolution of the sexual subject (the experience of jouissance) achieved through sadomasochism, viral sex is not so much a shattering force as it is an additive one. Viral sex could include all or none of the sexual practices traditionally associated with gay jouissance, since what defines viral sex is whether it carries the risk of infection with HIV. This difference highlights the status of HIV as a gift, the sign of a certain excess, or a token of exchange, that alters the traditional economy of male sexual subjectivity in which masculinity must be maintained, conserved, and guarded. In the context of viral sex, the self-shattering of jouissance becomes less important than the process of subjective *supplementation* in which the transmission of the virus (in gift giving, bug chasing, and viral "breeding") or the "raw" exchange of semen permitted by condomless sex (in barebacking) do not so much destroy the masculine subject as alter it by adding something foreign (and potentially fatal) to it.

Research conducted by social scientist Damien Ridge bears out this claim. The following is a description of barebacking offered by "Nic," a participant in a qualitative study of the meanings of male-male sex: "And it's like . . . it's almost like this man is injecting some of his masculinity into me . . . giving me some of that. And so I find it [receptive anal sex] a very augmenting experience as opposed to a diminishing experience. . . . In a sense, it's sort of like me taking something from him."[21] From the perspective of political economy, Nic's response is striking because it highlights the economic terms in which he experiences the thrill of another man's masculinity. Echoing the outlaw economies of bugs and gifts described earlier, Nic suggests here an economy in which masculinity might be "taken" according to the terms of a symbolic order in which semen metonymically stands in for "something" much more valuable, if intangible, perhaps an idealized or authentic masculinity. The thrill of barebacking results from adding to or "augmenting" one's own limited stores of a precious and desired commodity. Here, the transfer and acquisition of sperm functions as a type of commodity fetishism in which sperm magically

accesses the fantasmatic ideal of masculinity, creating meanings and pleasures far in excess of sperm's clinical existence as a potentially dangerous
bodily excretion. While tightly bound to economic logic and to the structure of the commodity fetish, viral sex resists the intensification of neoliberal subjugation by fully embracing its terms. The economic metaphors of
excess—theft, breeding, gift, and augmentation—that distinguish viral sex
demonstrate the centrality of economic rationality to the erotics of viral and
seminal exchange that are crucial to the seemingly individual experience of
masculinity.

Despite their differences, the practices of sadomasochism and viral sex
serve as good examples of what Foucault calls "becoming homosexual."[22]
Becoming homosexual—or, more specifically, "coming out" as gay—is not,
in Foucault's view, about adopting a fixed identity, aesthetic style, or psychology, but is about forging new "relational possibilities"[23] or new "affec-
tive and relational virtualities."[24] He therefore emphasizes the deliberate
choices men might make in the practice of sadomasochism to forge new
relations with others that can lead to a new way of life ("mode de vie") ("Triumph," 158). The same could also be said about viral sex, but not without
taking stock of the changes in homosexual life due to HIV and AIDS and of
the intensification of neoliberal and biopolitical controls in the conduct of
everyday life.

As compelling as Foucault's thinking about becoming homosexual
remains today, it nevertheless emerges from a particular moment in the
history of homosexuality that, just before the dawn of AIDS, is arguably
more optimistic than today's. To remain useful, his ideas need to be read
in the context of his own historical analysis of liberalism and subject to
the very same scrutiny that Foucault himself brings to other forms of
discourse. Specifically, the conflict between individual liberty, achieved
through the minimization of government, and "reason of state," expressed
through biopolitics, became the point of departure for Foucault's later work
on the ethics of self-care, which includes his thinking about the conduct
of homosexual life. At the heart of Foucauldian ethics is the practice of
freedom. "Freedom," he once said, "is the ontological condition of ethics.
But ethics is the considered form that freedom takes when it is informed
by reflection."[25] Yet in his interviews on homosexuality, Foucault does not
often pause to elaborate philosophically or historically on the nature of this
freedom. Is sexual freedom, for example, a specifically liberal freedom for

Foucault? The answer to this question seems to be yes, at least to the extent that Foucault makes clear in his interviews that homosexual becoming begins with individual freedom achieved in the liberal sense.

Foucault's problem with liberation politics, and what has been called for almost two decades "identity politics," begins when those politics become an end unto themselves. He repeatedly points out that the recognition of sexual identity and of the basic rights of sexual choice should be the beginning, not the end, of homosexual life. In particular, Foucault notes that the danger of liberalism is not that it offers the possibility of freedom, but that it too frequently links the idea of freedom to a discourse of "natural" rights that are thought to be immanent to the liberal subject. As an alternative to the struggle to liberate this mythical force, Foucault suggests that the discourse of liberal rights be altered to encompass "a new relational right that permits all possible types of relations to exist and not be prevented, blocked, or annulled by impoverished relational institutions" ("Triumph," 158). This view helps to explain why Foucault did not necessarily advocate for liberal rights such as gay marriage, since he viewed marriage as an "impoverished" form of social relation.[26] Once a certain measure of liberal freedom has been achieved, Foucault argues that fighting for liberal equality in areas such as the right to marry constitutes only "slight" progress ("Triumph," 158). Thus, it seems fair to say that liberal rights and liberal freedom were not in and of themselves contradictory to Foucault's understanding of homosexual ethics; rather, their achievement constitutes an essential and ongoing part of those ethics, but only insofar as liberalism refrains from positing a natural essence internal to the liberal subject and from imitating the form of existing social institutions.

Viral Sex as Biopolitical Resistance

The enduring political "good" of viral sex is that it points to the possibility of specifically biopolitical forms of resistance to coercive regimes of power. Furthermore, it suggests that the goals of biopolitical resistance will be to challenge the meanings of health or of illness whenever those concepts place unwelcome restrictions on the practice of sexual freedom. Biopolitical resistance moves toward the horizons of life, inhabiting those places where life takes on political meaning, and contests, at their thinnest points, the discourses and practices through which life becomes subjected to political power. This is quite different from seeking "a place at the table" in the liberal body politic.[27] Thinking about resistance biopolitically makes sense today, when liberal appeals to the state seem to be, at best, an endgame. The aim of biopolitical resistance is not liberation from power but a *better form of rule* in which the body and its pleasure can be fruitfully reimagined, experimented with, and rendered unfamiliar.[28]

Surrounding viral sex today is not what Foucault once called the "empty space" of sexual freedom but a bitter political struggle over the meaning of life itself ("Triumph," 160). If biopolitical "reason of state" aims to preserve and foster life for the sake of strengthening the state and sustaining its economic well-being, viral sex presents an immediate challenge to those aims. It resists neoliberal, biopolitical governmentality by calling into question the meanings of health and survival, mobilizing those concepts in direct opposition to the state-supported aims of public health. Eric Rofes has argued that the decision to engage in unsafe sex exposes "fundamental distinctions in the ways gay men conceptualize life in the epidemic," adding that it is "difficult for many to imagine a moral system which prioritizes pleasure or whatever meaning one derives from unprotected anal sex over long-term survival."[29] For this reason, viral sex is likely to remain an intractable problem in contemporary political life, very much like abortion in the United States. Unlike abortion, however, viral sex poses equal challenges to all ideological constituencies, regardless of one's attitude toward "homosexuality" and regardless of whether one espouses a traditional liberal or neoliberal view of government. For those on both the political Right and Left, men who put themselves at risk tend to elicit one of two essentially sentimental responses: either condemnation or compassion. For conservatives, such men appear to be beyond "our" reach and deserve their fate; for progressives, gay men desperately need "our" help. In both instances, those who engage in viral sex become sentimentally bound, by compassion, hate, or fear, to a position of high visibility on the margins of mainstream political life.[30]

Historically speaking, it comes as no surprise that viral sex has emerged as a "problem" at this particular point in time. The early twenty-first century is a time in Western history when the very concept of life itself has been significantly opened to political struggle. In areas such as abortion rights, assisted suicide and vegetative life support, genetic screening and therapy, and stem cell research—to name just a few examples from the United States—the concept of life is a political battleground. While it would be impossible to do justice here to the distinctive but often overlapping histories of these examples, what they suggest is that the early twenty-first century is a time in which a new "vital politics," or a politics of life itself, has begun to emerge.[31] Distinct from but emerging out of the life politics of the eighteenth and nineteenth centuries that focused on birth and death rates, sanitation, and hygiene, this new politics of life, according to Nikolas Rose, "is concerned with our growing capacities to control, manage, engineer, reshape, and modulate the very vital capacities of human beings as living creatures."[32] Especially important to this new politics is the concept of risk. The management of life today focuses on "those individuals, groups or localities where risk is seen to be high. The binary distinctions of normal and pathological, which were central to earlier biopolitical analyses, are now organized within these strategies for the government of risk."[33] The biopolitical problem of viral sex is, quite clearly, a case in point, offering up for biopolitical management a whole new class of risky individuals (barebackers, bug chasers, gift givers, virus breeders, tweakers) as well as the larger and more familiar "risk group" of gay men in general.

The technological and epistemological changes that have, in recent decades, contributed to this new politicization of life have, in the United States, been accompanied by the intensification of an ideological claim on life that links the sustenance of life to the health and strength of the nation. Evidence of this fact can be found in what President George W. Bush calls the "culture of life," something he routinely cites as one of America's most cherished political and moral goods.[34] This particular ideology represents the union of neoconservative social values and biopolitical governmental imperatives whose recent manifestations include the South Dakota legislative challenges to abortion, the acrimonious legal battle over sustaining the life of Terri Schiavo in Florida, and the decision to force-feed prisoners on hunger strike at the U.S. prison camp at Guantánamo Bay, Cuba. Each of these highly politicized events highlights a now familiar, conservative valuation of life frequently defended in the terms of its sanctity, divinity, and preciousness, even in the midst of war. As Dr. William Winkenwerder Jr., U.S. assistant secretary of defense for health affairs, said in defense of the force-feedings at Guantánamo (which many onlookers described as torture), "The objective in any circumstance is to protect and sustain a person's life."[35] As a chief proponent of the culture of life, Bush has used the phrase literally hundreds of times as part of his official presidential rhetoric. He has, for example, spoken of the nation's "commitment to building a culture of life where all individuals are welcomed in life and protected in law," adding elsewhere that this will be "a welcoming culture, never excluding, never dividing, never despairing and always affirming the goodness of life in all its seasons."[36] The gestures to universality here—"never excluding," "always affirming," "life in all its seasons"—are limited, however, because of their narrow grounding in a conservative vision of liberal inclusiveness that opposes abortion, promotes heterosexual "family values," cuts social services to the poor and needy, and requires abstinence advocacy as a precondition for AIDS relief. Bush's language highlights the way in which neoconservative valuations of life have been naturalized both as moral "goodness" and as properly belonging to the domain of government whose work, it seems, is to ensure that life is "protected in law." Through rhetorical linkages like this one, the biopolitical imperative to preserve and foster life becomes a silent warrant for the neoconservative defense of life.

One might say that, as a political gesture, the power of viral sex lies in its ability to deconstruct the opposition between life and nonlife as it operates within the culture of life. By putting life at risk, viral sex opens the space of *différance* between political life—life as it is explicitly defined through discourses of neoliberalism and biopower, as it is in the culture of life—and bare life. Life deliberately exposed to risk *differs* from healthy life as defined by neoliberal rationalism, as it *defers* from precious, inviolable, and divinely sanctioned life mandated by the culture of life. Thus, life-at-risk, especially when that risk is deliberate, more closely resembles bare life: life that cannot be counted as life in the political sense, yet life that also cannot be adequately mourned, since many see it as life that has been squandered, a death synonymous with suicide or murder.[37] In opposition to this way of thinking, viral sex demonstrates how the meaning of life is violently conflicted and open to revision.

Perhaps the best starting point for biopolitical resistance will be new experiences of mourning.[38] This includes acceptance of the fact that seeking an end to viral sex entails the death of the new pleasures and human relations occasioned by the exchange of HIV. The pursuit of health produces, as a kind of by-product, a certain melancholia. The fact that biomedicine and rational health promotion cannot bring about an end to AIDS is one of the many failures of modern biopolitics, one that produces an unfulfillable longing alongside its most heroic efforts. As the starting point of biopolitical resistance, mourning's most important aim would be to acknowledge biopower's broken promises.

If health, productivity, and longevity mark the success of biopolitical rule, then chronic illness represents the limits of that rule through its detrimental claims on health, work, and life span. Although Foucault argues that death is the ultimate limit to power in the age of biopower, I would add that chronic illness and especially the deliberate choice to become chronically ill are highly effective forms of resistance against such power.[39] One might call out the limit of biopower by choosing to end one's existence, thereby refusing the modes of subjugation associated with the bureaucratic administration of life, but death will always remain a fixed signifier in this particular economy of life. Death is not, in this sense, strategic, but rather is absolute: it marks the limit of power without necessarily intervening in its continued operation. By contrast, chronic illness and HIV infection, in particular, remain a threatening and therefore potentially powerful mode of embodiment. The long, slow engagement with illness that frequently characterizes HIV infection mobilizes, even as it threatens to exhaust, the vast individual and collective resources stockpiled in the name of the biopolitical management of life. While biopolitics aims at optimization of the workforce, ensuring the availability and productivity of labor, chronic illness and death are not, to put it bluntly, good for the bottom line.[40]

Not since the late nineteenth century has chronic illness possessed such strong connections to both cultural and economic capital. Entire industries have sprung up around the management of chronic illness on a global scale, while the cultural integration of chronic illness into the practices of everyday life has been so pervasive that chronicity is now regarded as a "lifestyle" as much as it is a medical condition. These cultural developments coincide with a rising tide of economic complaints—legitimized by the expertise of the social sciences and fiscal watchdogs—that point to the fact that chronic illness is one of the most expensive of all social problems, leading to exorbitant costs for governments, private citizens, hospitals, and insurers. Chronic illness functions, therefore, as a kind of engine within the domain of political economy, affording the movement of capital—measured today in the billions of dollars—while helping to incite new identities and a wide range of cultural productions. The aim of biopolitical resistance is to intervene within this political economy, not to "contain costs" or to "promote health" (the only solutions that ever seem to gain much recognition) but to more fully comprehend HIV as a part of life that must, for the foreseeable future, be endured. In this way, viral sex functions as a "noninstrumental affirmation" of life, that is, of life affirmed not in hopes of an impending cure, or in terms of a "compassionate" reintegration into bour-

geois society, or even in those of reincorporation into the optimized workings of capitalist productivity.⁴¹ To the extent that viral sex works against
the standards of life's normalization, it poses an alternative to the paucity of
options for those whose lives might very well be managed out of existence
in societies acutely focused on the containment of risk. The metaphors
of bugs and gifts that mark the intransigence of HIV are harbingers of a
future in which HIV has not been vanquished by biomedicine and public
health. Instead, they function as an imposition, one that insists on making
HIV more ubiquitous. They are a sign of the fragility of time, acting counter
to the future seen through the biopolitical and neoliberal optimization of
life. Coming to terms with the enormity of HIV and AIDS means imagining a time when large numbers of bodies may not be fully optimized for
work, for rational living, or for liberal "happiness."

Notes

1   *Barebacking*: intentional unprotected anal sex between two men. *Bug chasing*: intentional
    unprotected anal sex performed in order to become infected with HIV. *Gift giving*: inten-
    tional unprotected anal sex performed in order to infect another person with HIV. *Virus
    breeding*: the deliberate sexual exchange of HIV between men. *Tweaking*: using crystal
    methamphetamine, which many see as contributing to unsafe sex among gay men. For
    more on these practices, see Tim Dean, *Unlimited Intimacy: Reflections on the Subculture
    of Barebacking* (Chicago: University of Chicago Press, forthcoming); Perry N. Halkitis
    et al., *Barebacking: Psychosocial and Public Health Approaches* (Binghamton, NY: Haworth,
    2006); David M. Halperin, *What Do Gay Men Want? An Essay on Sex, Risk, and Subjec-
    tivity* (Ann Arbor: University of Michigan Press, 2007); Dave Holmes, Patrick O'Byrne,
    and Denise Gastaldo, "Raw Sex as Limit Experience: A Foucauldian Analysis of Unsafe
    Anal Sex between Men," *Social Theory and Health* 4.4 (2006): 319–33; David A. Mosko-
    witz and Michael E. Roloff, "The Existence of a Bug Chasing Subculture," *Culture, Health,
    and Sexuality* 9.4 (2007): 347–57; Frank Sanello, *Tweakers: How Crystal Meth Is Ravaging
    Gay America* (Los Angeles: Alyson Books, 2005); Michael Shernoff, *Without Condoms:
    Unprotected Sex, Gay Men, and Barebacking* (New York: Routledge, 2005); and Gregory
    Tomso, "Barebacking, Bug Chasing, and the Risks of Care," *Literature and Medicine* 23
    (Spring 2004): 88–111.

2   See Larry Kramer, *The Tragedy of Today's Gays* (New York: Tarcher, 2005); Dan Savage,
    "Bug Chasers," Savage Love, *The Stranger* (Seattle), January 30, 2003, www.thestranger
    .com/seattle/SavageLove?oid=13241; Gregory A. Freeman, "In Search of Death," *Rolling
    Stone*, February 6, 2003, 44–48; and *The Gift*, written and directed by Louise Hogarth
    (Los Angeles: Dream Out Loud Productions, 2000).

3   I am not the first to use the phrase "viral sex." Most notably, it is the title of a book by
    Jaap Gaudsmit, *Viral Sex: The Nature of AIDS* (New York: Oxford University Press, 1992).
    I take up the phrase in a different context here.

4   See, for example, Barry D. Adam et al., "AIDS Optimism, Condom Fatigue, or Self-Esteem? Explaining Unsafe Sex among Gay and Bisexual Men," *Journal of Sex Research* 42.3 (2005): 238–48; Mark Davis, "HIV Prevention Rationalities and Serostatus in the Risk Narratives of Gay Men," *Sexualities* 5.3 (2002): 282–99; Perry N. Halkitis and J. T. Parsons, "Intentional Unsafe Sex (Barebacking) among HIV-Positive Gay Men Who Seek Sexual Partners on the Internet," *AIDS Care* 15.3 (2003): 367–78; Susan Kippax and Kane Race, "Sustaining Safe Practice: Twenty Years On," *Social Science and Medicine* 57 (2003): 1–12; Kane D. Race, "Revaluation of Risk among Gay Men," *AIDS Education and Prevention* 15 (2003): 4369–81; Damien Thomas Ridge, "'It Was an Incredible Thrill': The Social Meanings and Dynamics of Younger Gay Men's Experiences of Barebacking in Melbourne," *Sexualities* 7.3 (2004): 259–79; and Nicolas Sheon and G. Michael Crosby, "Ambivalent Tales of HIV Disclosure in San Francisco," *Social Science and Medicine* 58 (2004): 2105–18.

5   Andrew Barry, Thomas Osborne, and Nikolas Rose, *Foucault and Political Reason: Liberalism, Neo-Liberalism, and Rationalities of Government* (London: University College London Press, 1996), 1.

6   Michel Foucault, "The Ethics of the Concern for Self as a Practice of Freedom," in *Ethics: Subjectivity and Truth*, ed. Paul Rabinow (New York: New Press, 1997), 281–301.

7   Bareback.com, www.bareback.com (accessed August 3, 2007).

8   The phrase is the title of a book by Andrew Sullivan, *Virtually Normal* (New York: Vintage, 1996).

9   As Wendy Brown defines it, *neoliberalism* is a political rationality that "while foregrounding the market, is not only or even primarily focused on the economy." Rather, "it involves *extending and disseminating market values to all institutions and social action,* even as the market remains a distinctive player." Brown, "Neoliberalism and the End of Liberal Democracy," in *Edgework: Critical Essays on Knowledge and Politics* (Princeton, NJ: Princeton University Press, 2005), 39–40. Neoliberalism, then, is more than a set of economic priorities; it, too, might best be understood in terms of Foucauldian governmentality, as a rationality "that produces subjects, forms of citizenship and behavior, and a new organization of the social" (37). For more on neoliberalism, see Michel Foucault, "The Birth of Biopolitics," in *Ethics*, 73–80, esp. 74. (This reference is to Foucault's summary of his lectures at the Collège de France in 1979. The full English translation of the lectures on biopolitics has not yet appeared but is forthcoming by Palgrave Macmillan.) For the full version of the lectures in French, see Foucault, *Naissance de la Biopolitique: Cours au Collège de France (1978–1979)* (Paris: Gallimard and Seuil, 2004). For a useful and readily accessible English overview of these lectures, see Thomas Lemke, "'The Birth of Biopolitics': Michel Foucault's Lectures at the Collège de France on Neo-liberal Governmentality," *Economy and Society* 30.2 (2001): 190–207. For more on neoliberalism, see Lisa Duggan, *The Twilight of Equality? Neoliberalism, Cultural Politics, and the Attack on Identity* (Boston: Beacon, 2003); and David Harvey, *A Brief History of Neoliberalism* (New York: Oxford University Press, 2005).

10   Erick Eckholm, "Medicaid Plan Prods Patients toward Health," *New York Times*, December 1, 2006.

11   For a further elaboration of this point, see Adam et al., "AIDS Optimism, Condom Fatigue, or Self-Esteem?"; and Davis, "HIV Prevention Rationalities." See also Deborah Lupton,

ed., *Risk and Sociocultural Theory* (Cambridge: Cambridge University Press, 2005), especially the essay by Mitchell Dean, "Risk, Calculable and Incalculable," 131–59; and Alan Petersen and Robin Bunton, eds., *Foucault, Health and Medicine* (New York: Routledge, 1997).

12 In his 1979 "The Birth of Biopolitics" lectures at the Collège de France, Foucault explores a fundamental tension between "reason of state" and liberalism. One, he says, has always "haunted" the other (79). While liberalism presupposes that government always "governs too much," the rationale of "reason of state" advocates strengthening the state through forms of governmentality that require both growth and more intensive regulation in regard to issues of population (74). Foucault, "The Birth of Biopolitics."

13 For a detailed analysis of the "new" (versus traditional) public health, see Alan Petersen and Deborah Lupton, *The New Public Health: Health and Self in the Age of Risk* (Thousand Oaks, CA: Sage Publications, 1997). See also Alan Petersen, "Risk, Governance, and the New Public Health," in Petersen and Bunton, *Foucault, Health and Medicine*, 189–206.

14 On the rebuilding of gay sexual culture, see Eric Rofes, *Dry Bones Breathe: Gay Men Creating Post-AIDS Identities and Cultures* (New York: Haworth, 1998).

15 The phrase is also the title of a book by Simon Watney, *Practices of Freedom: Selected Writings on HIV/AIDS* (Durham, NC: Duke University Press, 2004). See also Foucault, "The Ethics of the Concern for Self," 284.

16 "BB Bottom seeking tops to breed my ass. Anonymous scene cool," personal ad, Men Seeking Men, Craigslist San Francisco Bay Area, http://sfbay.craigslist.org/cgi-bin/personals.cgi?category=m4m, posting ID 385782984 30 July 2007, 9:31 p.m. PDT (accessed August 1, 2007); and "Looking for a Raw top this AM (concord/pleasant hill/martinez)," personal ad, Men Seeking Men, Craigslist San Francisco Bay Area, http://sfbay.craigslist.org/cgi-bin/personals.cgi?category=m4m, posting ID 381435613 25 July 2007, 7:41 a.m. PDT (accessed August 1, 2007).

17 For the standard explanation of gift economies, see Marcel Mauss, *The Gift: The Form and Reason for Exchange in Archaic Societies* (New York: W. W. Norton, 2000). For an application of Mauss's thinking to online cultures of viral sex, see Michael Graydon, "Don't Bother to Wrap It: Online Giftgiver and Bugchaser Newsgroups, the Social Impact of Gift Exchanges, and the 'Carnivalesque,'" *Culture, Health, and Sexuality* 9.3 (2007): 277–92.

18 Linda Singer, *Erotic Welfare: Sexual Theory and Politics in the Age of Epidemic* (New York: Routledge, 1992). Hereafter cited parenthetically by page number. This is also an example of what Paula Treichler describes as the "epidemic of signification" characteristic of AIDS. Treichler, *How to Have Theory in an Epidemic* (Durham, NC: Duke University Press, 1999).

19 Judith Butler, introduction to Singer, *Erotic Welfare*, 7.

20 David Halperin, *Saint Foucault* (Durham, NC: Duke University Press, 1995), 88, 90.

21 Ridge, "'It Was an Incredible Thrill,'" 266.

22 Michel Foucault, "Friendship as a Way of Life," trans. John Johnston, in *Ethics*, 135–40, 136.

23 Michel Foucault, "Social Triumph of the Sexual Will," in *Ethics*, 157–62, 160. Hereafter cited parenthetically by page number as "Triumph."

24 Foucault, "Friendship," 138.

25 Foucault, "The Ethics of the Concern for Self," 284.

26 Michel Foucault, "Sexual Choice, Sexual Act," in *Ethics*, 141–56, 143.

27 The phrase is a title of a book by Bruce Bawer, *A Place at the Table: The Gay Individual in American Society* (New York: Simon and Schuster, 1994).

28 I am extending here Barry et al.'s claim that freedom, in the Foucauldian sense, is a "formula of rule." See Barry, Osborne, and Rose, *Foucault and Political Reason*, 8.

29 Eric Rofes, *Reviving the Tribe: Regenerating Gay Men's Sexuality and Culture in the Ongoing Epidemic* (New York: Haworth, 1996), 164, 196.

30 These basic responses are an updated version of the logic that, according to Cindy Patton, underwrote first-wave safe-sex education campaigns that identified members of "risk groups" (gays, intravenous drug users, etc.) as opposed to an undifferentiated "everybody else." Patton, *Fatal Advice: How Safe-Sex Education Went Wrong* (Durham, NC: Duke University Press, 1996). One problem with this way of thinking is that it perpetuates a specific form of epistemological violence that, in its need to identify those at risk, discursively produces sexual subjects who, by definition, are categorically different from the undifferentiated subjects who occupy the political center.

31 This argument has been made by Nikolas Rose, from whom I take the term *vital politics*. See Rose, *The Politics of Life Itself: Biomedicine, Power, and Subjectivity in the Twenty-First Century* (Princeton, NJ: Princeton University Press, 2007).

32 Ibid., 3.

33 Ibid., 70.

34 George W. Bush, "National Sanctity of Human Life Day, 2006: A Proclamation by the President of the United States of America," January 20, 2006, www.whitehouse.gov/news/releases/2006/01/20060120-5.html; and George W. Bush, "Remarks by the President at Dedication of the Pope John Paul II Cultural Center," March 22, 2001, www.whitehouse.gov/news/releases/2001/03/20010322-14.html. I am indebted to Troy Urquhart, a participant in a spring 2006 seminar on poststructuralism and sexuality that I taught at the University of West Florida, for these sources and for alerting me to Bush's use of the phrase "culture of life."

35 Tim Golden, "Tough U.S. Steps in Hunger Strike at Camp in Cuba," *New York Times*, February 9, 2006.

36 Bush, "National Sanctity of Human Life Day, 2006"; and Bush, "Remarks by the President at Dedication of the Pope John Paul II Cultural Center."

37 For more on the notion of bare life, see Giorgio Agamben, *Homo Sacer: Sovereign Power and Bare Life*, trans. Daniel Heller-Roazen (Stanford, CA: Stanford University Press, 1998).

38 See Douglas Crimp, "Melancholia and Moralism: An Introduction," in *Melancholia and Moralism: Essays on AIDS and Queer Politics* (Cambridge, MA: MIT Press, 2004), 1–26.

39 Michel Foucault, *The History of Sexuality*, vol. 1, *An Introduction*, trans. Robert Hurley (New York: Vintage, 1990). Foucault writes that in "a society in which political power had assigned itself the task of administering life" (139), death accordingly becomes "power's limit, the moment that escapes [power]" (138). But making this argument comes dangerously close to affirming a belief that Foucault spent much of his late career unraveling, namely, the idea that "sex is worth dying for" (156). To buy into that idea is to participate, Foucault argues, in a naive politics of sexual liberation based on what he calls the "repressive hypothesis," or the idea that sex is something that requires liberation from repression

in order to be made free. Thus, embracing death as a queer strategy of resistance to power remains an unsatisfying political option, however much it might expose the limits of biopower.

40   It is for such reasons that Foucault could argue that the rise of biopolitics is closely linked with the advent of capitalism: "Bio-power was without question an indispensable element in the development of capitalism; the latter would not have been possible without the controlled insertion of bodies into the machinery of production and the adjustment of the phenomena of population to economic processes." Foucault, *History of Sexuality*, vol. 1, 140–41.

41   The phrase comes from Butler, introduction to Singer, *Erotic Welfare*, 3.

Megan Brown

Somehow We All Survived:
The Ideology of the U.S. Backlash
against Risk Management

One of the best-selling books in the United States in 2007 was a large, red volume—reminiscent of a well-thumbed tome of magic spells—with old-fashioned gilt letters spelling out a surprising title: *The Dangerous Book for Boys*.[1] Authors Conn and Hal Iggulden fill the book's pages with instructions and illustrations teaching boys all sorts of boisterous outdoor and rainy-day activities, many of which have nearly been lost to time. Readers can learn techniques for playing stickball, making a bow and arrow or slingshot, and skinning a rabbit. Asked by an Amazon interviewer why he and his brother/coauthor embarked on this *Dangerous Book* project—also a huge success in the United Kingdom, where it was first published—Conn Iggulden explained: "We've become aware that the whole 'health and safety' overprotective culture isn't doing our sons any favors. Boys need to learn about risk. They need to fall off things occasionally, or—and this is the important bit—they'll take worse risks on their own. If we do away with challenging playgrounds and cancel school trips for fear of being sued, we don't end up with safer boys—we end up with them walking on train tracks."[2] Iggulden's sentiment is a popular one, as the book's impressive

South Atlantic Quarterly 107:2, Spring 2008
DOI 10.1215/00382876-2007-067 © 2008 Duke University Press

sales figures and enthusiastic reviews suggest.[3] *The Dangerous Book for Boys* taps into a growing nostalgia in the United States for a more carefree, less cautious, and less litigious era. Many of the activities advocated in the book could lead to skinned knees or broken bones.

The desire to set aside concerns about physical safety—and the regulations stemming from those concerns—also comes through clearly in a popular e-mail message that has been circulating ("Send to 10 friends!") since at least early 2006 and has been posted on hundreds of Web sites ranging from MySpace to parenting support group sites to Libertarian Party information pages. The subject line, "TO ALL THE KIDS WHO SURVIVED the 1930's, 40's, 50's, 60's and 70's!!" heads a long and sharply worded description of the good old days, implicitly and favorably comparing such beloved highlights of childhood as riding bicycles without wearing helmets and drinking supersugary fruit punch to today's helmet- and knee pad–wearing, 100 percent organic juice–sipping, hypervigilant, boring risk-free times.[4] Readers of this message are encouraged to shake their heads with regret for lost freedoms as they remember fighting for the front seat of a family car without seat belts or air bags, building go-carts without brakes, and even—as babies—sleeping on their stomachs in cribs coated with lead-based paint. The repeated refrain is that the children of these less strictly regulated and less micromanaged times survived just fine, without all of the interventions now deemed necessary by politicians, administrators, educators, board-certified experts, and parents. Indeed, the rancor of this message seems directed at a few major groups: the governments that officially regulate products and activities, the organizations that recommend embracing or avoiding certain practices (the American Medical Association, the American Lung Association, and so forth), and the individuals who choose to follow such regulations and recommendations.[5]

Late-twentieth- and early-twenty-first-century shifts in attitude toward individual risk have become the subject of parody. The oft-cited specters of big government and greedy trial lawyers are alluded to in Conn Iggulden's interview responses and in the e-mail message, which fondly recalls what childhood was like "before the lawyers and the government regulated so much of our lives for our own good." These vilified parties share the blame with members of the public who have bought into the culture of "risk management." Loosely following the work of Ulrich Beck, I define risk management as a collection of preventive measures attempting to shield people from the widespread consequences of industrial development—

including production and consumption—and scientific advancement. Recent years have seen an increasing backlash against risk management and the enforcers (official and unofficial) of the values of caution, preparedness, and vigilance. Right-wing pundits sneer at the so-called nanny state, and grassroots organizations spearhead protests against state and local laws that they feel to be oppressive. Certainly, there have always been critics of state attempts to regulate citizens' lives, but the current backlash has disturbing ideological underpinnings worth analyzing. The hostility toward risk management is troubling because it often perpetuates problematic notions of personal freedom, champions self-defeating stoicism, and absolves corporations from responsibility for the consequences of their actions. Indeed, as suggested by the childhood theme in *Dangerous Book* and the "TO ALL THE KIDS" message, risk management backlashers often contrast a mythical, "innocent" age of enjoying risks (and ignoring or being blissfully unaware of consequences) with an overcautious, overly regulated adulthood. The backlashers want to be kids again, but simultaneously—like rebellious teenagers—they don't want to be "nannied" or coddled. To examine the ideology of the risk management backlash in more detail, this essay will focus on health and safety regulations and their detractors. The first section centers on discourses about smoking tobacco, the second is about consuming food containing or cooked in trans fats, and the third considers consumer safety, with particular emphasis on scandals involving products from Procter and Gamble and Mattel.

Smoke Gets in Your Eyes: Freedom and Its Costs

Many scholars, including Beck and François Ewald, have focused on the issue of response to risk. In *Risk Society*, Beck claims that one of contemporary society's most pressing problems is how to manage risks—how to mitigate or reduce dangers and how to make the personal, environmental, health-related, and economic hazards of everyday life seem negligible or natural ("you win some, you lose some" or "that's just the way things go").[6] These risks are both individual (people suffering from illnesses caused by pollution) and national or global (the rising costs of illness in terms of medical prevention, insurance, and lost work time). In an era when ideal solutions to widespread socioeconomic and environmental problems seem impossible to find, the concept of risk management becomes especially important. Risk management, which works in part through shifting the responsibility for handling risks away from groups (most notably, corporations) and to individuals, is central to many organizations, including insurance agencies, state government bodies or committees, and medical research groups. These organizations set up various regulatory apparatuses for managing risks with the expectation that individuals will internalize, or even expand on, the rules and regulations. In this way, risk-reducing and risk-avoiding practices have become increasingly central to individuals' everyday lives. According to Beck, risk management is deemed crucial in contemporary society because, without it, not only would everyday life be more dangerous, but also, future scientific, technological, and economic "progress" might be impeded by a justifiably angry, frightened public.

For example, if U.S. consumers were informed about the water contamination caused by paper mills, they might take it upon themselves to protect their health, their families, and their communities. Such protective strategies could range from personal decisions (installing a home water-filtration system, avoiding the consumption of fish caught in rivers near paper mills) to broader actions, such as publicizing the issue in newsletters, lobbying politicians, or organizing protests. All of these strategies require some diligence and effort from individuals, but, except in rare circumstances where bad publicity trumps concerns about expenditure, the corporations that own paper mills and other pollution-producing facilities do not have to spend much time, money, or energy to change their ways. Instead, the people affected by companies' risky practices must make the effort to find out about the risks and try to counteract or avoid them. This effort can be time-consuming, expensive, and ultimately unrewarding, but it may help individuals to avoid suffering such consequences as chronic or life-threatening illness.

Of course, paper mills do not inherently have to dump toxic waste into waterways, and if consumers were fully informed that the environmental risks of manufacturing might well outweigh the benefits of paper production, some might demand changes in corporate practice, which might in turn create new costs for corporations. The new manufacturing costs in this scenario are precisely the type of impediment that group risk management seeks to avoid or downplay. Citizens (living near paper mills and elsewhere) may have to suffer the consequences of paper manufacturing, but the manufacturers themselves will be spared having to outlay additional capital for redesign of facilities or development of environmentally friendly processes. Meanwhile, some people might feel helpless in the face of mass risks—the "everything gives you cancer so why fight it" attitude often cited by smokers who refuse to quit. As the constant downplaying and management of risks often contribute to consumer apathy and cynicism, risks become more global and ubiquitous—even countries with the greatest commitment to reducing pollution are affected by the lax environmental policies of other countries—and the responsibility for handling risks is increasingly shifted from governing bodies and corporations to individuals. *You* have to make sure that the local factory isn't dumping toxic waste into your town's waterways; *you* have to research which products are detrimental to your family's health. Overall, members of the public are encouraged by this set of circumstances to become increasingly careful about protecting their safety. Individuals are also encouraged—or coerced, sometimes—into protecting their health when they are confronted with local ordinances, bans on certain products deemed harmful, consumer recalls, and prohibitively high insurance costs.

In this context, debate about government regulation of human health risks, which in and of itself is nothing new, has become especially intense. Recent developments in the discourse about smoking tobacco illustrate this intensification and engage with a crucial question: why do people object to risk management? Since 1948, when physiologist Richard Doll published his studies suggesting a link between smoking habits and health problems, medical research has found overwhelming evidence that regular exposure to cigarette smoke has detrimental effects on the human body, particularly on the lungs and the heart. Doll's was not the first research about the effects of tobacco consumption, but his findings were considered credible enough to be widely disseminated and eventually to inspire government responses. One early smoking regulation was Minnesota's Clean Indoor Air Act of 1975, which required all restaurants in the state to include "no smoking" dining areas. In the United States, smoking-related laws continue to be enacted at the local or state level. The regulations at the center of today's backlash against risk management include, most notably, California's and New York's bans of smoking in bars, California's attempt to make entire cities (except for private residences) "smoke free," and various states' bans of smoking in workplaces, shopping malls, and parks.

While many people—consumers, restaurant employees, and medical professionals, among others—have voiced their support of such antismoking legislation, opponents are also common, and often vocal. The ban on smoking in New York bars met with a flurry of protests and angry editorials.

Editorials in the *New York Daily News* referred to "anti-smoke fascists" and called the ban "Prohibition redux."[7] Nick Gillespie, writing about bans on tobacco and other "bad for us" substances, opined, "New York used to pride itself on being the toughest city in the world. . . . it has just become one of the most annoying."[8] Even Pat Buchanan weighed in, describing New York City Mayor Michael Bloomberg as "a blindly intolerant man who does not understand freedom, but thinks himself a great progressive . . . like the Puritans of old of whom it was said they opposed bear-baiting, not because of the suffering it caused the bear, but because of the pleasure it gave the spectators."[9] As indicated here, one major argument against such smoking bans is that governments should not impinge on individuals' "freedoms." In short, the argument goes, adults who choose to smoke should be allowed to do so in public places such as restaurants and bars and should be able to enjoy a park or beach without suppressing their urge for a cigarette. More important, smokers' rights advocates suggest that prohibitions on the use of cigarettes should be seen as warning signs, indicating that future prohibitions on other personal habits are sure to follow.

Writers such as Christopher Hitchens and Richard Klein have helped to popularize the smokers' rights stance. Hitchens, an unapologetic smoker, has bluntly called smoking bans "un-American."[10] In *Cigarettes Are Sublime*, Klein laments the possibility that cigarettes' "cultural significance is about to be forgotten in the face of the ferocious, often fanatic or superstitious, and frequently suspect attacks upon them that are often, but not always, conducted by well-meaning people."[11] He focuses on the dark allure of cigarettes and the hypocrisy of government prohibitions of tobacco, contending that America's "dominant ideology" is "healthism"—emphasizing longevity and survival above enjoying one's life and one's freedoms.[12] Examining the ban from a somewhat different angle, a group called CLASH (Citizens Lobbying Against Smoker Harassment) claims that smokers are treated like second-class citizens: "Freedom is not a matter of popularity. The true measure of our society is how we protect the freedoms of the minority."[13] Other smokers' rights groups, such as Smokers United and FORCES (Fight Ordinances and Restrictions to Control and Eliminate Smoking) International, make comparable statements about liberty and rights.

Certainly, the language of personal freedom is compelling, and such language tends to appeal to people across the political spectrum. The idea of risk management through increasing government intervention in citizens' lives tends to conjure up disturbing images of Big Brother–like surveil-lance and censorship for right- and left-wingers alike, with some concerned about individual rights to bear arms and others worried about protecting a woman's ability to have an abortion. Along these lines, Beck warns that risk management itself poses risks, specifically those to the notions of per-sonal sovereignty and will: "With the increase of hazards totally new types of challenges to democracy arise in the risk society. It harbors a tendency to a legitimate totalitarianism of hazard prevention, which takes the right to prevent the worst and, in an all too familiar manner, creates something even worse."[14] In this passage, Beck implies that the costs of risk manage-ment can potentially be as steep as the costs of risks themselves. Unfor-tunately, the discourse of "freedom" can also become sinister, expedient, and biopolitically dangerous. Why has it become more important, to some people, to exercise the right to smoke than to avoid a high risk for lung cancer? Why would some individuals prefer to be able to enjoy a Marlboro at the local bar than to lower their likelihood of suffering from emphysema or heart disease?[15] Who pays—and does anyone benefit—from these deci-sions? Might the antiregulation crusaders, with their worries about losing their liberties, actually be playing into the hands of the authority figures they criticize?

In *Powers of Freedom: Reframing Political Thought*, Nikolas Rose points out that the concept of "freedom" is not the opposite of government or regulation, as some might assume, but is instead central to the workings of state power, used as a technique in governing: "To govern humans is not to crush their capacity to act, but to acknowledge it and utilize it for one's objectives."[16] Basing his argument on Michel Foucault's concepts of "governmentality" and "technologies of the self," Rose describes the diverse ways in which strategies of governing act at a distance on everyday activi-ties. By encouraging people to live "freely" rather than expressly forbidding certain practices, liberal government works by fostering the idea that indi-viduals have autonomy and should enjoy and exercise their free will:

> People were to be "freed" in the realms of the market, civil society, the family: they were placed outside the legitimate scope of politi-cal authorities, subject only to the limits of the law. Yet the "freeing" of these zones was accompanied by the invention of a whole series of attempts to shape and manage conduct within them in desirable ways. . . . the private conduct of free citizens was to be civilized by

equipping them with languages and techniques of self-understanding and self-mastery. (69)

Rose, following Foucault, emphasizes activities and practices thought to be healthy or otherwise "good for you." Everyday existence is a series of investments, in Rose's view—all of one's mundane decisions are oriented toward the goal of improving one's life (and lifestyle). Individuals are "being urged by politicians and others to take upon themselves responsibility for the security of their property and their persons" (247). Governing is not only concerned with maintaining law and order, bolstering the economy, and establishing relations with other nations, but also with improving the health and extending the longevity of the citizenry. As such, gently guided by expert advice and the occasional nudge in the right direction from government, individuals learn to regulate their own behavior when met with outside criteria from some sort of authority, and they feel that they are freely deciding to take care of themselves. For example, individuals must discipline themselves to regulate their health: to get the recommended amount of exercise per week, wear the appropriate sunscreen, and drink alcohol only in moderation. As suggested above, Rose argues that such "technologies of the self" have made governance and management efficient and effective because the process seems to be good for everyone involved. Personal goals and the values of government seem to be smoothly aligned, connecting "public objectives for the good health and good order of the social body with the desire of individuals for personal health and well being" (74).

So, what about the risk management backlash, in which people seem to rail against what's good for them, choosing instead to embrace habits (such as smoking) that have been proven *unhealthy*? Here is the twist on Rose's formulation of freedom: smokers' rights discourses infer that smoking is actually good for individuals' emotional well-being and mental health, and for the United States as a whole. Rather than being mindless conformists, sitting idly by as individual rights are stripped from Americans, members and supporters of smokers' rights organizations are brave dissenters—the staunch defenders of freedom and justice. Smokers are "healthy" because they are exercising their free will, whereas supporters of bans are repressed. The point of view of unrepentant smokers, so antithetical to established views on tobacco consumption, is also a proud rebel stance—one with cultural cachet. Smoking is a mark of insubordination, the glamorous act of the rebellious teen. As Klein contends, "Understanding the noxious effects of cigarettes is not usually sufficient reason to cause anyone to stop smoking or resist starting; rather, knowing it is bad seems an absolute precondition to acquiring and confirming the cigarette habit."[17]

The recourse to the rhetoric of individual freedom is troubling because, as Ewald notes, risk is collective: "[It] implies a kind of active as well as passive solidarity among the individuals composing a population: no one may appeal to a good driving record [for insurance purposes] to escape the constraints of the group. All must recognize their constitutive weakness or, better, recognize that by their very existence they are a risk to others."[18] The smokers' rights groups only grudgingly mention the dangers of second-hand smoke (and sometimes even deny those dangers) in their publicity materials, downplaying the fact that more is at stake than individual rights in the debate about smoking bans: the physical health of smokers and of people frequently exposed to smoke, employees' rights to a healthy work-place, and so forth.

Many people can be hurt when individual freedom is valued above all other concerns, but who benefits? Such cigarette manufacturers as Philip Morris and R. J. Reynolds—and the U.S. government, which continues to subsidize tobacco farmers—have certainly benefited from the redirection of smoking-related health risks toward consumers who, despite being increasingly cognizant of the risks associated with tobacco usage, continue to smoke. Indeed, Beck might not have anticipated the active, almost eager response of Philip Morris to risk management culture; the corporation has produced slick television commercials about ways to quit smoking, in which attractive, middle-class people of various ethnic backgrounds smile with satisfaction at their accomplishments. These advertisements refer interested parties to the company's official Web site, where one can learn about QuitAssist, a cessation program devised as "a free information resource . . . a voluntary effort by Philip Morris USA."[19] The company even acknowledges the irony of QuitAssist: "It may seem contradictory for a cigarette manufacturer to help smokers who have decided to quit succeed. But, smoking causes serious diseases and is addictive. It can be difficult to quit smoking and many smokers who try to quit do not succeed."[20] So, when someone claims that Philip Morris is culpable for lung cancer deaths (or when someone attempts to sue for damages), the company can easily point to the cessation resources it so generously advertises and provides, thus garnering favorable publicity and avoiding potentially expensive lawsuits. But Philip Morris and similar corporations can *also* benefit from the *backlash* against risk management. Thanks in part to the appealing rebel stance of the smoker in today's culture, even antismoking advertisements may serve to strengthen cigarette sales. Klein notes: "The more vividly the abyss is opened beneath the traveler's feet, the more awesome is his satisfaction at playing with life and death and the more acute his pleasure at defying the negativity before him. From that logic, it follows that the surgeon general's warning on every pack of American cigarettes actually serves to advertise their charms and promote their use."[21] Indeed, according to the 2006 financial report of Philip Morris's parent company, Altria, net revenues for Philip Morris USA went up 1.9 percent to $18.5 billion, with the Marlboro product line enjoying a retail market share of 40.5 percent—its highest ever.[22] The freedom to choose Marlboro also comes with costs. According to the American Lung Association, approximately 342,000 U.S. citizens die of lung disease each year, and more than 35 million suffer from chronic lung disease.

I Want My KFC: The Trans Fat Ban and the Nanny State

One of the smokers' rights groups mentioned earlier—NYC CLASH—has recently taken on another health-related issue, trans fat. Consumption of this now-notorious unsaturated fat—usually found in the form of human-made, partially hydrogenated oils and often used in industrial baking, cooking, and frying—has been linked to increased levels of LDLs in the human body. High levels of this type of cholesterol can lead to coronary heart disease. Due to these alarming findings, the National Academy of Sciences, World Health Organization, and Center for Science in the Public Interest, among others, have declared that people should avoid eating foods containing trans fats. This recommendation quickly led to action. In 2003, the Food and Drug Administration began requiring packaged food producers to include trans fat statistics in the "Nutrition Facts" labels on their products. The Center for Science in the Public Interest sued Kentucky Fried Chicken in 2006 because of the fast-food chain's use of trans fats; KFC has since replaced its partially hydrogenated cooking oil with a healthier substitute in its U.S. restaurants. In December 2006, after an unsuccessful attempt to convince restaurant owners to phase out oils containing trans fat from their kitchens, New York City's Board of Health unanimously voted to ban trans fats in city restaurants. Affected businesses must completely eliminate these fats from their foods by July 2008.[23]

The New York City ban has been welcomed by many health-related organizations but remains controversial. Predictably, the restaurant industry has complained about potential costs, but much of the uproar has been focused on the "freedom" issue described above. This angle is precisely the one found in the discourse of CLASH. As CLASH founder Audrey Silk once testified to the New York City Department of Health and Mental Hygiene, the ban on trans fat is "not public health. That's social engineering. Eliminating choice and coercing behavior is not the American way."[24] In CLASH's "Library of Information," found on the group's Web site, there is a section about smoking, trans fat, and other health-related regulations called "Let's Get Crazy: What the Nannies Are Up To." Here, readers will find an overview of the actions of health "crusaders" banning smoking in nursing homes, removing images of smoking from old cartoons, and filing lawsuits about exposure to secondhand smoke. A section of the CLASH Web site titled "The Taxonomy of Anti-Smokers" parodies people who object to smoking.[25]

Derogatory images of the "nanny" and the "nanny state" frequently appear in critiques of risk management. These images help to illuminate the backlash discourse's lionizing of the ideal of the "tough guy" who takes risks and braves the consequences without whining. In short, backlashers contend that Americans learn to be stoic, toughen up, and take care of themselves rather than depending on, or even tolerating, intervention from outside authorities when making health-related decisions. Backlashers contrast the nanny, who wants to regulate people "for their own good," with the fiercely independent citizen who wants to be fully responsible for his or her own decisions and face any consequences that arise. Certainly, the emphasis on responsibility seems reasonable, and even admirable, but this stance comes with costs. Accepting full responsibility for all life circumstances can be dangerously misguided, because doing so may discourage or prevent active responses to the problematic consequences of risk.

The term *nanny state*, which is used to criticize governments seen as overly protective of citizens, has been in circulation since the mid-1960s and is now strongly associated with various aspects of risk management. A nanny state regulates people's lives in a wide variety of areas, including some traditionally conceived of as personal or private. It illustrates Foucault's concept of governmentality: "To govern a state . . . means exercising towards its inhabitants, and the wealth and behaviour of each and all, a form of surveillance and control as attentive as that of the head of a family over his household and goods."[26] Concerned about the encroachment of government into their "private" affairs, critics of the nanny state focus their rancor on a constellation of regulations outlawing or discouraging individual practices. Detractors of the trans fat ban, for example, claim that eating fatty foods does not harm anyone but the consumer, so he or she should be allowed to choose an unhealthy diet. (Some people, however, have countered that the obesity that can result from a diet with too much fat raises nationwide insurance costs and negatively affects the obese person's family and friends.) Nanny state critics tend to lean right politically. Republican Congressman Ron Paul has written about "The Therapeutic Nanny State," and conservative/libertarian commentator John Stossel argues, "The people who have the biggest passion for restricting other people's behavior are the people we should worry about most."[27] In his book *Nanny State: How Food Fascists, Teetotaling Do-Gooders, Priggish Moralists, and Other Boneheaded Bureaucrats Are Turning Americans into a Nation of Children*, David Harsanyi attacks legislators and supporters of smoking regulations, the trans fat ban, rules forbidding schoolyard tag in several Massachusetts towns, and various local ordinances forbidding the use of mini-motorbikes and aluminum baseball bats. With a nostalgic tone echoing that of the "TO ALL THE KIDS" message, he writes: "The fact that politicians, bureaucrats, and activists long to be our parents is not new. What is inexplicable, though, is the swiftness with which Americans have allowed these worrywarts to take the job. It's a dramatic about-face from our traditional attitudes towards overreaching government."[28] Interestingly, advocates of this anti–nanny state position rarely complain about the government bailing out struggling businesses and industries; their emphasis on freedom reaches its limit when the "free market" needs a safety net.

While many of the bans and laws cited by Harsanyi, Stossel, and other critics of the nanny state seem absurd and well worth a skeptical sneer, the backlashers' stance smuggles in problematic ideas about individual responsibility, sovereignty, and will.[29] The tough guy ideal ignores the substantial power of circumstances on people's day-to-day lives.[30] To cite an extreme and traumatic example, a passage from the No Nanny State blog chides the victims of the 2007 Virginia Tech massacre for being cowardly, having learned helplessness from government coddling: "Some nut is slaughtering people and (with one exception, holocaust survivor Liviu Librescu) all they could think to do was to hunker down, cower in the corner, and wait for someone else to come and fix their problem."[31] The writer pays no heed whatsoever to the terrifying, tragic circumstances in which the Virginia Tech students and faculty found themselves, nor does he acknowledge the fact that a so-called nanny state policy—stricter gun control—might have eliminated the tragedy in the first place. Instead, he compares the Virginia Tech victims to children who have learned helplessness from an overbearing parent.

Less extreme examples of this antinanny way of thinking are common and widely accepted. As previously noted, diet and smoking regulations are two targets of the backlash, but many other issues (and related regulations) have also been subject to scrutiny. Driving-related risk management strategies, such as using seat belts, placing children in car seats, and wearing a helmet while riding a motorcycle, are common targets of backlashers. Some people and organizations objecting to mandatory helmet laws claim that helmets actually decrease rider safety—a legitimate complaint, if accurate—but others simply object to helmets as markers of weakness or wimpiness.

The nanny state critics who focus on children's safety regulations are also disturbing. Returning to the "TO ALL THE KIDS" e-mail, the message's sarcastic commentary on changes in children's lives during the twentieth century clearly suggests that today's kids are being weakened and (s)mothered into submission, thanks to the nanny state. But why would a parent—knowing full well, as we do now thanks to research, that lead-based paint can be toxic to children—buy a crib without making sure that it meets current safety standards? Since a helmet can prevent brain damage in a bicycle accident, why not encourage children to wear helmets? Is doing so really a sign of weakness and a capitulation to the nanny state, or is it just a reasonable response to potential danger? As noted earlier, the backlash discourse's emphasis on an ideal of individual freedom is problematic because it ignores the power of circumstances. The "TO ALL THE KIDS" e-mail is one example of this problem, because the stoical "we" who "survived" intact is an exclusive club. What about the kids who died or were injured in car accidents before the advent of car seat and seat belt regulations, or the inner-city children suffering brain damage from the lead-based paint in their families' old, dilapidated apartments, or the residents of dangerously polluted areas who don't have the financial resources to move? Due to economic circumstances or geographic location, some individuals are far more likely to be exposed to certain risks than others; the so-called nannies may give such people a chance to survive.

Caveat Emptor Redux

For all of their distrust of big government regulations, risk management backlashers show remarkably little distrust of the corporations that create so many everyday risk factors in the first place. Anger at the so-called nanny state seems misdirected when one considers the serious impact that corporate risk taking may have on people's health. Rather than working together to combat corporation-created risks, many people have become cynical about government attempts to regulate businesses, bitter about what they perceive as frivolous lawsuits (and disdainful of the lawyers and plaintiffs involved) and, often, unwilling to take seriously the impact of corporate decisions on their lives. As Brian Massumi points out, however, "In complicity with capital, a body becomes its own worst enemy."[32] While risk management can be frustrating, attempting to avoid it is ill-advised, because corporations may not be held sufficiently accountable for their actions.

Thus, according to Beck, risk is dispersed among individuals (consumers and members of the public) and distributed away from corporations and organizations taking the actual risks, such as putting products on the market without extensive testing, destroying the environment with industrial waste, or outsourcing manufacturing to countries without quality control or factory safety checks. Individuals are then responsible for learning about the risks and consequences surrounding them in their everyday lives. In this formulation, individuals tend to be aware of the initial sources of the problems: the paper mill, the factory, Mattel selling toys decorated with lead-based paint. Risk management backlash discourse, however, suggests that the individual is not supposed to point a blaming finger at a corporate entity distributing dangerous products or polluting air and water. Instead, the individual is supposed to "tough it out," even though he or she may pay a steep price for such business practices as rapid expansion, sped-up product development and proliferation, and unregulated or underregulated production. Backlashers excuse corporate risk taking at the expense of those affected by the risks. Consider Jacob Sullum's commentary on what he perceives to be unfair stereotyping of the tobacco industry. Sullum argues that the common claim that "the tobacco companies hid the truth about the hazards and addictiveness of cigarettes from the American public" is unfair and inaccurate because "warnings about the health risks of smoking go back hundreds of years."[33] His examples of such warnings come from England's King James I and Sir Francis Bacon, who in the fifteenth century wrote about the dangers of smoking. These examples are entirely unrelated to the problematic twentieth-century policies of Philip Morris or R. J. Reynolds. In his argument, Sullum thereby lets these corporations escape from blame, dismissing corporate dishonesty to the public as inevitable "industry double-talk."[34]

Thanks to the backlash, consumers become more complicit in the risks of capitalism. Corporations may have created problems along with their products, but consumers ask for those products and keep buying them, often without protest if a recall (or worse) arises. Corporations continue to operate without changing their practices because what they do works—no one seems to be complaining, because to complain is to be a nannied wimp or the puppet of some greedy trial lawyer. A risk-taking company can thrive while an antiregulation citizenry stays fairly silent. For instance, despite several major scandals, Procter and Gamble continues to appear near the top of the Fortune 500. Procter and Gamble has a long history of product innovation, and many of its successes have been accompanied by consequences for the public, such as environmental and health problems caused by the production and distribution of the company's products.

Procter and Gamble justifies many of its particularly controversial decisions by alluding to the enthusiastic response of consumers to its products. In the 1970s, when research scientists hypothesized that the phosphates in household laundry detergents were destroying American lake ecosystems, many companies, in response to local and state bans and consumer outrage, quickly removed their phosphate products from the market. Procter and Gamble, however, claimed that the removal of phosphates would significantly decrease the cleaning action of detergents. The company justified its refusal to switch to more eco-friendly ingredients by saying that it did not want to sell inferior products to its customers, who had come to depend on the company for its reliability. The controversy culminated in a lawsuit, wherein Procter and Gamble charged that the city of Chicago's 1972 ban on detergents containing phosphates—driven by a desire to protect Lake Michigan and the Illinois Waterway from "nuisance algae"—was unconstitutional, in that it obstructed interstate sales.[35] A decision in favor of Procter and Gamble's claim was later reversed in a court of appeals. Today,

Procter and Gamble and its apologists still defend the decision to continue selling phosphate detergents, saying that the public had been misled by incomplete or incorrect scientific findings. As one such corporate booster wrote, "P&G refused to pander to the consumer hysteria."[36] Despite the environmental impact of phosphates and many consumers' concerns, the company continued to prioritize profits by taking risks despite potentially disastrous consequences; apparently, the loss of some customers was worth saving the research and development expenditure needed to develop new, phosphate-free products.

Today, Procter and Gamble continues to refer to customer desires when justifying its risky decisions, but with a difference: there is little evidence of consumer "hysteria," outrage, or even significant protest. In recent years, the company has been criticized for testing products on animals, polluting the Fenholloway River in Florida, attempting to influence independent product research, and continuing business operations in countries led by regimes accused of human rights violations. These serious issues have not been met with the widespread consternation that one might expect, at least not in the United States. Organized protests against Procter and Gamble's animal testing are largely based in the United Kingdom; concern about the Fenholloway (and the connection between the pollution and the sky-high local cancer rates) seems confined to residents of Taylor County, Florida; the research ethics question appears in a few scattered newspaper articles and on some researchers' blogs; and the human rights issue has warranted an occasional boycott. The company seems well aware of what it can get away with thanks to lax industry regulations, powerful corporate lobbies, and an indifferent public. As former CEO Ed Artzt once said at a banquet awarding Procter and Gamble's corporate citizenship, "Conscience is a wonderful thing. It can change the world. It can do what no laws, no rules, no threat of punishment or penalty can ever do, because it is an enduring, self-regulating force."[37] This comment is probably more telling than Artzt would have liked—it actually suggests the disturbing depths of the company's extreme version of risk management: a laissez-faire philosophy that flaunts regulations and truly lets the buyer beware. In today's backlash climate, cynical buyers, scoffing at the nanny state and at alleged government encroachment on their personal freedoms, may not even beware at all.

To return to a childhood-related example of risk management backlash like the ones with which the essay began, toy manufacturer Mattel announced a massive product recall in mid-2007. According to the company's statement, the recall of 9.5 million toys in the United States and 11 million toys in international markets was "voluntary" and due to "impermissible use of lead paint and risks associated with small, high-powered magnets."[38] At least three children were injured after swallowing poorly affixed magnets on Polly Pocket play sets, and the effects of the potential toxins in the lead-based paint on the other toys is as yet unknown. All of the recalled toys were manufactured in China. Unlike the Procter and Gamble case, Mattel appears to be suffering some consequences. The Consumer Product Safety Commission is investigating the company's response to the crisis—specifically, allegations that the company did not act quickly enough when first apprised of the hazards.[39] Also, soon after the initial recall, Senator Dick Durbin of Illinois recommended that all toys made in China be tested for unacceptable lead levels. The scandalized response to this massive recall is heartening in a sense; at least commentators are not professing nostalgia for a time when tough kids were free to choke on their toys. Risky business decisions are being blamed for the problem. However, much of the rancor is being directed at Chinese manufacturers rather than the U.S.-based companies that outsource production to said manufacturers (precisely because of low costs, which stem in part from not having to meet certain standards already common in the United States). Certainly, for the sake of its citizens as well as its trading partners, China should institute stronger quality control measures, but the backlashers want to send the "babysitters"—the regulators—to other countries. Nannying, it seems, is good enough for Chinese companies but not for American ones.

Given the advances in industrial development and the concomitant proliferation of potential risks, it is easy to be cynical about risk management—and to condemn the alleged loss of personal freedom, to rail against the nanny state, or to side with corporations rather than with their victims. It is even tempting to become nostalgic for a responsibility-free past and envision oneself as a rebel, standing apart from the overcautious risk society. The backlash position is complex; backlashers idealize children, living life without fear of consequences, gently guided by parents (rather than lawmakers), but they also envision themselves as rebellious adolescents free to refuse all advice from authority figures ("I'll smoke if I want to") and likely to prioritize their desires over the needs of the community around them ("My right to smoke is more important than their right to smoke-free air"). Also, for much of the right-leaning, antinanny crowd, vigilance is disdained, but caution—even paranoid overcaution—is reserved for protecting Americans against "outsiders," such as terrorists, Mexicans crossing the southern border, and products stamped "Made in China."

Beck himself articulates the contradictions of the backlash position as he describes a frustration similar to that of the backlashers: "Risk positions create dependencies which are unknown in class situations; the affected parties are becoming incompetent in matters of their own affliction. They lose an essential part of their cognitive sovereignty."[40] Here, Beck laments the loss of individual "sovereignty"—the same concern articulated in back-lash discourse—even though much of his work suggests the relative help-lessness of humans in the face of natural risks. Zygmunt Bauman also warns of the negative consequences of risk management on personal free-dom: "History . . . teaches us that the price for survival is practical involve-ment, the transformation of ideas into domination. Is this price, however, worth paying?"[41] In these passages, Beck and Bauman presuppose that there is an outside to risk society, an ideal place of liberty where people are unfettered by risk. But can an individual—even one who protests risk management—opt out of risk society? Even a vehement opposition to such risk management regulations as smoking prohibitions or trans fat bans is a response to risk—a wholehearted acceptance of risk rather than an attempt to avoid it. There is no outside. Asserting one's sense of individuality by criticizing regulations embraces rather than mitigates risks, and chances are that the backlasher may suffer in the end. Maybe we all can benefit from the work of nannies, who will at least try to prevent corporations from get-ting away with murder. Maybe we all need the risk managers—the doctors, lawyers, nonprofit organizations, state and local officials, government com-mittees—who attempt to keep power, be it corporate, state, or any other form thereof, in check.

Notes

1   Conn Iggulden and Hal Iggulden's *The Dangerous Book for Boys* (New York: Harper Collins, 2007) was number two on the August 12, 2007, *New York Times Book Review* best-sellers list, in the advice section. As of that day, it had been on the list for thirteen weeks. Advice, How-To, and Miscellaneous category, *New York Times Book Review*, August 12, 2007.

2   Amazon.com, "Questions for Conn Iggulden," www.amazon.com/Dangerous-Book-Boys-Conn-Iggulden/dp/0061243582/ref=pd_bbs_sr_1/102-6008224-3468138?ie=UTF8&s=books&qid=1188499399&sr=8-1 (accessed August 30, 2007).

3   As of May 2007, there were 405,000 copies of *The Dangerous Book for Boys* in print, and the book was projected to sell a minimum of four million copies in the United States.

Jeffrey A. Trachtenberg, "'Dangerous Book for Boys' Soars to Dizzying Heights," *Wall Street Journal*, May 18, 2007.

4   The message can be read at the following Web sites, among many others: www.free republic.com/focus/f-chat/1405663/posts; http://forums.military.com/eve/forums/a/tpc/ f/2401981206/m/2290019341001; and www.dvo.com/newsletter/weekly/2007/05-18-182/ random_musings.html (all accessed September 17, 2007).

Here are some other highlights of the e-mail message:

> First, we survived being born to mothers who smoked and/or drank while they were pregnant. They took aspirin, ate blue cheese dressing, tuna from a can, and didn't get tested for diabetes. . . . We had no childproof lids on medicine bottles, doors or cabinets and when we rode our bikes, we had no helmets, not to mention, the risks we took hitchhiking. As infants & children, we would ride in cars with no car seats, booster seats, seat belts or air bags. Riding in the back of a pick up on a warm day was always a special treat. . . . We ate cupcakes, white bread and real butter and drank Kool-aid made with sugar, but we weren't overweight because, WE WERE ALWAYS OUTSIDE PLAYING! We would leave home in the morning and play all day, as long as we were back when the streetlights came on. No one was able to reach us all day. And we were O.K. We would spend hours building our go-carts out of scraps and then ride down the hill, only to find out we forgot the brakes. After running into the bushes a few times, we learned to solve the problem. . . . We fell out of trees, got cut, broke bones and teeth and there were no lawsuits from these accidents. . . . The past 50 years have been an explosion of innovation and new ideas. We had freedom, failure, success and responsibility, and we learned HOW TO DEAL WITH IT ALL!

5   Former *American Idol* finalist Bucky Covington has released a single based on this e-mail forward. Called "A Different World," the song includes such lyrics as "No childproof lids / No seat belts in cars / Rode bikes without helmets / And here we still are." Covington, "A Different World," *Bucky Covington*, Lyric Street Records, 2007.

6   Ulrich Beck, *Risk Society: Towards a New Modernity*, trans. Mark Ritter (1986; London: Sage Publications, 1992).

7   Sidney Zion, "Mike's Blowing 2nd-Hand Smoke," *New York Daily News*, October 10, 2002, available at www.data-yard.net/10u/zion.htm (accessed October 8, 2007).

8   Nick Gillespie, "The Race to Ban What's Bad for Us," *Reason*, December 11, 2006, www .reason.com/news/show/117171.html.

9   Patrick Buchanan, "The Unfree Society of Michael Bloomberg," Townhall.com, August 19, 2002; text available at www.theamericancause.org/pattheunfreesociety.htm (accessed September 17, 2007).

10   David Holman, "Smoking Room," *American Spectator*, June 23, 2005, www.spectator.org/ dsp_article.asp?art_id=8343.

11   Richard Klein, *Cigarettes Are Sublime* (Durham, NC: Duke University Press, 1993), xi.

12   Ibid., 185.

13   NYC CLASH, www.nycclash.com (accessed October 8, 2007).

14   Beck, *Risk Society*, 80.

15   Or, for that matter, why would one individual's right to smoke a cigarette outweigh the health of bar and restaurant workers?

16 Nikolas Rose, *Powers of Freedom: Reframing Political Thought* (New York: Cambridge University Press, 1999), 4. Hereafter cited parenthetically by page number.

17 Klein, *Cigarettes*, 1.

18 François Ewald, "Two Infinities of Risk," in *The Politics of Everyday Fear*, ed. Brian Massumi (Minneapolis: University of Minnesota Press, 1993), 221.

19 Philip Morris, "About QuitAssist," www.pmusa.com/en/quitassist/about/index.asp (accessed October 8, 2007).

20 Ibid.

21 Klein, *Cigarettes*, 189.

22 Altria, "2006 Annual Report," www.altria.com/annualreport/ar2006 (accessed October 8, 2007).

23 Similar bans on trans fat have been passed in Philadelphia; Montgomery County, Maryland; and Albany County, New York.

24 Audrey Silk and Linda Stewart, "Testimony to NYC on Trans Fat Ban," NYC CLASH, www.nycclash.com/TransFatTestimony.html (accessed September 17, 2007).

25 NYC CLASH, "Let's Get Crazy: What the Nannies Are Up To," www.nycclash.com/unreasonable.html (accessed September 17, 2007); "The Taxonomy of Anti-Smokers," www.nycclash.com/Psych101.html (accessed September 17, 2007).

26 Michel Foucault, "Governmentality," in *Power: Essential Works of Foucault, 1954–1984*, vol. 3, ed. James D. Faubion, trans. Robert Hurley et al. (New York: New Press, 2000), 202.

27 John Stossel, "Trans Fat Ban Is 'Nanny State' Intrusion," *20/20*, ABC, December 6, 2006, http://abcnews.go.com/2020/Story?id=2705411&page=1. While most nanny state criticism comes from right-wing commentators, in a recent book Dean Baker argues that the conservative stance about unregulated markets belies the benefits that conservative officials actually glean from government regulations. See Dean Baker, *The Conservative Nanny State: How the Wealthy Use the Government to Stay Rich and Get Richer* (Lulu.com, 2006); and Ron Paul, "The Therapeutic Nanny State," LewRockwell.com, www.lewrockwell.com/paul/paul204.html (accessed September 17, 2007).

28 When this essay was written, Harsanyi's book was not yet published, but advance excerpts were available online. David Harsanyi, *Nanny State: How Food Fascists, Teetotaling Do-Gooders, Priggish Moralists, and Other Boneheaded Bureaucrats Are Turning Americans into a Nation of Children* (New York: Broadway Books, 2007), www.davidharsanyi.com (accessed September 17, 2007).

29 Beck suggests a similar reason for impatience with the nanny state: "There occurs . . . an overproduction of risks, which sometimes relativize, sometimes supplement and sometimes outdo one another." Beck, *Risk Society*, 31.

30 I use the word *guy* on purpose here. Though it snippily dismisses political correctness, the nanny state discourse is usually "correct" enough to avoid explicitly gendered language, but one need not look too closely at its language and imagery to notice resentment toward the perceived coddling of Americans by lawmakers and medical authorities, which is configured as mothering or babysitting. In addition, even though men are hired as nannies these days, women still disproportionately bear the responsibility for child care, and it's safe to assume that people are likely to be envisioning women when they use the phrase *nanny state*.

31 "All Nanny, All the Time," No Nanny State blog, April 26, 2007, http://nonannystate .blogspot.com. The same blogger contends that people left homeless by Hurricane Katrina's destruction are still struggling because "they're programmed [by government nannying] to be helpless." "Quiet Riot????" No Nanny State blog, June 5, 2007.

32 Brian Massumi, "Everywhere You Want to Be: Introduction to Fear," in *The Politics of Everyday Fear*, 12.

33 Jacob Sullum, *For Your Own Good: The Anti-Smoking Crusade and the Tyranny of Public Health* (New York: Free Press, 1998), 277.

34 Ibid.

35 A summary of the court case *Procter and Gamble Co. v. Chicago*, U.S. Court of Appeals, 7th Circuit, 1975, written by Memory Machingambi, can be found at www.rpts.tamu.edu/ courses/renr662/cases/ProcterandGamble.pdf (accessed October 8, 2007).

36 Charles L. Decker, *Winning with the P&G 99: 99 Principles and Practices of Procter & Gamble's Success* (New York: Pocket Books, 1998), 108.

37 Alecia Swasy, *Soap Opera: The Inside Story of Procter & Gamble* (New York: Times Books, 1993), 308.

38 Bob Eckert, "Because Your Children Are Our Children, Too," Mattel.com, www.mattel .com/safety/us (accessed October 8, 2007).

39 Mattel may still benefit in the long run. In an interview with the Associated Press, financial analyst Sean McGowan suggested that the company's straightforward, apologetic response to the recall will help to recuperate and even strengthen Mattel's trustworthy image. Anne D'Innocenzio, "Mattel Defends Itself on Safety of Toys," *Daily Sentinel* (Grand Junction, CO), August 14, 2007.

40 Beck, *Risk Society*, 31.

41 Zygmunt Bauman, *Mortality, Immortality, and Other Life Strategies* (Stanford, CA: Stanford University Press, 1992), 70.

Robert Harvey

Safety Begins at Home

Proud, Prepared, Protected.
—Nevada Department of Homeland Security motto

Quick, a place. With no way in, no way out, a safe place.
—Samuel Beckett, *The Unnamable*

Ever since its post–World War II rise to the status of superpower, the United States and its citizens have had a conflicted attitude toward safety. Those of us who grew up here in the 1950s and 1960s can undoubtedly still remember those junior high school hygiene classes in which we received training in health safety that seems quaintly bizarre today. With our examination gloves, goggles, and safety shutoffs, our warnings about microwavable pets and Styrofoam coffee cups between legs, we convince ourselves that we have made a safe place in this land of ours—safe, at least, from work-related accidents. With regard to enemies that may lurk within, we are still armed to the teeth with handguns and automatic rifles. Since we became a superpower during the cold war, we have practiced and perfected a combination of fastidious self-defense and reckless foreign policy.

South Atlantic Quarterly 107:2, Spring 2008
DOI 10.1215/00382876-2007-068 © 2008 Duke University Press

Such "precautions" notwithstanding, until 9/11 we apparently did not realize how unsafe a somewhat isolationist population—increasingly convinced it constitutes an exception among nations—really is. Though spontaneously recalled when the World Trade Center went up in flames, filled the pristine sky with smoke, then collapsed, Pearl Harbor suddenly paled by mental comparison. In 1941, Hawai'i had been a distant possession; whereas, in 2001, the WTC was the behemoth double spinal column of capitalism at the very heart of *Kapital*. Nevertheless, the tacit discursive program to assimilate the subsequent "war on terror" to the United States' World War II is symptomatic of a temporal dystopia wherein the United States hallucinates that it was a victim of the ultimate weapon of mass destruction used, in reality thus far, uniquely by the United States itself. This discursive program is part collective psychosis, part policy of the federal administration. Its dynamics is situated at the safety-danger nexus, which results, inevitably, in historical blindness and misguided relations to the world outside.

Are We Safer?

"Are we safe now?" This is what we Americans are relentlessly being told we want to know. Yet, is it really imperative that we regain at all cost some nebulous level of safety that we took for granted before we heard much about al-Qaeda or anything at all about Mohammed Atta? How many people in this country ask themselves these questions? We've actually already forgotten how vulnerable we suddenly felt—suddenly, collectively, vicariously, and for the first time—in 2001. But for the few who continue to ask the questions that many so easily forget, quick and easy answers-meant-to-soothe can be had by consulting the Web site of the U.S. Department of Homeland Security (on whose name I shall soon comment). Before the House Committee on Homeland Security, back in May 2003, former DHS secretary Tom Ridge asserted, "Today, we are significantly safer than we were twenty months ago."[1] Several years later, with the Taliban back at operating strength in Afghanistan and al-Qaeda flourishing in Iraq, where none of significance existed prior to 9/11, we might be moved to wonder what Ridge's assurances meant. Or we might consider this declaration made by New York Mayor Michael Bloomberg at the Republican National Convention in 2004, also proudly displayed on DHS's Web site: "New York is the safest big city in the nation, and there will be no letup in law enforcement anywhere in this city."² It is not necessary to be a New Yorker to understand that control of the murder rate and enforcement of traffic and parking codes have nothing to do with keeping a city or the nation in which it is situated safe from the desperate actions of groups and individuals from a world where anti-U.S. resentment is partially justified. From yet another angle, in case we were in any doubt as to an intrinsic and necessary link between national safety and that other conservative project, the preservation of the heteronormative nuclear family, here is former New York governor George Pataki in 2004: "I've had people, as I've been around the country, say, 'Should I come here the week of the Convention?' The answer is, unequivocally, yes. I will be here, my wife Libby will be here, our kids are going to be here as much as they can, consistent with their school schedules, because this is the safest large city in America, and next week, it will be as safe as any place in America can possibly be."³ Meanwhile, the former chairman of the House Homeland Security Committee, Congressman Peter King, a Republican from New York, overtly endorses racial profiling as a sensible safety measure in our troubled times.⁴ "Are we safer today?" King asked in 2006 at my university.⁵

We must remind ourselves that the safety we are told we aspire to is doomed to fail as a project because it is always safety *from* something. There always must be an enemy to safety against which would-be guarantors of safety must struggle. We long to be safe from them—whoever they may be.

What's in a Name?

Unifying all the U.S. policing agencies might have been an otherwise acceptable or even advisable reorganization in most people's view, yet we may ask why that meta-administration needed to be christened the Department of *Homeland* Security. To get right to the point: What has changed in *this* America so bent on being safe that it has moved to embrace a term fraught with fascist baggage?

Post-9/11 safety is a function of our conviction that terror and terrorism are by definition *extrinsic* to our world. Our world is our people, however diverse they may look. Increasingly we think of our people as speaking English only and with one generic accent. Terror comes from the outside other or the other who has not assimilated. In the hours before we learned about "homeboy" Timothy McVeigh, we assumed that the Murrah Federal

Building in Oklahoma City was blown up by Arabic-speaking brown others. Terror is alien and aliens out there and among us incarnate terror. *Terror is other and we naturally "other" terror.* A terrorized population must therefore seek stability, familiarity, and comfort, however infantile and futile those efforts may appear. A "war on terror" is no time for regime change at home. Only elsewhere. The powers that be must don their masks of stern decision, take on responsibilities of apocalyptic scale, separate the patriotic wheat from the terrorist chaff, and distinguish between Bushian Allies and Axis powers: "You're either with us or against us."[6] "We" shall "stay the course" and be the sole restorers and guarantors of consolation for a wounded nation. Patriots of the *mère-patrie* will swaddle us and inoculate us against foreign bodies.

No wonder, then, at this historical conjuncture turned evangelical that a name like "Homeland Security" was chosen to designate the magnificently grandiose and vast bureaucracy that now unites all national and international U.S. policing agencies. "Homeland Security": This notorious case of semantic perversion declares, to all who will open ears and listen, our collective regression, our having taken refuge, our retreat to hearth and home, to warmth of womb.

We may have referred for centuries to our national territory as the "land of the free, and the home of the brave," but we have never before in our history called it the "homeland." In and of itself, the term is rather innocuous, and if it didn't have a history of its own—a "certain" history—it might be altogether unobjectionable. However, it has apparently disconcerted few (including the few "progressives" and "radicals" left in the United States) that the only other notable uses of this term in world history appeared in Nazi Germany and in South Africa under apartheid. True, our sense of our "homeland" striving for security under the enlightened leadership of Michael Chertoff appears to most folks to have little to do with the racist foundations of Bantustans and the Reich's *Heimatland*. Yet the sudden centrality of the term *homeland* in the United States would appear indicative also of the politics of safety and security at all costs that has been adopted and universally accepted, for better or for worse, against the other.

The homeland that was Nazi Germany was an ever-spreading *inside* whose safety was to be ensured by purging it of perceived parasites, vermin, and disease. Similar dispositions and gestures have been making their way into official U.S. policy over the past six years in order to appease the zealots of safety that we have become. But just how pathological has our terrorized madness become when we resort to the erection of barriers to keep brown others from their southern infiltration—barriers whose scale would rival China's Great Wall. This is the brown other who supposedly would take my job, he who would make my kid a drug addict or surely, one day, slip in a dirty nuclear bomb, he who might have the audacity to speak only Spanish (or, worse, Arabic or Farsi). Little wonder that we simplistically adjudge as nasty but necessary the security barrier erected by that other nation run by safety demagogues to keep their nasty brown others out.[7]

Anyone who has traveled anywhere since 2001 by any means other than foot, bicycle, or Hummer is acutely aware of a panoply of devices and measures to secure the homeland. We have almost fully interiorized the gesture of removing our shoes and forgoing our liquids and gels at airport safety checks. Because we have become a people who seldom question authority, we adapt for the sake of homeland security. It is not that difficult to pack differently so that we shall all feel safe. Yet, in our unchallenged madness, as long as we put them with our checked baggage, unload, and lock them, we can still travel with our rifles, handguns, and ammunition.[8] The advent of a supposedly secure homeland has dramatically altered the face of the Transportation Security Administration's personnel. No longer do we encounter all those friendly, bumbling, slightly incompetent, well-meaning agents casually inspecting hand luggage and waving us through the security gate. Now it is only surly Transportation Security Administration agents who appear to come from the same economically stressed origins as those who populate our all-"volunteer" armed forces treating everyone the same. For the sake of a safe "homeland," we are all just *this far* from being denounced as enemy combatants. The USA PATRIOT Act, which became permanent law in March 2007, provides for the suspension of habeas corpus as well as the detention and "extraordinary rendition" of terrorist suspects, including U.S. citizens.

By consecrating the nation in which the fantasy of absolute security must be achieved with the word *homeland*, we have reaffirmed the historical myopia and collective amnesia from which we have been suffering ever since we emerged as a superpower. It is as if making security that of the "homeland" we were consecrating our having achieved the status of sole superpower. This is an achievement devoid of fulfillment, however. It is an apotheosis immediately threatened with undermining by forces absolutely at odds with our conception of "home."

A Nation in Denial

Hawai'i was integrated into our "homeland" on August 21, 1959. With Pearl Harbor, however, the U.S. collective conscious has never come to terms that are grounded in some reasonable grasp of historical reality, as it can and should now, finally, be constituted. That is why we have never recognized what the rest of the world did immediately, fourteen years before Hawai'i was told to get rid of that glottal stop and was folded into the homeland: *On August 6 and 9, 1945, state-sanctioned crimes of war (if not against humanity) were perpetrated at Hiroshima and Nagasaki by the United States of America.* Yes, of course, the United States was at war with an intransigent imperial Japan. But impressively demonstrative scenarios for atomic bomb drops *other* than the ones that wiped out some 200,000 unwarned nonmilitary Japanese people were scrapped: *they simply would not have terrorized the population enough.*[9] Hundreds of thousands of civilian lives were deemed expendable when they were those of others (others "othered" as a fanatic civilian population). Vice President Dick Cheney's infamous "We don't do body counts"[10] indicates that for the powers that be today, little has changed. I therefore contend that it is our refusal to recognize "Hiroshima" *specifically* as a crime against humanity that fuels our delusion that crimes against humanity like the "kamikaze" attacks that took place in New York on September 11, 2001—attacks that we rightly, but endlessly and obsessively, call unspeakable—are only perpetrated against us. "Why do they hate us?" we whine, when deep down, somewhere, we know that it is because we occupy ourselves solely with *home* safety. Is Manhattan the ground zero to which the now-sanctified term *Ground Zero* will forever be anchored? The answer to this question bears the most egregious of semantic perversions in an age of terrorism rife with discursive subterfuge.

With Tom Ridge having passed the Homeland Security baton to Michael Chertoff and universal acceptance—in the form of oblivion—of the USA PATRIOT Act,[11] we have slowly made our way back to a bovine sense of safety.[12] We satiate ourselves by chewing our national cud. Yet we delude ourselves: we are as vulnerable and impermanent as the versatile rhetoric that will get George W. Bush's successor—from either party—through the next election and into the White House. We continue to be singularly unsafe in a world that is changing right *beyond* the tips of our upturned noses and in ways we refuse to imagine. Thanks to our psychosis, whose principal symptom is the semantic perversion that has taken hold in our twenty-first century and of which even the election of some fresh new face cannot ensure a cure, we are victims-in-waiting, on the installment plan, *morts à crédit* as Céline put it in the title of his first novel. (And Céline knew something of psychosis translated into the political realm.) Many of the terms in this lexicon of self-deception are fed to us by the Bush-Cheney White House. But some of the key terms, behind which aspects of our ailment lurk, are of our own handicraft. If we have taken false comfort in accepting that our security is to be in the hands of a megabureaucracy whose name starts with *Homeland*, we, as a collectivity, seem solely responsible for having declared that it all began at "Ground Zero."

The bombs that the United States dropped on Japan in 1945 were instruments of terror. The atomic bomb has been used by one state—the one state that first developed it in a secret project named "Manhattan"—for the exclusive and officially sanctioned purpose of terrorizing the population of an enemy state. This *repressed and disfigured fact* alone should suffice to explain the spontaneously sudden currency of the term *Ground Zero* to consecrate the site of an act of *alien* terrorism perpetrated *within* the expansive borders of the United States.

Yet the evidence of the connection between 9/11 Manhattan and August 1945 Hiroshima is compromised by the collective denial subtending the origins of the term. The magnitude of the lock securing this state of amnesia may be measured by the vigorous censorship of an exhibition planned in 1995 for the National Air and Space Museum on the Washington Mall. Unit 4: Ground Zero was to be the first honest and complete display of the Manhattan Project's results, of the military and civilian options for use of the new weapon of mass destruction, and of its eventual use. The exhibit was abruptly cancelled when various pressure groups—notably U.S. veterans of the war in the Pacific—determined the White House to intervene. As a result, not only has the U.S. public yet to learn that a WMD detonated at 800 meters above *ground zero Hiroshima* at 7:58 a.m. on a weekday without warning was *not* the only way to use the new tool, but Martin Harwit, museum director, lost his job by presidential fiat in 1995.[13] Once again we find ourselves safe and sound . . . from ugly but ultimately healthy truths.

Just like the assimilation of 9/11 to the attack on Pearl Harbor or Bush's identification of an "axis of evil," *Ground Zero* is one of those terms from World War II that the present administration has exploited to the hilt in order to orient public opinion toward acceptance of holy vengeance. But with *Ground Zero*, they are playing with fire. For to have embraced this term is to have avowed, finally if still unconsciously, that *Ground Zero* signifies the trauma of a people, a place where a terrorist crime against humanity was committed that no punishment can expiate. In pronouncing *Ground Zero*, we simply have not yet realized that what we are also affirming is that we tacitly recognize that we, the just and the true, did this to the Japanese people. A return of this repressed historical fact could be explosive and revolutionary for both ethics and politics in the United States. If I were working in the interest of the powers that be in Washington, I would advise them to redouble their efforts at extreme caution with this repressed truth.

Home Safety

The USA PATRIOT Act notwithstanding, we are not yet compelled to think along the lines suggested to us by network television and the experience of perception through that filter. Witness, by imagining the speaker's authoritative voice, what television in "our homeland" has become:

> January 2007. CNN. "The Most Trusted Name in News." The network's "Special Investigation Unit." The unit's spokeswoman: Christiane Amanpour, CNN's chief international correspondent. [Tough; husky voice; war-zone fatigues; the authority that U.S. citizens feel viscerally through that British accent.] The report: "The War Within."

We might have guessed that rampant paranoia would bring us to this: we are not even safe from *those who are already here*. It is one thing to take precautionary measures against an "axis" consisting of a few "rogue states" by means of "preemptive wars"; it is quite another to attempt to guard against incursions by saboteurs who may come from anywhere—even from within! Hence Guantánamo, the USA PATRIOT Act, the unbridling of executive power, and the concomitant emasculation of a willing Congress. The safe and "sweet land of liberty" to which we sang in grammar school is neither safe nor free. The very mandatory patriotism, which requires a certain mindlessness, that consists of coercing kids to pledge or sing to a nation (as if it were their mother) has anesthetized us to the point of accepting the USA PATRIOT Act as the rightful substitute of the old U.S. Constitution and shiny new "law" of the homeland. Carl Schmitt, the historian of law and legal philosopher, developed the concept of *exception* to describe in legal terms how political regimes driven solely by ideology give birth to themselves. When *laws of exception*—such as the USA PATRIOT Act, which indeed was openly presented to Congress as a corpus of laws of exception—*permanently* replace the *rule of law*, even the individual liberty the U.S. Constitution was meant to protect is no longer safe from suspension. Executive power is then safe to resume its mask of magnanimity by accepting judicial oversight of eavesdropping when every telephone in the land of the free is already wiretapped. Laws that we blindly believe will guarantee our safety and security will do so at the cost of turning citizens into enemy combatants the day after the next Ground Zero.

It is far—tragically far—from ironic that early in 2006 Congress made laws of exception the rule. Over the past twenty years (perhaps beginning in the Reagan years and the collapse of the Soviet Union), a mentality of exceptionalism has increasingly taken hold in this country. Whereas French exceptionalism has become a quaint residue of bygone colonial power, our sense that we are exceptional is current, fully operational, and expanding. The arrogant exceptionalism of twenty-first-century U.S. citizens is fueled by our obsession with fastidious safety: safety from the swarming hordes of Latinos pressing to enter the lower body of our nation; safety from the French, whose former president, however right-wing, vehemently opposed the second invasion of Iraq; safety, especially, from our own weakly repressed memory of terroristic trauma inflicted on a people of others.

When it comes to relations between disparate human groups, to regulating their relative peacefulness or bellicosity, there is nothing new under the sun. Isolationism is a main ingredient in most recipes for war. Some nation somewhere is always ready to think that by closing its borders and holding a cross (or other fetish) up in the face of an axis of evil it will exorcize the threat of invasion. Focusing first and exclusively on home—*my* parking space for *my* Hummer in front of the convenience store—blinds me to the picture everywhere else.

So, are we safer? In 2001, only a few dozen people in the world had either the will or the way to carry out a suicide attack on the scale of the one that brought down the World Trade Center towers. Now, thanks to the egregious destabilization of the Middle East by the "coalition of the willing," hundreds and probably thousands are literally dying to copy what Mohammed Atta's motley crew carried out. While candidates to renew the White House dither and equivocate, chaos, hypocrisy, and despair are spreading irreversibly, inexorably for the foreseeable future. Meanwhile, Iran's Mahmoud Ahmadinejad has convinced more than a few as to the legitimacy of his country's atomic aspirations: after all, even the cynics say, *our* great allies, the righteous Pakistan and Israel, have the bomb (unconfirmed, of course, in the second case cited).

Peace Instead of Safety?

We are and will remain for the foreseeable future far, far from safe. But let us not end on such a dire note. Achieving the sense of well-being, peace, calm, and security that the word *safety* harbors may be approached in two diametrically opposed ways. One would involve and indeed *does* involve the conceptualization, elaboration, and deployment of safeguards; the other way would require "continuing education" in cultural difference, economic and social divergence among peoples, diplomatic conversation, and magnanimity. The verb forms I have chosen for contrasting the two should indicate which has prevailed at exorbitant expense and with paltry results. The position from which the United States has been attempting to achieve safety since 9/11 consists almost exclusively of defensive measures accepted unquestioningly by a population that lives in a political dystopia fueled by historical amnesia. We have retracted into a patriotic shell in which we can only see the world myopically. This attitude, massively favoring defensive tactics over offensive ones, aligns us with Bush's moronic mantra, "You're either with us or you're against us." But an alternative vision is always possible. It is a vision *of* and *with* the other—one that includes cultural difference in peace. Against myopia, specifically, I am tempted to call it *panoptism*, or maybe even *panoptimism*.

If I am right that the topos of a global terrorist threat, inaugurated at Ground Zero, has led in the direction of monumentally botched wars for regime change and lamentably misguided safety programs managed by Homeland Security, there remains a utopian vision for a way out. The measures to take in order for us to be cured of our myopia, acquire 20/20 *foresight*, and work *with* the world instead of against it from our fragile bubble all involve the armed forces.

The first step is to advocate for and implement a return to the draft. Why, progressives ask, are there no mass protests against the Iraq quagmire when it is clearly as much a failure without aim as the Vietnam War? The answer is that the armed forces have been "voluntary" since the 1970s, and therefore, only the sons and daughters of the most alienated, poor, disaffected, and therefore blindly compliant of our population make up those same armed forces. The danger that more privileged sectors of our society might be drafted would precipitate the inevitable withdrawal from Iraq. Then, once a full withdrawal of U.S. armed forces in Iraq is completed and we apologize for having led Mesopotamia into wrack and ruin, we need to convert the quasi-totality of U.S. armed forces into a *weaponless force* whose mission would be strictly (for lack of a better term) humanitarian. John F. Kennedy was on the right track when he created the Peace Corps, except that the Peace Corps has always been an accessory to the U.S. Army. My idea is for the U.S. Army *to be* the Peace Corps. This would require a revolution in foreign policy transcending a conversion from aggression to negotiation, diplomacy, and compromise: it would require that "humanitarians" jettison their naïveté. Such a utopia would serve, finally, to reinforce the mission of the United Nations rather than antagonize it.

One *more* last word. I would like to pay tribute to citizens of the world too easily forgotten. *Safety first* is the last thing the defenders of liberty, equality, and justice take into consideration. If Anna Politkovskaya had had safety first and foremost on her mind, she would never have become the most prominent critic of political corruption in Russia and Vladimir Putin's autocratic ways.[14] If Hrant Dink had had safety first and foremost on his mind, he would never have become the most prominent revisionist of Turkey's official account of the Armenian Genocide.[15] May such boldly intelligent journalists spread their words and their ways in the United States, and may they be safe.

Notes

1   Tom Ridge, "Statement of Department of Homeland Security Secretary Tom Ridge before the House Select Committee on Homeland Security," U.S. Department of Homeland Security, May 20, 2003, www.dhs.gov/xnews/testimony/testimony_0013.shtm.

2   Tom Ridge, George Pataki, and Michael Bloomberg, "Remarks by Secretary of Homeland Security Tom Ridge, Governor of New York George Pataki, and Mayor of New York City Michael Bloomberg at a Press Conference Regarding Security at the Republican National Convention," U.S. Department of Homeland Security, August 25, 2004, www.dhs.gov/xnews/releases/press_release_0499.shtm.

3   Ibid.

4   J. Jioni Palmer, "King Endorses Racial Profiling," *Newsday*, August 17, 2006.

5   Radeyah Hack and Jeff Licitra, "Congressman Peter King Talks, Students Protest," *Stony Brook Independent*, October 11, 2006, www.sbindependent.org/node/1267/.

6   "'You are either with us or against us,'" CNN, November 6, 2001, http://archives.cnn.com/2001/US/11/06/gen.attack.on.terror.

7   I have written this allusion to Israel and its policy with regard to Palestinian Arabs and

Christians in such a way as to suggest the radical equivalency of both groups under the one term *Semite*. I have argued for this equivalency elsewhere, notably in *Témoins d'artifice* (*Witnessworks*) (Paris: L'Harmattan, 2003), as have others, in their own ways. Two further references for this way of thinking are Denis Guénoun, *Un Sémite* (Paris: Circe, 2003), and Gil Anidjar, *The Jew, The Arab: A History of the Enemy* (Stanford, CA: Stanford University Press, 2003).

8   When a friend read this, she was incredulous. I urged her to read the TSA's page on "permitted and prohibited items": U.S. Transportation Security Administration, www.tsa.gov/travelers/airtravel/prohibited/permitted-prohibited-items.shtm (accessed June 15, 2007).

9   See, for example, Gene Ray, *Terror and the Sublime in Art and Critical Theory: From Auschwitz to Hiroshima to September 11* (New York: Palgrave Macmillan, 2005), in particular chapter 3, "Ground Zero: Hiroshima Haunts '9/11,'" 51–60.

10   General Tommy Franks may have been the first to use the expression in response to questions about how many Iraqi civilians had died in the "coalition" bombing and subsequent invasion. Former secretary of defense Donald Rumsfeld, however, is most famous for using the expression. He first pronounced it publicly in an interview with Tony Snow on *Fox News Sunday*, November 2, 2003, www.foxnews.com/story/0,2933,101956,00.html.

11   It is worth remembering that *USA* in this acronym does not stand for the United States of America and that *PATRIOT* should be written in capital letters because not only does it complete the acronym, but also it stands as the fetish term for mandatory unanimity cowing our country's legislators into blindly passing these laws of exception. The acronym unpacked is Uniting and Strengthening America by Providing Appropriate Tools Required to Intercept and Obstruct Terrorism.

12   See Robert Harvey and Hélène Volat, *De l'exception à la règle: USA PATRIOT Act* (Paris: Lignes-Essais, 2006).

13   In addition to Ray, *Terror and the Sublime*, see also Martin Harwit, "Academic Freedom in 'The Last Act,'" *Journal of American History* 82.3 (December 1995): 1064–84.

14   Anna Stepanovna Politkovskaya (1958–2006) was a Russian journalist and political activist. In her criticism of Vladimir Putin's autocratic and authoritarian methods, she was perhaps most well known (and reviled) for her persistent opposition to Russia's policy in Chechnya. She was assassinated in the elevator of her apartment building.

15   Hrant Dink (1954–2007) was a Turkish journalist of Armenian ethnicity. He was founder and editor in chief of the bilingual newspaper *Agos*. He was a defender of minority rights and steadfastly struggled for the Turkish government to officially recognize the death of some several hundred thousand to more than a million Armenians between 1915 and 1917 as genocide. He was tried three times for "denigrating Turkishness." "Hrant Dink's Final Article," BBC, January 20, 2007, http://news.bbc.co.uk/2/hi/europe/6283461.stm. He was assassinated in broad daylight in a street in downtown Istanbul.

James Mandrell

"It Couldn't Happen Here":
A Cross-Cultural Rhetoric

So prepare, say a pray'r,
Send the word, send the word to beware.
We'll be over, we're coming over,
And we won't come back till it's over
Over there.
—George M. Cohan, "Over There," 1917

Now it almost seems impossible
We've found ourselves back where we started from
I may be wrong, I thought we said
It couldn't happen here
—Pet Shop Boys, "It Couldn't Happen Here," 1987

Before the Democrats retook both chambers of Congress (November 2006/January 2007), before George W. Bush admitted to secret CIA prisons (September 7, 2006), before the revelation of abuses in Abu Ghraib (April 2004), before Bush triumphantly marched across the deck of the carrier USS *Abraham Lincoln* to announce "Mission accomplished!" (May 2003), before Colin Powell's address to the United Nations in which he presented proof of weapons of mass destruction (February 2003), before Bush declared Iraq part of an axis of evil in a State of the Union address (January 2002) . . . before all of this, there was the simple fact of September 11, 2001.[1]

South Atlantic Quarterly 107:2, Spring 2008
DOI 10.1215/00382876-2007-069 © 2008 Duke University Press

I was in my office at the university, in Waltham, Massachusetts, that morning, doing whatever it is that we do in our offices, when I received an e-mail from a colleague in the Midwest. "What's going on with the WTC?" I immediately checked with CNN.com and then headed out to find a television. So it was that I saw the second plane, United flight 175, hit the South Tower at 9:02 a.m. Spellbound, I remained in front of the television until shortly after the South Tower collapsed, at which point I returned to my office. In something like a state of shock, I picked up the phone to call my mother in Phoenix. I could tell when she answered the phone that I had awakened her, but I proceeded to assure her that neither my partner, Rob, nor I was traveling that day and that my sister and her husband were also going about their business in New Hampshire. There was no need to worry. Groggily, she thanked me, not understanding the import of the call, and hung up. Later, when she called me back after realizing why I had called in the first place, she said quietly, "I never thought it could happen here."

Versions of this phrase were heard everywhere in the United States, and perhaps understandably.[2] The closest major assault on U.S. territory by someone other than U.S. citizens occurred when the Japanese attacked Pearl Harbor in 1941, and even that felt somewhat remote, given that it was off in the Pacific Ocean, some 2,500 miles west of the mainland. Subsequent attacks—such as the USS *Cole* bombing in 2000, even the eerily prescient World Trade Center bombing in 1993, the bombings of various U.S. embassies—seemed but minor blips in a history of "over there," even when over here.

The historical fact of keeping trouble far away, when taken with the notion of what is commonly referred to as "American exceptionalism," had the effect of making the attacks of September 11 all the more shocking, and not simply in terms of the violence and tragedy they brought, nor merely because of the extraordinary diplomatic and military reactions to which they gave rise.[3] Rather, the attacks and their aftermath revealed a surprising rhetorical inability on the part of the United States to come to grips with the event, as if we had been rendered speechless and uncomprehending, were suffering from a kind of aphasia. Even President George W. Bush initially reacted, perhaps characteristically, with silence when informed of the assaults, and continued with his photo opportunity at the Emma E. Booker Elementary School in Sarasota, Florida. Then he seemed to disappear from the face of the earth for the rest of the day.

To be sure, television broadcasts were in an all-disaster-all-the-time mode and certainly not without speech, and newspapers offered exhaustive and exhausting coverage. But the uncertainty, expressed as hesitancy and a loss of words, provoked by the events of September 11 was easily detected in the articles, editorials, letters, and op-ed pieces that were published over the next several days. Throughout the extensive commentary ran a litany of questions—why? why us? why now?—and baffled attempts at explanation that explained whatever was known at a particular moment. Thus, Bush, in a broadcast speech on September 11 that did little but paint a picture of U.S. resolve, spoke of "disbelief, terrible sadness, and a quiet, unyielding anger."[4] The next day, the lead editorial in the *New York Times*, entitled "The War against America: An Unfathomable Attack," included statements such as "Remember the ordinary, if you can," and "Every routine, every habit this city knew was fractured yesterday."[5] Letters to the editor in the same newspaper on that same day qualified the sadness as "unspeakable," and someone writing from Germany asked, "Who has words for what happened? What can we say—we are far away?" as if the possibility of speech were somehow linked to physical and/or geographical proximity.[6] Similarly, Maureen Dowd's commentary bore the title "Liberties: A Grave Silence," noting, "Manhattan had the noise of the grave. Washington had the silence of the grave." More acutely, she began, "If you called yesterday afternoon to the White House switchboard, that famously efficient Washington institution, you would hear a brief recording saying to hold for an operator and then the line would go dead."[7]

In many respects, Bush's address to the United States during the evening of September 11 was remarkably effective, as many commentators affirmed. Although short on analysis and explanation, since little was known beyond the disaster itself, Bush rallied people of all political stripes to gather around the flag in a show of unity. He also made clear that it wasn't a question only of people in the United States, since he laid down this rhetorical gauntlet: "We will make no distinction between the terrorists who committed these acts and those who harbor them."[8] Over the days that followed, people around the world and across the political spectrum stood solid with the United States. As a political leader in a time of extraordinary events, Bush swiftly divided the world into us and them, good and evil.

Bush also made it clear that he, as the commander in chief, would look to the security and safety of the people of the United States—hence, the division into us and them. In these terms, security and safety were physical things, pertaining to the impenetrability of our borders and airspace, our ability to lead our lives without fear or—in the lexicon of the Bush administration and much of the U.S. media—terror, that is, terrorists and terrorism. Yet, as many have noted, Bush used the rhetoric of fear, and continues to do so, as a means of instilling in the citizenry an almost irrational preoccupation with issues of safety,[9] such that, I would argue, we need to consider that questions of safety and security are not merely physical or tangible, but they also lurk in the language of reporting, explaining, defending, calling into question . . . in short, everywhere.

As pertains to the matter of us and them, good and evil, however satisfying and facile these Manichaean distinctions proved to a majority of the United States, there were dissenters, among them Susan Sontag, Dinesh D'Souza, and Bill Maher, at least two of whom paid a high price for pointing out the obvious. Sontag, in a much-vilified commentary published in the *New Yorker*, noted: "The voices licensed to follow the event seem to have joined together in a campaign to infantilize the public."[10] Her gravest sin was to call into question application of the word *cowardly* to the actions of September 11: "And if the word 'cowardly' is to be used [as in 'cowardly attack'], it might be more aptly applied to those who kill from beyond the range of retaliation, high in the sky, than to those willing to die themselves in order to kill others. In the matter of courage (a morally neutral virtue): whatever may be said of the perpetrators of Tuesday's slaughter, they were not cowards."[11] Sontag's commentary on the question of cowardice was joined by an exchange between D'Souza and Maher on the latter's *Politically Incorrect*, and all three were subsequently involved in conversations over semantics and what was in essence seen as treason.[12] Whereas Bush saw no difference between terrorists and "those who harbor them," the notion of harboring terrorists was expanded to include any speech that could possibly be interpreted by anyone as undermining the U.S. effort. Speech was being monitored for ideological conformity. Slowly but surely, people fell into line, and the doubters and naysayers fell to grumbling more or less quietly.

As the days became weeks, months, and years, we became accustomed to fitful speech, partial explanations, and revisions of events, including dizzying shifts in cause and effect. Indeed, it was as if everyone around us had been overtaken by fits of stammering and stuttering, that is, in the words of the *Oxford English Dictionary*, had begun to "falter or stumble in one's speech . . . to make one or more involuntary repetitions of a consonant or vowel before being able to pass from it to the following sound," or to "speak with continued involuntary repetition of sounds or syllables, owing to excitement, fear, or constitutional nervous defect" (cf. *stammer* and *stutter*). In retrospect, it is clear that excitement, fear, and constitutional defects—rather, defects in constitutionality—were all involved in the stammered explanations and excuses that swept around us: weapons of mass destruction, secret contacts with Osama bin Laden, violations of UN sanctions, terrorist cells, liberation of the Iraqis, safety in the "homeland," democracy and stability in the Middle East. Yet, as the years went by and evidence mounted that, in fact, stammering aside, the U.S. response to the assault on the World Trade Center was, if not misguided, certainly misrepresented time and again, people continued to listen and to believe, and therefore, they reelected George W. Bush and Richard B. Cheney to a second term in office.

What people failed to recognize is the degree to which this story, which began on September 11, 2001, could not be brought to an end.[13] There were simply too many loose ends to be tied up, much less tied up neatly. I am reminded of Barbara Johnson's discussion of Melville's *Billy Budd*, in which she notes of the novella:

> Far from totalizing itself into intentional finality, the story in fact begins to repeat itself—retelling itself first in reverse, and then in verse. The ending not only lacks special authority, it problematizes the very *idea* of authority by placing its own reversal in the pages of an "authorized" naval chronicle. To end is to repeat, and to repeat is to be ungovernably open to revision, displacement, and reversal. The sense of Melville's ending is to empty the ending of any privileged control over sense.[14]

In the case of September 11 and what followed, the narrative becomes the quintessential never-ending story that stutters and stammers on without end precisely because the endings we've been given—for example, "Mission accomplished!"—however authoritatively uttered, lack any authority, "any privileged control over sense."

The degree to which public discourse and political action in the United States have declined can be gauged by considering the events in Madrid on Thursday, March 11, 2004, known as 11-M, and their aftermath. Just after 7:30 a.m., three bombs exploded on a commuter train in Atocha, a major transportation hub in the center of Madrid. Shortly after, four additional bombs went off on a train as it entered that same station, two more bombs went off on a double-decker train in the station at El Pozo del Tío Raimundo, and another in a train arriving at Santa Eugenia. In all, ten bombs exploded and another three explosive devices were located and safely detonated. Within a matter of minutes, 190 people were killed—or more, depending on how and when the counting took place—and more than 2,000 were wounded.

To put this into perspective, the attacks on March 11, 2004, were the deadliest acts of terrorism in the modern history of Spain and the worst in Europe since the bombing of Pan Am flight 103 by Libyan terrorists over Lockerbie, Scotland, in 1988, facts that did not go unremarked in the Spanish press, ditto the comparison to September 11, 2001.[15] The day after the bombings, which occurred just three days before national elections were to be held, the announcement of the suspension of campaigning included historical comparisons found in the major national daily newspaper, *El País*: "Representatives of the democratic parties appeared shocked after learning the scope of the terrorist massacre, without precedent not only in Spain, but in Europe. They were clearly aware that this event will in some way affect the results of the elections on Sunday and the direction of the new legislature. By 10:00 am it was already known that March 11 was the European version of the North American September 11."[16]

As was the case in the United States, the various news media paid close attention to the situation and constantly updated the public with new information and reports, but attention quickly focused on official attempts to attribute responsibility for the bombings to the Basque separatist group ETA (Euskadi Ta Askatasuna—Basque Homeland and Freedom). As early as March 12, signs were pointing to al-Qaeda or another Islamic group, but Prime Minister José María Aznar's conservative government stuck to denouncing ETA. In a general overview of the bombings, doubts were cast on the link to ETA:

> From the beginning yesterday, sources in the antiterrorist fight in Spain believed that the attack was not in "the style" of those committed by ETA and that they had to have been planned for at least a month by a group of between 12 and 30 terrorists. Until now, the Interior Ministry has maintained that the infrastructure of ETA in Madrid was minimal. Moreover, the criminals did not give any warning of their deadly intentions, as ETA customarily does before its attacks.
>
> Despite all of this evidence, Interior Minister Ángel Acebes dispelled any doubts during a press conference held at 1:00 pm: "ETA has

realized its goal. The government has no doubt whatsoever that ETA is behind this." And he added: "It is absolutely unacceptable for anything to be directed at turning attention away from those responsible for this tragedy," in reference to information that pointed to Islamic groups as authors of the attacks.[17]

Another article clarifies that there were doubts from the beginning, but that these were set aside by senior officials: "The Interior Ministry singled out ETA from the first as the possible author of the attacks perpetrated yesterday against four trains in Madrid, but last night it already believed that the assassins might have been a radical Islamic group. . . . ETA became the only official hypothesis, despite the fact that investigators had said from the beginning, 'This is not their style.'"[18]

It was not just a question of the interior minister acting on his own, although some did call for his resignation.[19] Malén Aznárez, the ombudsperson at *El País*, explained the paper's source for the connection between ETA and the bombings as reported in a special edition that appeared on March 11: "The five-column headline is overwhelming: Massacre by ETA in Madrid. On what did *El País* base such an assertion if the interior minister had not yet confirmed it? It is very simple. Although different sources in the Department of the Interior had indeed affirmed it, the president of the government, José María Aznar, called the director of the newspaper, Jesús Ceberio, to confirm the attribution."[20]

Over the next two days, a kind of tug-of-war took place regarding information about and attribution of the attacks. It soon became clear that Aznar's government had taken control of the investigations and had shut out all other investigative authorities, in effect openly politicizing the attacks and their aftermath. As reported in *El País*, Interior Minister Acebes continued to insist on ETA as the responsible party and treated as "mere 'doubts' the possibility that an organization like Al Qaeda could have been responsible for the attacks."[21] At the same time, *El País* ran an article with the title "Radical Islamists Assure That the Claims of Al Qaeda Are 'Authentic,'" based on information from the Italian daily *La Repubblica*.[22] Even more critical and telling was the "investigative blackout," which led to increasing skepticism about the integrity of the government's interests in the bombings.[23]

Everything came to a head—the bombings, the elections, the misleading reports from Aznar's government—at a demonstration on March 13, the day before the elections. The government had originally organized a demonstration for March 12, in which around 11.5 million people across the country protested the bombings, chanting slogans such as "We were all on that train," "We're not all here; 200 are missing," "It's not raining, Madrid is crying," "The blood that was spilled will never be forgotten," "A united Spain will never be vanquished," "ETA and Al Qaeda are the same shit," as well as, quite pointedly, "We want to know who it was" and "We want the truth before Sunday."[24] In Madrid alone, it was estimated that more than half of the urban population, 2.3 of 4 million people, showed up for the demonstration, including government leaders from all parties and the three children of King Juan Carlos and Queen Sofía, Elena, Cristina, and Felipe, an appearance that was unprecedented in Spain's history.

The actions of the Spanish royal family bear some scrutiny, since they were, by the standards of the United States, noteworthy. Upon learning from Aznar of the attacks, King Juan Carlos, Queen Sofía, Prince Felipe, and his fiancée, Letizia Ortiz, watched from the king's office in his home as the first images appeared on television. At noon, while the king stayed behind to receive updates on the situation, the queen, joined by Felipe and Ortiz, began to visit hospitals in Madrid where victims had been taken and their families had gathered. Throughout the afternoon, the queen visited four hospitals, offering to the people she met "hugs, kisses, and words of encouragement." At one hospital, she consoled a woman who was waiting for her daughter-in-law; the queen was so moved that "tears rolled down her cheek." The woman she was consoling was heard to say, "The queen really cries." That same day, the king and queen's two daughters and sons-in-law together visited two hospitals after Cristina and her husband, Iñaki Urdangarín (who is himself of Basque and Belgian descent), arrived in Madrid from Barcelona and met up with Elena and Jaime de Marichalar.[25]

The evening of March 11, King Juan Carlos addressed the nation in a recorded message. With the exception of his annual Christmas broadcasts, it was only the second time that he had done something like that. The first was when, in response to an attempted coup by various military officers on February 23, 1981, he spoke as commander in chief of the armed forces against the perpetrators and in defense of the Spanish Constitution. In recognition of a similarly serious event, he once again spoke directly to the people, to rally them, of course, but also to express his own solidarity in personal terms:

> In these tragic times, I want to convey to the families of the victims my deepest affection and that of my family. I wish I could join with you all in an embrace of consolation and sadness. I will always be with

you, with all those who suffer the consequences of a macabre madness without any possible justification. These repugnant attacks merit
the most energetic and absolute condemnation. I also direct myself to
the wounded and their families, to express to them our affection, our
closeness, and our wish for a speedy recovery. Your king suffers with
you, and shares your indignation.[26]

Although it would be a mistake to sentimentalize the words and deeds of
members of the Spanish royal family, it is important to note the degree
to which they moved quickly on two fronts. First, King Juan Carlos was
understood to be involved from the first in discussions of the attacks and
to be regularly informed of developments. Second, Queen Sofía and the
children were visible presences in the community as they consoled those
who were most affected. In what might be described as a sacramental rendering of the relationship between the Spanish royal family and the people
of Spain, the words and deeds of the former joined together to symbolize
their commitment to and even their corporeality as part and parcel of the
latter.

The relatively calm demonstration of March 12, in which the royal children joined, was followed the next day by a much smaller but more political
action. Traditionally, the day before elections is a "day for reflection" (día
de reflexión), without campaigning or political activities. This tradition—
and law, according to Aznar's Partido Popular (PP) with the concurrence
of the courts—was broken by thousands of people throughout Spain who
protested against the government in central locations in major cities as well
as in front of the PP's various headquarters.[27] By this time, many felt it was
clear that the PP had been manipulating information in order to benefit at
the electoral urns.[28] When the elections were held the following day, the
PP was stripped of its power, and after being elected, José Luis Rodríguez
Zapatero, leader of the Partido Socialista Obrero Español, began to form
a new government. Although opinion polls up to the last days before the
election showed a tight race with the nod going to the PP, commentary
subsequent to the elections consistently noted the effect that the March 11
bombings had on the results.

Part of the issue in the outcome of the elections had to do with Aznar's
support—and, by extension, the support of his government and of Spain—
for the invasion of Iraq, which included sending Spanish troops to Iraq
as part of the international forces. For many, the bombings were seen as
an attempt to intimidate Spain into changing governments and thus with-

drawing its troops from the Middle East. But analyses of the elections pointed to a different conclusion. Even when the invasion of Iraq was adduced as a factor, it was the rhetoric about the war and its causes, coupled with the government's response to the bombings, that brought about the change in leadership: "The terrorist attack on March 11 as well as, above all, the conduct of José María Aznar's government when faced with the attack, brought back memories of the war. A lie, the weapons of mass destruction, and then another, that ETA, without any proof, had caused the massacre."[29] Yet there was an even simpler explanation that laid the failure of the PP at the feet of the party itself: "It is possible that on this occasion citizens have punished the government, withdrawing their support or voting for the opposition, because of what for many national and international observers has been a terrible reaction to the tragedy of March 11. The government of the PP did not act with transparency and it paid for that."[30]

On this side of the Atlantic, reaction to the events in Spain was, unfortunately, all too predictable. The initial outpourings of sympathy—the lead editorial in the *New York Times* concluded with the words "We are all Madrileños now"[31]—were quickly followed by reproofs: for comparing March 11 to September 11, for failing to be prepared for the bombings, for the results of the elections. Alan Riding chided those who would make a connection between the two attacks because it was something that people over there should be used to and should have expected: "After the murderous bombings in Madrid on Thursday, Spanish newspapers immediately compared 11-M—March 11—to 9/11. But there was a flaw in the analogy. On Sept. 11, 2001, the United States was caught off guard. In contrast, Spain and several other European countries have experienced terrorism for more than three decades. And lately they had been bracing for a big terrorist action somewhere in the region." Of course, Riding ignores the fact that, from all reports, the United States should have been bracing for "a big terrorist action somewhere in the region" of the continental United States, but did not pay heed to all of the intelligence pointing to that.[32]

Regarding the Spanish elections, there were indeed some moderate voices in the United States, but the loudest by far were of those who decried Spain's acquiescence to the threats of al-Qaeda and the withdrawal of troops. David Brooks, Thomas L. Friedman, and Edward N. Luttwak were particularly vitriolic. Brooks suggested up front that he did not want to think ill of Spanish voters, but then, even though he admitted he did not have all the facts, he chastised them:

I am trying not to think harshly of the Spanish. They have suffered a grievous blow, and it was crazy to go ahead with an election a mere three days after the Madrid massacre. Nonetheless, here is what seems to have happened:

> The Spanish government was conducting policies in Afghanistan and Iraq that Al Qaeda found objectionable. A group linked to Al Qaeda murdered 200 Spaniards, claiming that the bombing was punishment for those policies. Some significant percentage of the Spanish electorate was mobilized after the massacre to shift the course of the campaign, throw out the old government and replace it with one whose policies are more to Al Qaeda's liking.[33]

Condemnation followed upon an uninformed explanation ("Here is what seems to have happened"), which included the notion that Spanish voters were responding to the concerns of al-Qaeda and not their own reservations ("The Spanish government was conducting policies in Afghanistan and Iraq that Al Qaeda found objectionable").

Friedman was equally indignant but somewhat more historical in his assertions: "Spain is planning to do something crazy: to try to appease radical evil by pulling Spain's troops out of Iraq." Then he noted the futility of such a gesture: "The notion that Spain can separate itself from Al Qaeda's onslaught on Western civilization by pulling its troops from Iraq is a fantasy. Bin Laden has said that Spain was once Muslim and he wants it restored that way."[34] That is, because Spain was once the home of Muslims—before 1492 and the Spanish Reconquest—it must understand the bombings as part of an ongoing religious and territorial struggle. Luttwak made the same point, but in a fit of high dudgeon:

> Osama bin Laden and other Islamists had identified Spain as a priority target years before the Iraq war. Under Muslim law, no land conquered by Islam may legitimately come under non-Muslim rule. For the fanatics, Spain is still Al Andalus of the Middle Ages, which must be re-claimed for Islam by immigration and intimidation. Even if the bombs were placed by Islamists, the idea that Spain was attacked solely because of Mr. Aznar's support for the Iraq war is simply wrong.[35]

To be sure, others offered more judicious and reflective opinions. The *New York Times* saw the election as an "exercise in healthy democracy, in which a change of government is simply that, and not a change in national character."[36] Different people wrote in to correct the flaws in fact and logic by Friedman and Luttwak. Apropos of Friedman's article, one person wrote, "If he wants to blame someone for the sea change in Spain, he should blame the 'coalition of the willing' and its dishonest policy making. . . . We should thank the Spanish people for standing up to the Bush administration while we Americans sit idly by in silence."[37] Of Luttwak's strained logic, someone from Spain wrote, "Asserting that the Spanish people have allowed terrorists to 'dictate the outcome' of our national election is as dangerous as saying that the United States government fulfilled Al Qaeda's wishes by invading Iraq and providing more innocent dead for 'the cause.'"[38] Maureen Dowd noted acidly, "House Republicans haven't suggested an embargo on olives and paella yet, but it's probably just pocos minutos away. By the time these guys are through, it will be unpatriotic to consume any ethnic food but fish and chips and kielbasa, washed down with a fine Bulgarian wine."[39]

Yet it took two others to put the Spanish election into the kind of perspective that begins to elucidate important differences between reactions in the United States and Spain to September 11 and March 11, respectively. Elaine Sciolino noted that the Aznar government's manipulation of the truth of the attacks, whether perceived or real, "unleashed demons lurking in Spain's history. It was only 29 years ago that General Francisco Franco died, bringing to an end nearly four decades of dictatorship." For Sciolino, "history and current events combined to produce a whirlwind of resentment. Perceptions that the government had misled the public about weapons of mass destruction in Iraq blended with misleading public declarations about the investigation into the Madrid bombings, and both fed memories of the manipulations of truth under dictatorship decades ago." Thus, the election was not about the bombings or Spanish involvement in Iraq per se. It was "a referendum on the government's commitment to democratic rule."[40]

Paul Krugman made a somewhat similar point when he drew a distinction between voters in Spain and those in the United States that had to do with the obligations of democracy. According to Krugman, in the best democratic tradition, voters in Spain were holding their government accountable for actions, policies, and words. Yet, "in the world according to Mr. Bush's supporters, anyone who demands accountability is on the side of the evildoers." He summed up the opposing views of Spain in this way: "So there you have it. A country's ruling party leads the nation into a war fought on false pretenses, fails to protect the nation from terrorists and engages in a cover-up when a terrorist attack does occur. But its electoral defeat isn't democracy at work; it's a victory for the terrorists."[41]

Whereas Friedman and Luttwak took Spain to task for its *lack* of historical memory, Sciolino located the change in the government in the *persistence* of memory. Whereas Bush and his supporters had divided the world in Manichaean fashion into good and evil, Krugman implicitly pointed to the possibility that evil can be found in more than one place, on more than one side of an issue, including in a democratically elected government. Thus, in Spain, it appeared that people listened carefully to what had been said, considered what had been done, and made a decision that security was not simply a matter of borders and airspace, of the ability to lead lives without fear or "terror." Rather, the rhetorical dimensions of safety revealed a more troubling threat to security, the stutter, authoritative and/or authoritarian, that could be cured only by silence. To put it in slightly different terms, what Johnson referred to as the "privileged control over sense" ultimately rests not in the government but in the body politic, as Aznar and the PP learned to their dismay.

A persistence of memory in the United States in the weeks, months, and years following September 11 would have noted similarities to McCarthyism and the witch hunts of the 1950s; the struggle for ideological conformity, both politically and socially; perhaps the perfidy of Richard M. Nixon; and the more recent "culture wars" and discussions of "political correctness." The powerful insights provided by a historical perspective would have enabled people in the United States to realize that the gauntlet that Bush threw down when he addressed the nation on the evening of the attacks — "We will make no distinction between the terrorists who committed these acts and those who harbor them"—was not a statement of fact but instead a rhetorical strategy, the purpose of which was to place evil "over there" so that we could remain good. And safe. Because we responded to Bush, and to all of the language of patriotism swirling around us, by accepting what he said at face value, we failed to recall, as they did in Spain, that evil is not an either/or proposition, but that evil can exist among the good as well as over there, its rhetoric to be recognized and it effects resisted.

For all that Donald Rumsfeld disparaged "Old Europe"—meaning in that instance Germany and France, which would be joined by Spain's Zapatero government some fifteen months later in its opposition to the invasion of Iraq—there is a degree to which the United States could learn much about political discourse and process, to say nothing of the complex nature of safety.[42] Despite remarking on Spain's inability to recognize the long-term Islamic threat to the integrity of the country that stemmed from the

Middle Ages, both Friedman and Luttwak conveniently forgot about far more recent historical events in the United States that would have indicated the necessity for a change not merely in direction but of horses and riders. It is possible that the shifts occurring in U.S. political life since the beginning of 2007 will bring with them a renewed attention to language and its effects. And yet, unlike in Spain, I fear that, to quote the Pet Shop Boys, "It couldn't happen here."[43]

Notes

1   There are many easily accessible timelines for the events prior to, on the day of, and after September 11, 2001. Among those, some of the most useful are the following: CNN, "September 11: Chronology of Terror," September 12, 2001, http://archives.cnn.com/2001/US/09/11/chronology.attack/ (accessed December 15, 2006); Wikipedia, "September 11, 2001, Timeline for the Day of the Attacks," http://en.wikipedia.org/wiki/September_11,_2001_timeline_for_the_day_of_the_attacks (accessed February 23, 2007); Cooperative Research, "Complete 911 Timeline," September 14, 2006, www.cooperativeresearch.org/project.jsp?project=911_project (accessed December 15, 2006); and U.S. Army, "Timeline of Terrorism," September 11, 2007, www.army.mil/terrorism/ (accessed September 20, 2007).

2   Ronald Steel wrote in an op-ed in the *New York Times*:

> This is the end: the end of an era, the era of our invulnerability. We will recover physically and even psychologically, but nothing will ever quite be the same again. A barrier has been irrevocably breached: a barrier against the world outside. Until this week our enemies never seriously penetrated our continental shores. But in the attacks on the World Trade Center and the Pentagon, the proud symbols of our global power and influence were violated. Our invulnerability lasted for more than 200 years.

   Steel, "The Weak at War with the Strong," *New York Times*, September 14, 2001. See also "It Happened Here," *New Republic*, September 24, 2001, 10–12.

3   On American exceptionalism, see Seymour Martin Lipset, *American Exceptionalism: A Double-Edged Sword* (New York: W. W. Norton, 1996); Deborah L. Madsen, *American Exceptionalism* (Jackson: University of Mississippi Press, 1998); Michael Ignatieff, ed., *American Exceptionalism and Human Rights* (Princeton, NJ: Princeton University Press, 2005); and Byron E. Shafer, ed., *Is America Different? A New Look at American Exceptionalism* (Oxford: Clarendon Press, 1991).

   In an essay on American exceptionalism in the world after September 11, Stanley Hoffman writes:

> The United States has had much leeway to be original. The main component of its exceptionalism has been, for more than a century after its independence, its geographically privileged position: far enough away from Europe and Asia to be able to be safe and uninvolved, yet capable of expanding into contiguous territories easily and without much of a contest. A second component was its institutions: it grew

into being the greatest representative democracy, with greater participation of the public and of the legislative branch in foreign affairs than occurred anywhere else. Finally, American principles turned geography and institutions into guidelines for behavior: a distaste for the rule of force that characterized European diplomacy and colonialism, the repudiation of aristocracy and its wiles, enshrined in a sacred text, the Constitution, which served and still serves as the glue that amalgamates all the ingredients of the melting pot. (France, with its vast number of constitutions, could use only its language and culture as the glue of Frenchness.)

Hoffman, "American Exceptionalism: The New Version," in *American Exceptionalism and Human Rights*, 225–40, 225.

4 George W. Bush, "Statement by the President in His Address to the Nation," September 11, 2001, www.whitehouse.gov/news/releases/2001/09/20010911-16.html.

5 "The War against America: An Unfathomable Attack," editorial, *New York Times*, September 12, 2001.

6 Suzanne E. Evans, letter to the editor, *New York Times*, September 12, 2001; and Martin Meyer, letter to the editor, *New York Times*, September 12, 2001.

7 Maureen Dowd, "Liberties: A Grave Silence," *New York Times*, September 12, 2001.

8 Bush, "Statement."

9 See, for example, Paul Krugman, "Weak on Terror," *New York Times*, March 16, 2004.

10 Susan Sontag, Talk of the Town, *New Yorker*, September 24, 2001, 32.

11 Ibid.

12 On the exchange between D'Souza and Maher, see Celestine Bohlen, "Think Tank: In the New War on Terrorism, Words Are Weapons, Too," *New York Times*, September 29, 2001. For a reasoned appraisal of the situation, see Stanley Fish, "Condemnation without Absolutes," *New York Times*, October 15, 2001. For extreme versions of reaction, see Charles Krauthammer, "Voices of Moral Obtuseness," *Washington Post*, September 24, 2001, who asks and answers, "Why are we keeping Saddam in his box? Because we know he is developing nuclear, chemical and biological weapons"; and John Podhoretz, "America-Haters Within," *New York Post*, September 19, 2001, who demonstrates a breathtaking ability to misread, as when he cites Sontag as lamenting, "'Our country is strong,' we are told again and again. I for one don't find this entirely consoling. Who doubts that America is strong? But that's not all America has to be." He then asserts, "Our nation should be weak and defenseless, in Sontag's view, because that is the only fair thing for an immoral and hateful nation to be."

13 In this regard, Susan Sontag once again proved prescient. In an article in the *New Statesman* with the subtitle "Bush's endless 'war on terrorism' stops thought and releases the US from all bounds on its conduct," she opens: "Since last 11 September, the Bush administration has told the American people, America has been at war. But this war has a rather peculiar nature. It seems to be, given the nature of the enemy, a war with no foreseeable end. What kind of war is that?" Sontag, "How Grief Turned into Humbug," *New Statesman*, September 16, 2002, www.newstatesman.com/200209160021.

14 Barbara Johnson, "Melville's Fist: The Execution of *Billy Budd*," in *The Critical Difference: Essays in the Contemporary Rhetoric of Reading* (Baltimore: Johns Hopkins University Press, 1981), 79–109, 81.

15 "El atentado más sangriento en Europa desde 1988" ("The Bloodiest Attack in Europe since 1988"), *El País*, March 12, 2004. All translations are my own.

16 L. R. Aizpeolea and C. Valdecantos, "Los partidos suspenden la campaña electoral y el Gobierno convoca hoy una manifestación" ("Political Parties Suspend the Election Campaign and the Government Calls for a Public Demonstration"), *El País*, March 12, 2004. See also Timothy Garton Ash's commentary, in which he asserts that the March 11 bombings in Madrid were Europe's version of September 11. Ash, "Is This Europe's 9/11?" *Guardian*, March 13, 2004, http://politics.guardian.co.uk/comment/story/0,9115,1168578,00.html. This commentary was published that same day in *El País* in a translation by María Luisa Rodríguez Tapia.

17 José Manuel Romero, "Cuatro atentados simultáneos causan una matanza en trenes de Madrid" ("Four Simultaneous Attacks Cause a Slaughter on Madrid Trains"), *El País*, March 12, 2004.

18 Jorge A. Rodríguez, "Interior apunta a Al Qaeda y no descarta a ETA" ("The Interior Ministry Points at Al Qaeda and Does Not Dismiss ETA"), *El País*, March 12, 2004.

19 "IU sostiene que el PP manipula el atentado para ganar apoyos" ("IU Maintains That the PP Manipulated the Attacks to Gain Support"), *El País*, March 13, 2004.

20 Malén Aznárez, "Infomar en medio de la confusión" ("Reporting in the Midst of Confusion"), *El País*, March 14, 2004. This same information was reported in the *New York Times*: "Mr. Aznar personally called the editorial heads of newspapers and television and radio stations at 1:30 p.m. and said the government was sure it was ETA. He urged them to put out the information." Lizette Alvarez and Elaine Sciolino, "Spanish Government Seeks to Document That It Did Not Lie about Suspects," *New York Times*, March 19, 2004.

21 Ernesto Ekaizer, "'Apagón' sobre la marcha de las investigaciones" ("'Blackout' on the Progress of the Investigations"), *El País*, March 13, 2004.

22 "Radicales islamistas aseguran que las reivindicaciones de Al Qaeda son 'auténticas'" ("Radical Islamists Assure That the Claims of Al Qaeda Are 'Authentic'"), *El País*, March 13, 2004. See José Manuel Romero's timeline regarding the bombings, the government's reactions and public pronouncements, and what other sources had to say. Romero, "El desconcierto del Gobierno sobre la autoría del atentado" ("Confusion in the Government over the Authorship of the Attacks"), *El País*, March 13, 2004.

23 Ekaizer, "'Apagón.'"

24 N. Labari et al., "Millones de personas se manifiestan contra el terrorismo" ("Millions of People Demonstrate against Terrorism"), *El Mundo*, March 14, 2004, www.elmundo.es/elmundo/2004/03/12/espana/1079113316.html.

25 Mabel Galaz, "Las lágrimas de la Reina" ("The Queen's Tears"), *El País*, March 14, 2004.

26 "'Frente a la sinrazón y la barbarie, sólo cabe la unidad, la firmeza, y la serenidad'" ("'When Faced with Injustice and Barbarity, Only Unity, Steadfastness, and Calm Are Possible'"), *El País*, March 12, 2004.

27 L. R. Aizpeolea, "La Junta Electoral recuerda que en jornada de voto están prohibidas las concentraciones políticas" ("The Election Board Reminds People That Political Gatherings Are Prohibited on Election Day"), *El País*, March 14, 2004.

28 "Miles de personas exigen en las calles españolas que se les diga la verdad antes de votar"

("Thousands of People in the Streets in Spain Demand That They Be Told the Truth before Voting"), *El País*, March 14, 2004.

29 Ernesto Ekaizer, "Doble factura: guerra y manipulación" ("A Doubled Bill: War and Manipulation"), *El País*, March 15, 2004.

30 Belén Barreiro, "14-M: Y hubo sorpresa" ("March 14: And Then There Was a Surprise"), *El País*, March 16, 2004.

31 The editorial also included this startling statement: "Most of the hard work [of combating terrorism effectively] will be far less dramatic than the successful military campaigns in Afghanistan and Iraq." "Ground Zero, Madrid," *New York Times*, March 12, 2004.

32 Alan Riding, "Europe Knows Fear, but This Time It's Different," *New York Times*, March 14, 2004.

33 David Brooks, "Al Qaeda's Wish List," *New York Times*, March 18, 2004.

34 Thomas L. Friedman, "Axis of Appeasement," *New York Times*, March 18, 2004.

35 Edward N. Luttwak, "Rewarding Terror in Spain," *New York Times*, March 16, 2004. It is of interest to note in this context that on the one-year anniversary of the bombings in Madrid, Spanish imams declared a fatwa against Osama bin Laden and al-Qaeda. See "Bin Laden Fatwa as Spain Remembers," CNN.com, March 11, 2005, www.cnn.com/2005/WORLD/europe/03/11/madrid.anniversary/; "Imanes españoles declaran a Bin Laden y Al Qaeda fuera del islam en un edicto" ("In an Edict, Spanish Imams Declare That Bin Laden and Al Qaeda Are Not Part of Islam"), *El País*, March 11, 2005; and "La comunidad islámica en España condena el terrorismo y se suma al dolor por la tragedia" ("The Islamic Community in Spain Condemns Terrorism and Shares in the Pain Caused by the Tragedy"), *El País*, March 12, 2005.

36 "Change in Spain," *New York Times*, March 16, 2004.

37 Caleb M. Stewart, letter to the editor, *New York Times*, March 19, 2004.

38 David Loscos, letter to the editor, *New York Times*, March 17, 2004.

39 Maureen Dowd, "Pride and Prejudice," *New York Times*, March 18, 2004.

40 Elaine Sciolino, "In Spain's Vote, a Shock from Democracy (and the Past)," *New York Times*, March 21, 2004.

41 Paul Krugman, "Taken for a Ride," *New York Times*, March 19, 2004.

42 On the Rumsfeld remark, see "Outrage at 'Old Europe' Remarks," BBC New World Edition, January 23, 2003, http://news.bbc.co.uk/2/hi/europe/2687403.stm.

43 Pet Shop Boys, "It Couldn't Happen Here," *Actually*, Capitol, 1987 (song by Neil Tennant, Ennio Morricone, and Chris Lowe).

Dara E. Goldman

There's (Always) Something about Cuba: Security and States of Exception in a Fundamentally Unsafe World

Michael Moore firmly established himself as the agent provocateur of contemporary documentary filmmaking in films such as *Roger & Me* (1989), *Bowling for Columbine* (2002), and *Fahrenheit 9/11* (2004). In *Sicko* (2007), he unleashes his bag of tricks on the U.S. health care system. Moore's approach uses sardonic humor in order to lay bare the sometimes comic, yet all too frequently tragic discrepancies between the promise of American democratic values and the realities of U.S. democratic systems.[1] Not surprisingly, this film drew enthusiastic praise from leftist pundits and equally passionate vilification from right-wing conservatives. Of course, the responses from the majority of media and political critics fell somewhere between these extremes: many of the reviews commended the project while also calling attention to its perceived shortcomings. This array of responses is certainly familiar terrain for the filmmaker. In this case, however, the attention paid to the film's perceived shortcomings proved unusually consistent and focused.

Moore's film explores the state of health care in the United States. After commenting briefly on a few cases of uninsured patients and their

South Atlantic Quarterly 107:2, Spring 2008
DOI 10.1215/00382876-2007-070 © 2008 Duke University Press

plights, Moore announces that the film will focus on the experiences of patients who (purportedly) have medical coverage. The remainder of the film examines cases in which individuals in the United States were denied health care because of the restrictions or limitations imposed by their insurance providers. He compares these cases to some outside the United States, including those of patients in Canada, France, and Cuba. In the end, Moore emphasizes how the practices of U.S. insurance providers ultimately compromise the quality of health care—and, by extension, health—in the United States.

In the course of his investigations, Moore learns that rescue workers who had been in the vicinity of the World Trade Center on and immediately after September 11, 2001, have been unable to receive adequate medical care for ailments that ostensibly resulted from their exposure to dangerous and toxic substances at Ground Zero. Moore takes these individuals to Cuba so that they can receive treatment at the medical facilities at Guantánamo Bay Naval Base. Numerous critics of the film underscored the visit to Cuba as the film's most noteworthy point of extremity. Reviews in *Rolling Stone*, the *New Yorker*, and *Bright Lights Film Journal* all pay particular attention to this visit and its contribution to the project of the film. In *Rolling Stone*, Peter Travers discusses this episode and its (apparently astounding) implications: "Note to the president: Here's your chance to lock up Michael Moore. . . . Moore shows us how France, England, Canada, and—yikes!—Cuba actually help sick people instead of letting them wither and die for lack of health insurance."[2] In an interview conducted for Rotten Tomatoes, Tim Ryan questions Moore extensively about the decision to accompany the 9/11 rescue workers to Cuba and his depiction of health care in Cuba. Similarly, in an interview with Moore, Amy Goodman emphasizes this episode as a key feature of the film.[3]

The critics almost universally raise the question of whether a trip to Cuba "belongs" in *Sicko*. Of course, if the film is understood as a commentary on the larger relationship between capitalism and the human costs of consumerist culture (with health care as a symptom of that relationship), then the visit to a socialist country with a surprisingly successful track record in health care could easily be viewed as a logical component of the project. This, of course, raises the issue of how the responses to Moore's incorporation of Cuba figure as an exemplum—or, for some, a provocation—of the curious status of Cuba in U.S. popular culture. Why is the visit to Cuba such a noteworthy element of the film? Why do commentators so consistently feel compelled to condemn or justify this particular moment of international exploration in Moore's comparative observations about various national systems of health care? In other words, what is it about Cuba that seemingly sets it apart from every other locale depicted in *Sicko*?

Throughout the twentieth century (both before and after the Cuban Revolution in 1959), the United States has had a strange—and sometimes strained—relationship with the Caribbean island. Dominated alternately by fascination and fear, mainstream portrayals of Cuba in the United States have firmly situated our southern neighbor as a strategically convenient enemy that must be carefully monitored and controlled. Following the failed invasion at the Bay of Pigs and the Cuban missile crisis, Cuba has been consistently portrayed as a potential threat. As recently as 2005, Condoleezza Rice announced the federal government's plans for a transition to democracy in Cuba.[4] The U.S. Treasury's Office of Foreign Assets Control regulates travel to and from Cuba by individuals and organizations such as religious groups and schools, but the business of large corporations (i.e., American Express, Archer Daniels Midland, Coca-Cola, and so on) remains largely unchecked. The need to regulate such travel, moreover, has frequently been invoked in order to justify militant policies on and toward the island. This essay examines how the idea and threat of Cuba have been mobilized in recent years. I shall also contextualize this depiction of the island in terms of the history of U.S.-Cuban relations. This relationship points to a long-standing link between the rhetoric of security, a discourse of exceptionalism, and the status of the United States as a global and imperial power. Recent depictions of Cuba, as well as larger issues of security and safety, have frequently been linked to the events of September 11, 2001. As the historicized analysis of U.S.-Cuban relations reveals, however, recent policies constitute in part a larger continuum of foreign policy that significantly predates the putative raison d'être of current legal and rhetorical positions.

Forbidden Territory: Guantánamo Bay and the Curious Status of Cuba

Although the filmmaker eventually escorts the ailing 9/11 rescue workers to a hospital in Havana, the initial destination of Moore and company's trek across the Florida Straits is the U.S. naval base at Guantánamo Bay. Moore transports the group to the base because he has learned that the military offers complete health care to the enemy combatants held at Camp Delta.[5]

As the boats approach the entrance to the bay, Moore informs the guards — via megaphone — that he is merely trying to secure the same level of care for the rescue workers that the prisoners linked to al-Qaeda are receiving.

Of course, this attempt to enter the base is clearly a theatrical gesture designed to underscore the ironic discrepancies between the treatment afforded the Guantánamo prisoners and the lack of health care available to New York City rescue workers. Moore ostensibly obtained his information about health care on the base from congressional hearings. Footage in the film shows military officers testifying to a congressional committee about conditions at the prison camps (opened in 2001) housed on the base and the treatment of the detainees held there. Although the film does not specifically emphasize this point, representatives of the naval base offer this testimony about the treatment of prisoners in order to counter accusations of prisoner abuses.[6] In the wake of the Abu Ghraib scandal, investigations by international journalists and human rights activists have revealed that torture and other violations of civil rights have been commonly practiced at Guantánamo Bay. The quality of health care the prisoners receive from military officers is therefore presented as evidence of the supposed humane treatment they have received.

Indeed, the status of Guantánamo — both within Moore's film and beyond it — is particularly curious. According to the documents signed by Alberto Gonzales authorizing the creation of a prison camp on the base, Guantánamo and its detainees constitute a special case — especially exceptional, it seems, regarding health care.[7] The camp is outside the normal purview of international jurisdiction and agreements that generally govern relations between sovereign countries and their citizens. The special status of the enemy combatants imprisoned in the camp also places them beyond the normal protections of civil rights and international codes of conduct such as the Geneva Conventions. In the wake of 9/11 and the suspension of the rule of law instigated by the supposed exigencies of homeland security, Guantánamo becomes an ambiguous space that is not directly subject to the standing legal code of any sovereign nation. Prisoners may have access to quality health care, but they are not entitled to the rights, privileges, or protections usually afforded by U.S. juridical codes and systems — or the terms of the Geneva Conventions.

Consequently, it would seem that the special circumstances of Guantánamo — the very circumstances that make it worthy of increased attention and scrutiny — are directly tied to the changing landscape of security in the purportedly unsafe, post-9/11 world. At the same time, however, it could be argued that current conditions at Guantánamo are not as exceptional as they might seem. Recent events can also be understood as the latest install-ment in a well-established and consistent history of disenfranchisement realized in the name of national safety and stability. Since its creation in the early twentieth century, the naval base at Guantánamo Bay has been afforded a special status, and this status has been repeatedly justified by invoking the potential of imminent danger that the region poses to the security of Cuba, the United States, and, in some cases, both.

As Carl Schmitt has argued, political states often respond to perceived threats with a suspension of the rule of law and disenfranchisement of citizens. In his work, Giorgio Agamben has examined how contemporary governments have expanded on this trend. They enact purportedly tem-porary actions as contingent measures designed to address an urgent and specific situation. Of course, these measures remain in place and effectively become policy, thus allowing the state to achieve an extraordinary concen-tration of totalitarian powers without ostensibly compromising its demo-cratic status. He argues that throughout the twentieth century major events such as World Wars I and II led to an expansion of executive powers. Agam-ben traces how special measures invoked by European and U.S. adminis-trations during those historical periods have fundamentally reshaped West-ern democracy. In the case of George W. Bush, moreover, he argues that the tendency has been significantly expanded. Rather than a contingent response to a finite military conflict, the current rhetoric lays claim to an amorphous and seemingly omnipresent threat and thereby justifies a more sustained suspension of the rule of law.

> President Bush's decision to refer to himself constantly as the "Com-mander in Chief of the Army" after September 11, 2001, must be con-sidered in the context of this presidential claim to sovereign powers in emergency situations. If, as we have seen, the assumption of this title entails a direct reference to the state of exception, then Bush is attempting to produce a situation in which the emergency becomes the rule, and the very distinction between peace and war (and between foreign and civil war) becomes impossible.[8]

By declaring a perpetual state of peril against an ill-defined (readily inter-changeable) supranational enemy, the current administration has substan-tially eviscerated the restrictions on executive power and—by extension—

the protection of civil liberties. The suspension of the erstwhile rule of law has, in fact, become standard practice.[9]

In this sense, Guantánamo and Cuba constitute a symptom of a larger trend toward "states of exception" in the United States: the government has repeatedly stripped individuals of their human and civil rights. Despite the historical continuity of antidemocratic policies, moreover, the case of Cuba continues to be treated as an exception that lies outside the normal parameters of democracy. A close examination of the treatment of Guantánamo— in popular culture as well as in official policy—will reveal the underlying paradox between its supposed exceptionalism and its more permanent and quotidian role within the U.S. cultural and political landscape.

The Exceptional Evolution of Guantánamo and Its Role in Ensuring (Inter)National Safety and Stability

The complex and often paradoxical exceptionalism of Guantánamo has its roots in the U.S.-Cuban diplomatic relationship that evolved in the decades following the Spanish-American War. As it cultivated greater imperial ambitions throughout the Western Hemisphere during the second half of the nineteenth century, the United States developed strong economic and cultural interests in Cuba. The ties between the two countries were formalized in December 1898 through the Treaty of Paris, and territorial possession of the island formally passed from Spain to the United States in 1899. Cuba gained its independence from the United States in 1902; nevertheless, the conditions of that independence, including the Platt Amendment, further reinforced the connections between the two countries.[10] According to section 7 of the Platt Amendment, the United States retained the right to purchase or rent land from Cuba in order to protect the national interests, sovereignty, and stability of both countries. In 1903, President Theodore Roosevelt and the Cuban Senate agreed that the United States would rent the forty-five square miles of land and water in and around Guantánamo Bay "por el tiempo que las necesitasen" ("for as long as might be necessary").[11]

In 1934, President Franklin Roosevelt signed an agreement that eliminated most of the provisions enacted in the Platt Amendment. The allocation of the property for a military base, however, was renewed and renegotiated. According to the renewed amendment, the base was vital to the security of the region and therefore should be maintained. In fact, the document stipulated that the rental of the land could be terminated only through the mutual consent of both parties. Although Guantánamo remains the legal property of Cuba, the United States still retains the right/obligation to purchase or rent the lands as long as one of the two countries deems it necessary to ensure the safety and security of either.[12]

In the wake of the Cuban Revolution in 1959, the U.S. presence on the island was significantly reduced but not eliminated, thus producing rather strained relations between the two nations. Although direct references to this undesirable coexistence can certainly be found in political discourse, the post-1959 U.S. presence within the confines of the island has rarely been mentioned in U.S. popular or cultural representations. Instead, once again, the prolonged intimacy of these strange bedfellows was recast as a proximate threat by both U.S. and Cuban political leaders. After the Cuban Revolution, members of the Cuban Communist Party attempted to challenge the legality of the base, but their claims were rejected by arbiters of international law, such as the International Court of Justice, based on the absence of the requisite bilateral agreement necessitated by the 1934 modifications to the Platt Amendment. Following this failure, Cuban authorities no longer attempted to remove the base. Instead, they cited it (albeit occasionally) as evidence of U.S. imperialism and hostility.

In a 1963 report commissioned by the local government in Guantánamo, Gonzalo Bermejo insists, paradoxically, that the Cuban Revolution had saved Guantánamo from the untoward influence of the naval base. He cites the increased presence of bars, gambling, and prostitution (along with concomitant incidents of drunkenness, violence, and other criminal behavior) that developed between the opening of the base and the closing of the Guantánamo border. At the same time, Bermejo criticizes the inappropriate threat to that salvation engendered by the base's continued presence.[13] In his report, he also condemns the puerile behavior with which the guards on the U.S. side of the fence purportedly tormented their Cuban counterparts, while he criticizes them as ideologically indifferent mercenaries. He claims that the military presence was directly responsible for a sharp moral and sociocultural decline in the area, as evidenced by the prostitution, gambling, and disease found along the Guantánamo "border," and he argues that although the revolution and the consequent "closing" of this border had improved conditions significantly, only the complete removal of the U.S. military from the island would ultimately solve the problem of inappropriate influence. The author clearly positions himself as a pro-revolutionary advocate condemning U.S. imperialism and praising Fidel Castro's government for its redemptive salvation of Cuba. Bermejo's passionate argument for the elimination of the base despite the notable decline in evidence of its undesirable influence points to the rhetorical tension in his argument: if the success of the revolution was measured in terms of the eradication of U.S. cultural influence, the naval base indeed posed a significant threat to the complete and absolute realization of this success. In this manner, the rhetoric of national ideology cannot be fully reconciled with the coterminous occupation of a portion of the island by external and ideologically incompatible forces. In this sense, Cuban policy paradoxically reinforces—even celebrates—the isolation engendered by the U.S. embargo. Rather than present it as an undesirable obstacle, Cuban rhetoric valorizes insularity as affording the opportunity for alternative (and ultimately superior) development.

Given that this report was published in 1963, these contradictions could be understood as a product of their historical context. That is, the early 1960s constituted a period of transition in which Cuba both celebrated the triumph of the revolution and condemned the traces of U.S. imperialism that the revolutionaries were still working to eliminate or overcome. In the decades that followed, however, the discourse on Guantánamo Bay remained relatively unchanged. By the end of the twentieth century, there was still comparatively little discussion of the military base in public discourse in Cuba, and the analyses produced echoed the assertions of Bermejo's report. Noted Cuban legal scholar Olga Miranda Bravo, for example, published an extensive study of the U.S. naval presence and its international implications.[14] She argues that the base was anachronistic at best, and she analyzes several possible strategies for the eventual recovery of the "occupied territory." Miranda Bravo traces the history of the base and its role in U.S.-Cuban relations throughout the twentieth century and asserts that the military presence circumvented the expressed desire of the Cuban people to have the base closed and violated the right of Cuba as a sovereign nation to complete self-determination.

Military historians Felipa Suárez Ramos and Pilar Quesada also articulate a similar argument in *A escasos metros del enemigo* (*Mere Meters from the Enemy*).[15] Their study is one of the few analyses to focus on the extraordinary proximity of the United States and Cuba, separated as they are by only a few meters rather than ninety miles. As in Miranda Bravo's book, Suárez Ramos and Quesada highlight the inappropriateness (and untenability) of this relationship and underscore its negative impact on Cubans. In this case, not only do the authors decry the political and sociological implications of the base, but they also pay tribute to two Cuban soldiers who lost their lives on the Guantánamo border.[16] In fact, the book is primarily dedicated to the first two members of the Brigada de la Frontera (Border Brigade), who were killed by gunshots that emanated from the base in the 1960s: "A Ramón y Luis, cuyas jóvenes vidas fueron vilmente cesadas desde ese pedazo de tierra nuestra usurpado por los yanquis" ("To Ramon and Luis, whose young lives were vilely ended from within this piece of our land that has been usurped by the Yankees").[17]

Throughout its history, therefore, the base has always been afforded a special status, whether condemned as an illegitimate encroachment on Cuban sovereignty, touted as a necessary measure of protection by the United States, or cited as a potential threat to international relations by both countries. Along with the legitimacy of the base itself, potential threats have also been invoked in order to justify particular practices routinely realized in Guantánamo. The small strip of land that separates the base from the province of Guantánamo is filled with surveillance devices and other equipment generally reserved for zones marked by open military conflict. Indeed, the status of the base as an essential guardian against extreme conditions of potential peril has engendered dangerous conditions and caused the death of at least one U.S. soldier in addition to the two aforementioned Cuban border guards on the "front lines" between the base and the province (notably in the absence of any active warfare).

The depictions of the region in U.S. and Cuban popular culture reveal how it figures their respective national imaginaries. More important, these perceptions do not fully conform to the characterization of the base as a necessary condition of extraordinary conditions or policies. Of course, the base is inexorably linked to the extremist rhetoric that alternately justifies and denounces its existence. At the same time, by calling attention to everyday conditions engendered on and around the naval base, these examples underscore the contradictory intersections of the supposed purpose of the base and its impact.

Extreme Measures: The Extraordinary Conditions of Everyday Life in Guantánamo

As a dissident émigré, the protagonist in Reinaldo Arenas's autobiographical novel *Antes que anochezca* (*Before Night Falls*) recounts his persecution in Cuba as well as his attempts to escape from the confines of the post-1959

Cuban system.[18] At one point in the novel, Reinaldo—the protagonist—
tries to reach the naval base in order to seek asylum in the United States.
The description of this endeavor underscores the extraordinary militari-
zation of the narrow separation between Cuba and the base. His efforts
are thwarted by the overwhelming presence of geographical barriers, land
mines, alligators, armed guards, and trained dogs. He recounts how he
narrowly escapes from these perils during his failed attempt to reach the
base:

> En aquellos momentos empezaron a aparecer por los matorrales
> extrañas luces verdes. . . . A los pocos instantes, sonó el estruendo
> de una ametralladora; era una balacera que pasaba rozándome. Más
> tarde me enteré de que aquellas luces verdes eran una señal; eran
> rayos infarrojos. Se habían percatado de que alguien quería cruzar la
> frontera y trataban de localizarlo y, naturalmente, aniquilarlo. Corrí y
> me trepé a un árbol frondoso, abrazándome a su tronco todo lo más
> alto que pude. Carros llenos de soldados con perros se lanzaron a mi
> búsqueda; toda la noche estuvieron buscándome muy cerca de donde
> yo me encontraba. Finalmente, se marcharon.[19]

> Suddenly, strange green lights began appearing. . . . A few seconds
> later I heard machine-gun fire; the bullets seemed to be grazing me. I
> later found out that those green lights were signals; they were infrared
> lights. The guards had discovered that someone was trying to cross the
> border; they were trying to locate and, of course, to exterminate the
> intruder. I ran to a tree with a dense canopy and climbed as high as I
> could, hugging the trunk. Cars came, full of soldiers with dogs, look-
> ing for me. All night they searched, at times rather close to my hiding
> place. At last, they left.[20]

Arenas's description presents the policing of this area as both extraordinary and capricious. On the one hand, it calls attention to the multifaceted
technological and human mechanisms designed to make the Guantánamo
border impenetrable. On the other, however, it demonstrates how those
techniques can be utterly thwarted by simple luck and the unexpected
advantages afforded by the natural features of the region. Although the
geography of the area contains obstacles that impede Reinaldo's progress
and restrict human mobility, the landscape also protects him. In the end,
Reinaldo abandons this strategy and eventually travels to the United States
by concealing his identity and leaving Cuba via the Mariel boat lift.[21]

Arenas's novel thus renders the distance between Cuban national territory and the naval base more insurmountable than the separation between the island and the Florida peninsula.

Arguably, the most famous citation of the base as justification for extreme behavior comes not from Cuban but from U.S. popular culture. The Aaron Sorkin play (and subsequent film) *A Few Good Men* fictionalizes events that occurred on the naval base.[22] Sorkin's older sister had recently become an attorney with the Judge Advocate General's Corps when she was assigned to the court-martial on which Sorkin's play is based. In the play and film, two marines are tried for killing a member of their unit. They admit to having killed the marine but claim that it was an accident that resulted from an attack ordered by their superiors. According to Sorkin, this aspect is drawn directly from his sister's account of the facts: in the court-martial, ten marines were accused of killing a private in their company during a disciplinary action intended to punish the private for inappropriate conduct. Although such actions were officially condemned, the accused claimed that they were acting on the orders of their commanding officer.[23] In the movie, of course, this all leads to that famous outburst by Colonel Nathan R. Jessep, played by Jack Nicholson: "You can't handle the truth." That may be the very point of Guantánamo: it is the "truth" that is manifestly present and unpalatable to both the United States and Cuba—to the politically incommensurate enemies who are also, strangely, geopolitical allies in their commitment to keeping the truth of their unruly alliance silent.

Although many of the specific details and characters in the film are fictional, they underscore the complicated physical reality of Guantánamo. That is, the military base is just a few meters from Cuba, and the two nations are separated only by a no-man's-land filled with land mines and patrolled by soldiers on both sides of a fence. The members of the U.S. military indeed coexist with Cubans on the opposite side. As Colonel Jessep claims in Sorkin's script, "I eat breakfast seventy yards away from 3,000 Cubans who are trained to kill me."[24] Not only does this statement reflect a curious reality, but it is also used as a justification for exceptionality in *A Few Good Men*: the officers argue that, given their unique location, marines at Guantánamo cannot be expected to fully conform to norms established outside of Cuba. Guantánamo is, as it has always been, outside of any law—U.S., Cuban, international. Guantánamo is a law unto itself. At the very least, it is a place where Jessep wants only his law to obtain.

In both Arenas's and Sorkin's works, the conditions of the base and surrounding area are presented as simultaneously quotidian and exceptional. In fact, as the incident depicted in *A Few Good Men* aptly demonstrates, the extreme nature of everyday life on the base leads its inhabitants to believe that they must suspend normal codes of conduct in order to survive. Guantánamo Bay constitutes, in this formulation, a zone of ideological indistinction that is meant to mark the discrete: the border that is not a border but functions (precariously, historically, intransigently) as such.[25] In this sense, the treatment of prisoners at Guantánamo—including the paradoxical combination of abuses and privileges cited earlier—can be understood as the latest example in a long history of "extremist" yet strangely cooperative politics that have characterized the base. The very existence of the naval base, the measures deployed to ensure its protection, and the behavior of its inhabitants have all been shaped by the purported "special conditions" of the U.S.-Cuban relationship that is acutely dramatized on the eastern edge of the Caribbean island.

Guantánamo and the Trap of Exceptionalism

In this cultural-historical rendering, Guantánamo constitutes an instantiation of what Agamben has defined as a state of exception.[26] As mentioned earlier, he draws upon Schmitt's theories regarding states of emergency and their role in the evolution of political systems.[27] Agamben argues that contemporary politics has undergone a fundamental shift. Through the systematic suspension of the rule of law, ostensibly democratic nations such as the United States now function essentially as mechanisms of control and surveillance. The case of Guantánamo Bay acutely dramatizes this evolving trend in the U.S. political landscape and the consequences (and costs) that inevitably follow.

Guantánamo, moreover, points to the rhetorical traps of exceptionalism that can be traced throughout contemporary U.S. policies and politics. As Agamben asserts, one of the principal dangers of the "exception" enacted under a state of emergency is that the supposed exception often becomes the dominant paradigm. The suspension of civil liberties initially permitted only to redress a clear and immediate threat to national security is gradually accepted as standard practice, as demonstrated by the popularity of TV shows such as *24*.[28] Consequently, the suspension of liberties eventually becomes the new rule of law rather than a temporary measure. In other words, that which we accept as an exception ultimately evolves into the standard. Popular culture certainly reinforces the ideology that undergirds this process, yet it also highlights the way in which states of exception are often not seamlessly woven into the fabric of the cultural imaginary. Popular representations call attention to the contradictory status of the state's power as both limited and carefully circumscribed, on the one hand, and excessively ubiquitous, on the other. They therefore elucidate how the logic of the new legitimacy of the state of exception—as the only sustainable way to protect the state—now threatens not only to institutionalize but ethically to gird the U.S. state's increasingly repressive proclivities.[29]

At the same time, the other trap of exceptionalism is to accept the basic premise on which the suspension of the erstwhile rule of law had been predicated. The depiction of conditions as exceptional often obfuscates their connections to preexisting and/or ongoing patterns. As the case of Guantánamo demonstrates, the responses to current conditions—the emergency measures taken in order to ensure security in a world that has purportedly become unsafe—can often emerge from a larger history of disenfranchisement and reterritorialization. In this context, the fundamental substructure of the system can be obscured by the perpetual characterization of these components as new and emergent elements. The state of exception mitigates against the retention of political and ideological memory.

However obvious and banal it might seem, the essential lesson of Guantánamo is that it demands an interrogation of the supposed newness of the current conditions. To what extent are the immediate and unprecedented threats of a post-9/11 world merely old foes recast in the garb of terrorism and fanaticism? To what extent, moreover, do they constitute underlying dichotomies on which the current power structure fundamentally depends? The very circumstances that are so easily ascribed to the current exigencies of a purported atmosphere of unsafety may not be so exceptional after all. Instead, they may be the foundational myths on which the system has always been predicated—myths that are reinforced and reinvigorated in the current climate of states of exception. The unsafety of Guantánamo Bay, for both the United States and Cuba, has long been the rule and not the exception of relations between these two (antagonistic) states. Without recounting the history of these relations, Moore's *Sicko* does compel another look—arguably the first popularly critical investigation—at how the logic of safety and the rhetoric of health (public health, from a U.S. public health system unable to provide for its citizens) function. The Dick

Cheney–like question posted by Colonel Jessep in *A Few Good Men* still holds, only this time with a traumatic veracity. Who, exactly, can (and can't) handle the truth? The U.S. government? The Cuban government? The work of the popular, it seems, is to at least recognize the need for a complicated, historical truth that might begin with a critique of the lawlessness—the extraterritoriality that refutes the law as it claims to protect the safety and security of U.S. citizens—of Guantánamo. What kind of law is founded on the abrogation and negation of the law? What kind of law denies human rights and due process and yet affords the inmates good health care? What kind of *Sicko* society can live with those kinds of contradictions? That's the virtue of agent provocateurs: they have a strange way of getting at the very truths Colonel Jessep wants to keep hidden from the citizenry.

Notes

1   *Sicko*, directed by Michael Moore (New York: Weinstein Company, 2007).

2   Peter Travers, review of *Sicko*, *Rolling Stone*, June 13, 2007, www.rollingstone.com/reviews/movie/14706803/review/15039821/sicko. See also David Denby, "Do No Harm," Current Cinema, *New Yorker*, July 2, 2007; and Karin Luisa Badt, "Stay Well or Else . . . ," *Bright Lights Film Journal* 57 (2007), www.brightlightsfilm.com/57/mooreiv.html (accessed October 18, 2007).

3   Tim Ryan, "A Healthy Dose of *Sicko*: Michael Moore Talks *Sicko*, Heath Care, Edutainment, Cuba," Rotten Tomatoes, June 25, 2007; and Amy Goodman, "An Hour with Michael Moore on 'Sicko,' his Trip to Cuba with 9/11 Rescue Workers, the Removal of Private Healthcare Companies, and Clinton's Ties to Insurance Companies," *Democracy Now!* June 18, 2007.

4   Condoleezza Rice, "Announcement of Cuba Transition Coordinator Caleb McCarry," U.S. Department of State, July 28, 2005, www.state.gov/secretary/rm/2005/50346.htm.

5   Camp Delta is the permanent facility that was established in 2002 to accommodate enemy combatant detainees held at Guantánamo Bay. It replaced Camp X-Ray, a temporary facility established in 2001, since that facility had already exceeded its maximum capacity.

6   The footage is not identified or discussed in any detail. Moore simply incorporates clips from the hearings that feature testimony regarding the conditions in the camps and the quality of services provided therein.

7   Alberto Gonzales, memorandum to President Bush, Office of the White House Counsel, January 25, 2002, available at www.msnbc.msn.com/id/4999148/site/newsweek/.

8   Giorgio Agamben, *State of Exception*, trans. Kevin Attell (Chicago: University of Chicago Press, 2004), 22.

9   The illegal wiretapping would probably be the best example of the intensification Agamben identifies. The U.S. Foreign Intelligence Surveillance Court provisions, allowing the U.S. attorney general to authorize warrantless surveillance in cases of exigent circumstances and then obtain the legal authorization up to seventy-two hours after the fact,

would already qualify as an "emergency measure." The Bush administration, however, is now circumventing even those expansions of executive power that Schmitt and Agamben had identified in their analyses of nineteenth- and twentieth-century trends.

10 The Cuban Constitution and Platt Amendment favored exchanges between the two countries, and the United States enjoyed the privileges of singular political control (i.e., the ability to intervene in and manipulate national politics in Cuba) and economic access in Cuba until 1959. For the text of the Platt Amendment, see appendix A, Felipa Suárez Ramos and Pilar Quesada, *A escasos metros del enemigo: historia de la Brigada de la Frontera* (*Mere Meters from the Enemy: A History of the Border Brigade*) (Havana: Verde Olivo, 1996), 227–31. See also George W. Bush and Donald H. Rumsfeld v. Falen Gherebi, *petition for a writ of certiorari filed*, 28 U.S.C. 1254(1) (December 18, 2003) (no. 03-1245), www .usdoj.gov/osg/briefs/2003/2pet/7pet/2003-1245.pet.aa.pdf (accessed October 4, 2007), 23a–24a.

11 Suárez Ramos and Quesada, *A escasos metros del enemigo*, 216.

12 "Treaty of Relations between the United States of America and the Republic of Cuba," May 29, 1934; text available from the Avalon Project at Yale Law School, www.yale.edu/ lawweb/avalon/diplomacy/cuba/cuba001.htm (accessed October 4, 2007).

13 [Gonzalo?] Bermejo, "Guantánamo: A Fence between Two Worlds," in *Reporting on Cuba* (Havana: Instituto del Libro, 1963). The report is actually credited just to "Bermejo," but I have found other documents indicating that it was likely to have been written by a Gonzalo Bermejo.

14 Olga Miranda Bravo, *Undesirable Neighbors: The U.S. Naval Base at Guantánamo* (1998; Havana: Editorial José Martí, 2001).

15 Suárez Ramos and Quesada, *A escasos metros del enemigo*.

16 Ibid., dedication.

17 Ibid., front matter.

18 Reinaldo Arenas, *Antes que anochezca* (Barcelona: Tusquets, 1992); and Reinaldo Arenas, *Before Night Falls: A Memoir*, trans. Dolores M. Koch (New York: Penguin, 1993).

19 Arenas, *Antes que anochezca*, 190.

20 Arenas, *Before Night Falls*, 163–64.

21 In 1979, groups of Cubans seeking asylum stormed the Venezuelan and Peruvian embassies in Havana. After initial denials and protests, Castro announced in April 1980 that the individuals not supportive of the revolutionary project constituted an obstacle that the Cuban government neither needed nor desired. Consequently, all Cubans who wanted to emigrate were allowed to leave through the port of Mariel. Over the following month, the "freedom flotilla"—a group of ships provided by the U.S. military—transported close to 100,000 Cubans from Mariel to Miami. This mass exodus is commonly referred to as the Mariel boat lift. In the end, the émigrés included prisoners and mental patients that the Cuban government intercalated with asylum seekers as well as refugees who left despite the government's efforts to prevent their departure (as in the case dramatized by Reinaldo in *Before Night Falls*).

22 Aaron Sorkin, *A Few Good Men* (New York: Samuel French, 1990); and *A Few Good Men*, directed by Rob Reiner (Burbank, CA: Castle Rock Entertainment, 1992).

23 Sorkin recounts how he drew on this source material in an interview included on the DVD of the Rob Reiner film. *Exclusive Documentary: Code of Conduct*, directed by Michael

Gillis, edited by Chris Sias, on *A Few Good Men* DVD (Culver City, CA: Columbia Tristar Home Video, 2001).

24   Sorkin, *A Few Good Men*, 51. In the film, Colonel Jessep delivers an altered version of this line in which he claims to eat breakfast 300 yards away from 4,000 Cubans.

25   Grant Farred, "The Not-Yet Counterpartisan: A New Politics of Oppositionality," *SAQ* 103.4 (2004): 589–605.

26   Agamben, *State of Exception*.

27   Carl Schmitt, *The Concept of the Political*, trans. George Schwab, expanded ed. (Chicago: University of Chicago Press, 2007).

28   *24*, created by Joel Surnow and Robert Cochran (Universal City, CA: Imagine Entertainment, 2001).

29   However, TV shows such as *The Kill Point* (created by James DeMonaco [Santa Monica, CA: Lions Gate, 2007]) and *Saving Grace* (created by Nancy Miller [Century City, CA: Fox Television Studios, 2007) have become increasingly critical of the Bush regime's war on terror.

Susan Willis

Forensics of Spinach

> Spinach planting is an incredibly programmatic system.
> —Barry Eisenberg, River Ranch Fresh Foods

A lot is now known about the E. coli contamination of bagged spinach that threw the United States into a frenzy over food poisoning during the early days of September 2006. Such was not the case when the first reports of food-borne illness began to appear in newspapers and on the evening news. Indeed, wire service reporters peppered the media with a barrage of seemingly disconnected but apparently incriminating details. There were cows somehow adjacent to verdant fields of spinach, and creeks were suspect, as were the processing plants. Finally, a wild boar burst into the news. How to make sense of the situation?

Meanwhile, grocery stores and restaurants pulled spinach from their shelves and menus, as health-conscious consumers began to look askance at all leafy greens. To stem the tide of potential consumer flight into safe, processed junk food, chefs and food gurus touted the wonders of arugula, Swiss chard, and kale. Yes,

South Atlantic Quarterly 107:2, Spring 2008
DOI 10.1215/00382876-2007-071 © 2008 Duke University Press

America was in the throes of yet another media-fed frenzy over security—
even though bioterrorism was quickly ruled out (Health and Human Services Secretary Tommy Thompson's warning about the vulnerability of the
nation's food supply notwithstanding).

As an academic who divides her time between cultural criticism and the
uncertain rewards of backyard farming, I was immediately drawn to the
spinach incident for the way it promised to unite my two, generally separate
fields of practice. As a farmer, I know that E. coli is commonly found in animal excrement. Indeed, it is the single most important flora responsible for
mammalian digestive health. But how did it get in the bag of spinach, and
why was this particular outbreak so virulent? In the end, three people died
and nearly two hundred fell ill, some with kidney failure.[1] I approached the
scatter-shot reportage with dogged determination. I would treat the facts
as evidence and assemble a forensics of contamination. Would my case,
just like those tackled by the CSIs on television tell as much about our
culture as a whole as the autopsied body under investigation? Remark how
the investigators on CBS's *CSI* approach each week's homicide victims as
corpses to be tabulated and read as the sum total of their technologically
derived and screened data. Every televised episode provides a technological
fix both to the death at hand, as determined by the physical evidence, and
to the life itself, as inscribed in the sum of our digitized information. So,
then, will the forensics of spinach similarly reduce the culture to its data?
Or will it yield another, perhaps more socially significant explanation?

As with most things we eat, spinach is not endemic to the United States.
It arose in China, where 76 percent of the world's output is still grown.[2]
California is a distant but substantial second with the annual value of Mon-
terey County's crop at $188 million.[3] Salinas Valley spinach is planted and
harvested from March through November. The Salinas Valley epicenter of
the 2006 E. coli outbreak has been the point of origin for eight incidents
of contamination over the past ten years.[4] The topography of spinach cultivation demonstrates a high level of horticultural Taylorism. The same features of centralization and monoculture typify industrial corporate food
production the world over. They also explain the maximization of both output (bagged spinach everyday in every state of the Union) and contagion
(E. coli in twenty-six states in a matter of days).

Centralized production continues up the food chain to the processing
plant. According to Michael Pollan, renowned food and horticulture writer,
in the United States, "75 percent of the precut salads are processed by two

[companies]." Worse yet, "We're washing the whole nation's salad in one big sink."[5] Grisly! In the case of the recent contamination, Earthbound Farm under its Natural Selection label emerged as the culprit. This is precisely the brand I buy when I shop at Whole Foods. Is it ironic or just a fact of marketing that the idea of wholesome goodness that the name suggests may be in the name only? Another culprit was Dole, as it bagged up some Natural Selection spinach under its own label. Apparently, brand names have very little to do with a particular corporate entity's control over a product, nor do they appear to be tied to a product's point of origin. What, then, about the "organic" designation that appears on so many of the bagged greens that I buy? With all spinach sorted, washed, dried, and bagged in just a couple of processing plants, aren't inorganic leaves apt to fall in with the organic just as the contaminated ones did with the clean?

The earliest accounts of E. coli contamination raised questions about industrial hygiene. What about the processing plant—the vegetal killing floor, so to speak—and all those robotic conveyors and weighers? I wonder, do we as a gut reaction to calamity always betray a deep mistrust of industry, even while our lives depend on industrially produced goods? Attention then turned to the workers. Do they wash their hands? Do they wear gloves? What about hairnets? Somehow a hairnet does not seem to pertain to an E. coli outbreak. I wonder, too, if in singling out the workers at such an early stage of the investigation did the press betray an unconscious view of the working class (in this case, largely Latino) as somehow dirty? By comparison, is the consumer positioned as not just innocent but also more middle class and therefore more hygienic?

Not given to dwell on any subject longer than the time necessary to establish innuendo, the press quickly scoped out other, more lurid possible causes for contamination, including mice in the field.[6] The mere mention of mice and mouse droppings kindled instant revulsion. Not to be outdone, another report suggested that E. coli can be transported by "droppings from birds that swallowed manure"[7] or "a supervisor's dog in the back of his pickup, who might defecate in the field."[8] Finally, the press seized upon a truly exotic vector of biohazard contamination—a wild boar. Gleefully, U.S. and Canadian wire services reported the exploits of a fence-trampling wild boar that wantonly transported the E. coli from an adjacent pasture into the pristine, unsuspecting, and totally innocent rows of spinach. How convenient when the wild can be blamed for human and industrial culpability. Mother Nature did it just as she flattened New Orleans. Father

Capitalism had nothing to do with it. The pig as scapegoat lets everyone off the hook.

But not so fast! The most important piece of evidence has yet to be considered. The contaminant was no ordinary form of E. coli but instead a deadly mutant known as 0157:H7. The wild boar may have transported the bacteria, but was it the point of origin? In the end, 0157:H7 was found on one particular ranch in samples of cow dung, stream water, and the wild boar's gut (I guess they killed the pig). Genetic research establishes 0157:H7's unique history. It arose in the rumen of cows raised not on pasturage and hay but on a rich feedlot diet of grain. The excessive acidity needed to break down the grain creates an environment lethal to normal E. coli but one ripe for the natural selection of a strain capable of handling what is essentially an unnatural bovine diet. Doubtless, Earthbound Farm did not fully grasp the Darwinian implications of its Natural Selection label, nor the fact that the especially virulent nature of 0157:H7 dramatizes how natural processes can adapt to industrial settings.

"Industrial farming gave us this bug." This is how Pollan couches his condemnation of agribusiness. Cows "stand around in their manure all day long" eating an improper diet. "Industrial animal agriculture produces more than a billion tons of manure every year." Needless to say, some of it "ends up in places it shouldn't be,"[9] like bags of spinach. What might have been a single patch of contaminated plants in the field ends up being dispersed throughout the processing plant by way of the industrial wash cycle and then dispersed throughout the nation by way of a rapid, fully integrated food distribution network.

The forensic specificity of 0157:H7 as endemic to feedlot cows and exemplary of industrialized agriculture begs a reexamination of the wild boar. In their haste to pin the blame on something outside what Pollan calls the "vegetable-industrial complex," did journalists fail to recognize that the boar was not the originary source of the contamination? As an animal that forages for its food, the boar most likely consumed the 0157:H7 in the course of its rambles through cow and spinach fields. Undoubtedly, the boar's constitution was a good deal tougher than that of the humans who either sickened or died when they ate 0157:H7, but isn't the boar, as the consumer of impure food, something of a victim as well? Recognizing the boar as vector rather than originator casts blame back on the production process itself. But imagine how costly it would be to clean up the "vegetable-industrial complex," if not to dismantle it entirely, by dispersing rather than centralizing meat and vegetable production and thereby developing a regional—maybe even a local—food system. No, rather than adopt the slow food model, we buried the problem with the boar.

Thus concludes the case of the contaminated spinach. The boar—caught, killed, gutted, and autopsied—offers an incredibly pat solution wherein evidence and guilt come together in one tidy package. Like an Agatha Christie whodunit, an array of questionable characters was introduced (mice, birds, dogs) only to be discarded. Tight as a mathematical equation, the case narrowed to its denouement in which the revelation of the guilty party pulled the puzzle together. But real life is not nearly so tidy. In fact, it is more like a Sara Paretsky novel in which seemingly disconnected and disinterested players from corporations, labor unions, and political and philanthropic organizations can never be discarded because the final pinning of the blame that solves the case doesn't really end with the guilty party, but instead turns back on the larger society to reveal the sordid interconnectedness of all the powers that be.

So, back to the case—this time to view the evidence with a much wider lens, beginning with the boar. Isn't it unsatisfying to see the boar as no more than a conclusion? Think of the romance we attach to the wild. Don't we want the boar to be more than its guilt? What if we step back from the autopsy and attempt to grasp all the meanings that the boar conveys, not just those that sealed its fate. Can we suspend the need to pin the blame and instead consider the function of the boar in a larger narrative that is still about contamination but isn't necessarily tied to a specific case?

Significantly, a wild boar crossed paths with Pollan months before the 0157:H7 outbreak, and although he does not reference a boar in his comments on the spinach incident, he does make the wild boar a star player in his recent best seller, *The Omnivore's Dilemma*. Motivated by the desire to make a meal entirely from "scratch" and at the same time confront the moral and practical implications of what it means to be an omnivore in twenty-first-century America, Pollan decided that he had to go to the source of the meat component of his meal—and not on the farm or in the slaughterhouse but in the wild. Thus, he undertook to hunt a wild boar: "A little after 9 in the morning, we were walking together down a logging road cut into a steep hillside when we were stopped in our tracks by a grunt so loud and deep and guttural that it seemed to be coming from the bowels of the earth. A very big pig was very close by."[10] But just how wild is a boar in a state as densely populated as California, where so-called wildlands disappear daily under the developer's bulldozer? I suspect a boar is wild in the same sense as a deer, coyote, or turkey. These are animals that have claimed human topographies as their own. The coyote rummages in our trash, the deer browses our garden, the turkey takes a dust bath in our yard, and the boar roots about in Earthbound Farm's spinach. These are animals that are considered wild only because they are not domesticated (although the boar once was, its ancestors having escaped from the Spanish during California's hacienda period). Animals such as these are liminal in that we see them at dusk and dawn. They stitch together the margins of our notions of nature and culture as they articulate trajectories from more natural settings—an abandoned canyon, a deep thicket—into fully humanized terrains like suburban gardens and agribusiness fields. In the case of the wild boar found to be carrying O157:H7, it is a hybrid, that is, a nondomesticated animal that has been colonized by industrial bacteria.

It may be that as our own world becomes more suburbanized, we long to maintain a distinction between the postindustrial landscapes we inhabit and an elsewhere that we deem wild. But, as the wild boar makes clear, the purity of such categories depends entirely on how we define them and, then, how we police them. Consider the general distinction between animal and vegetable kingdoms that constitutes the multiple vegetarian foodways. It is a distinction borne out in the map of the ranch where the O157:H7 outbreak occurred: cows in one fenced area, spinach in another. Now consider the dilemma that many vegetarians confront when presented with a restaurant menu. What about the potato-leek soup—is it made with chicken broth? Are those bacon bits or pecans on the spinach salad? What are the telltale signs of meat contamination in foods served at restaurants? Are we to imagine that Burger King fries up its veggie burger on a separate grill? Remember the court case brought against McDonald's by a Sikh family who discovered that the french fries were cooked in a vat of lard, thereby infusing the vegetal with the animal. Myself a vegetarian, I worry that my own food policing practices may come to resemble those of truly pathological picky eaters who can't abide a plate of food on which one item comes in contact with another. God forbid the peas should roll into the mashed potatoes! Could it be that the invention of the TV dinner had only nominally to do with efficiency? After all, those oven-ready trays, with each food item plopped into its own discrete well, suggest a culinary version of field and fence.

Commenting on the distinction between us and so-called primitive peoples, anthropologist Mary Douglas stipulates, "Our experience is fragmented. Our rituals create a lot of little sub-worlds, unrelated."[11] By comparison, the rituals of primitive peoples "create one single, symbolically consistent universe" (*Purity*, 69). Nevertheless, I suspect that many of our practices—particularly those involving food—have their roots in the more coherent bodies of practice associated with the groups typically studied by anthropologists. Remark the Bible's interdiction of certain animals that might otherwise be food. "The camel, the hare, and the rock badger, because they chew the cud but do not part the hoof are unclean for you" (*Purity*, 41). And then there is "the swine, because it parts the hoof, but does not chew the cud" (*Purity*, 41).

The problem with rational explanations is their piecemeal approach to the total system of Biblical dietary restrictions. After working through the various scientific and legalistic accounts for why certain fliers, swimmers, and hoppers are clean and others are not, Douglas concludes: "Any interpretations will fail which take the Do-nots of the Old Testament in piecemeal fashion. The only sound approach is to forget hygiene, aesthetics, morals and instinctive revulsion, even to forget the Canaanites and the Zoroastrian Magi, and start with the texts. Since each of the injunctions is prefaced by the command to be holy, so they must be explained by that command" (*Purity*, 49). Thus, the solution is not in the particulars, which may, indeed, be contrary, but in allegiance to the order that the entire system enunciates. As Douglas explains, "Be ye Holy" means more than "Be ye separate": "By the rules of avoidance holiness was given a physical expression in every encounter with the animal kingdom and at every meal" (*Purity*, 57).

So, if holy means both separate and the steadfast adherence to order, might we now consider veganism—with its precise delineation of animal and vegetable kingdoms and strictly structured kitchen—as a secular enactment of the Old Testament? Both veganism and Biblical foodways dramatize that what is at stake is order itself and, by extension, the status of integrity of the people who adhere to order. From this point of view, contagion—what Douglas simply calls "dirt"—is what allows us to detect the system. But what about the larger world in which the majority of us live? Here, the categories appear to be muddied or disrupted. Recall the wild boar whose autopsy revealed its own species DNA as well as that of an industrial mutant bacteria and whose foraging habits upset idealized notions of the wild as separate from the suburban. Indeed, there are those who see the incursion of deer, coyotes, raccoons, and boars into cul-de-sac neighborhoods as a resurgence of the wild, a reprimitivizing of the planet. Who knows, homeowners may have to borrow a page from James Fenimore Cooper, especially when jogging.

The dilemma over categories is particularly fraught when it comes to vegetable production. We are currently witnessing a wholesale expansion in demand for organic fruits and vegetables. Even Wal-Mart has jumped into the organic market, thus undercutting the big purveyors such as Whole Foods as well as farmers' markets and food co-ops. While the definition of what it means to be organic has only recently been codified in federal guidelines, the popular imagination quite simply equates organic with purity. But organics are something of a conundrum, particularly as blemishes attest to purity, while beauty—like that of Snow White's poison apple—can signify a fruit steeped in carcinogens.

The question of purity versus contagion finally comes down to dirt. Most plants are in a cycle of exchange with the dirt, and healthy organic vegetables are often in a cycle of exchange with animal waste—usually the manure of herbivores, who are themselves in a cycle of exchange with plants (although the vegan equivalent of organic farming can rely solely on vegetal waste such as leaves and grass clippings). Hence, *organic* articulates a system of open exchange with the environment. That exchange is usurped in the case of fruits and vegetables raised according to so-called conventional methods, where chemical fertilizers supplant the function of dirt. By this line of reasoning, what's dirty is pure, and what's clean is impure.

But dirt in an organic garden is not the random wild boar patty. Manure may be a natural ingredient of organic farming, but before it is spread in the field it has to be composted in a pile that is turned five times over a fifteen-day period and cooked to 130°F to kill harmful bacteria.[12] Here, "cooked" embodies the Lévi-Straussian definition as composting converts a "raw" natural substance into a cultural product. (If raw manure is to be used at all, it must be spread 120 days before planting so that it can be cured—jerked, so to speak—by the elements.[13]) We tend to think of organic farming as a "natural" endeavor. Nothing could be further from the truth as it is an intensely cultural practice. Witness the plight of wild-caught salmon. They may not wear the organic label[14]—nor, indeed, might Pollan's shot-in-the-wild boar. Contrariwise, many farm-raised salmon may qualify as organic. The wild is excluded not because it might be impure but because it was not cultivated. At the other end of the spectrum, debate now focuses on whether industrial farming practices can be considered organic. Is Earthbound Farm's organic spinach truly organic when it is factory farmed, harvested, and processed? The answer turns on the extent to which we see technology as a vital aspect of human culture or more along the lines of Frankenstein's monster. If cultivation is a cultural practice, how do we construe the culture? Is it on the basis of a giant, computerized John Deere harvester that a farmer "drives" by pushing buttons and staring into a monitor? Or is it on the basis of a "chicken tractor," a contraption that allows a farmer to move chickens about a field so that their scratching cultivates the earth, their pecking harvests harmful grubs, and their droppings fertilize the soil?

In a world of contested and fluid categories, a fence is often the solution. Fences work on two levels: the real and the symbolic. Contrary to popular opinion, a fence almost never succeeds as a real barrier and is, hence, best considered for the symbolic messages it conveys. The fence that hemmed in Earthbound Farm's spinach gave the impression of the field's integrity, but as an impediment to movement, it probably did more to deter humans than the wild boar that conveniently trampled it. As an unaccomplished fence builder, I wonder how all the predators who torment my chickens perceive the fences I build. The black snake, the opossum, the raccoon, the owl, the hawk, and a number of stray dogs that have eaten my hens and their eggs—did my fence slow them down? Did they have to negotiate it as they would a troublesome thicket or briar patch? Or did they fail to remark it, intent only on a tasty meal?

Perhaps cognizant of the insufficiency of fences, many in the food industry propose buffers as a means for separating and ordering different aspects of agricultural production. In response to the E. coli outbreak, Robert Brackett of the U.S. Food and Drug Administration said the incident might be used to demonstrate "what the minimal distance" should be between crops like spinach and potential sources of contamination like cows.[15] Is half a mile enough? A mile? And what about the land in between? Does it simply lie fallow? What, then, of the vectors of contamination? How far might the water flow, the wind blow, a wild boar roam? Buffers are also touted as the means for preserving genetic integrity in a food industry currently seduced by the supposed benefits of genetically modified (GM) crops and simultaneously struggling to maintain order between modified and nonmodified forms. Plants may well be more mobile than animals as it only takes a milligram of pollen to transport a species from field to field and thereby across whole regions. Witness the plight of Percy Schmeiser, a Canadian canola farmer, who was sued by Monsanto when the corporation's genetically modified canola showed up in his field. Schmeiser was found guilty of illegally growing a patented crop that the wind or a passing canola-laden truck had most likely sown in his field. The case validated the intellectual property rights of the corporation over the farmer's old-style and out-of-date right to preserve his property against trespass. According to the judge, "A farmer can generally own the seeds or plants grown on his land if they blow in or are carried there by pollen—but . . . this is not true in the case of genetically modified seed."[16]

As a traditional farmer, Schmeiser had perfected his canola crop and seed over a period of forty years. He had not signed a contract with Monsanto or paid the required "$37-per-hectare fee for the privilege" of growing Monsanto's patented seed.[17] In an attempt to start fresh, Schmeiser

> removed his entire canola crop and bought non-GM seeds to replant his fields. To his shock, he discovered that a new crop of Monsanto's GM canola plants had re-germinated in his fields. When unwanted "volunteers" crop up in fields, the typical way the farmer deals with the problem is to apply herbicides. But these second-generation Monsanto seeds had been engineered in the lab to be "Round-up Ready"—i.e., designed to survive applications of Round-up herbicides (also made by Monsanto).[18]

Besides contamination in the field, GM crops have insinuated themselves with non-GM varieties in the processing plant. Such was the case when StarLink corn turned up in Kraft taco shells. Approved only for use in animal feeds, StarLink has been modified to include an insecticidal protein known as Bt (*Bacillus thuringiensis*) that "does not break down easily in the human digestive system."[19] Apparently, we would need four stomachs like a cow to eat a steady diet of StarLink.

According to Aventis (the corporation that holds the patent on StarLink), "four years is how long it could take for StarLink-contaminated corn to clear the food channels."[20] Methods to avoid future incidents of what the corporation prefers to call "commingling,"[21] rather than contamination, include separate grain elevators for the GM corn, carefully labeled seed bags, and of course buffer strips. But with StarLink turning up in snack foods in Japan and Korea—two countries that ban GM foods—the buffer may need to be wider than the Pacific Ocean.

For as long as people have tilled the soil, the planet's biological history has been intertwined with human culture. GM crops threaten the future precisely because they erase the past. Only genetic diversity can sustain a species against the calamities associated with weather and climate change as well as insect, fungal, and bacterial infestations. Efforts to preserve the planet's botanical and horticultural stores are severely challenged by the invasive nature of Frankenspecies, which infuse sameness where there was once diversity. The story of corn again offers a case in point. Originating in the Americas, corn is now an important source of protein the world over. This is particularly true as U.S. food aid consists primarily of corn (although this may change as corn is produced to meet the nation's fuel energy needs). As with most food crops, the seed stock has been bred and hybridized over time to produce a handful of important market varieties. But the future of corn, the possibility that there will always be corn, resides in the species' genetic bank—open-pollinated, heritage varieties still grown in their originary places. One such place is the remote highlands of Mexico, where farmers plant their milpas with seed saved over the years and across the generations. This genetic bank has now been infiltrated with GM corn. How did it happen? Researchers surmise that corn labeled for animal use only found its way into the region's marketplaces, where local farmers—not apt to make a distinction between what is appropriate for themselves but not their animals, or between kernels that may be eaten but not planted—sowed the GM corn alongside their own. So much for warning labels—borders, boundaries, buffers, and fences. Contamination was the result of two different and mutually incompatible ordering systems. Where ours is based on containment as defined by the notion of private property and a legal system to support it, theirs is based on open and free exchange between humans, animals, and plants. As the Frankenspecies exceed our containments, it remains to be seen if our system can continue to preserve order.

Our borders are porous. This is the oft-heard refrain from security-conscious politicians. The source of their anxiety is not the spread of GM materials wafting north to Canada and south to Mexico. No, America is itself besieged by tens of thousands of so-called illegals who yearly migrate north for jobs in our food and service sector paradise. Latinos have become a number one domestic issue. Whether or not they come bearing documents, these are the people who cultivate California's spinach, Arizona's melons, and North Carolina's cucumbers. For some, the promised paradise can become hell as it did for poultry workers trapped in a processing plant fire in Hamlet, North Carolina. Still, cost-conscious consumers accustomed to a bounteous and diverse food supply depend on such workers even while growing numbers of Americans want to "keep them out" or "send them back" as if we might achieve a free flow of goods and services without an equally free flow of labor.

What's lacking in the xenophobic worldview is a sense of how food gets from field to table. Anti-immigration furor focuses only on the bottommost rungs of a food production system that is shaped and controlled by giant corporations, not the people in the field. Profit at the top requires a low-wage pool of planters, pickers, and packers whose compliance is guaranteed by the risks they face in terms of poor housing, lack of health care, and the ever-present fear of deportation. It also requires an equally dependent pool of "farmers" who produce under contract to corporations with names like Monsanto, Purdue, and Smithfield. The corporation furnishes seed or starter livestock, fertilizer or feed, pesticides or antibiotics against return on a market-ready product, be it tomatoes or pigs. All risks are borne by the farmer, whose relationship to the corporation resurrects the same potential for debt peonage that defined sharecropping.

Perhaps as testament to a collective sense of powerlessness, we are fast becoming a nation of protectionists. Fearing cultural contagion, states and municipalities have issued punitive rulings against landlords who rent to presumed illegals (overturned at the district court level but pending appeal to the U.S. Supreme Court). We blame Latinos for all our domestic woes from job loss to failing public schools and collapsing health care systems. Taco Bell with its south-of-the-border menu items may have been Americanized by its merger with KFC under the greater PepsiCo corporate umbrella, but the Spanish language used in places other than menus constitutes a defilement of our national identity. Only English will be tolerated on drivers' license tests and voting ballots; only in English will the national anthem be sung. And immigrants who take to the streets to demonstrate against draconian anti-immigration legislation must be seen to wave only the American flag.

The height of our protectionism is the recently passed legislation to build a 700-mile "double set of steel walls with floodlights, surveillance cameras and metal detectors" along portions of the border with Mexico.[22] Helicopters and unmanned aerial drones are part of the security package, along with a beefed-up CBP Border Patrol and supplemental National Guard. Then, too, there are the Minutemen militias, who carry out their own border surveillance patrols and fence building activities. Declaring the federal government ineffectual and claiming that more Americans "were murdered this year by illegal aliens than the combined death toll of US troops in Iraq and Afghanistan," the Minutemen Civil Defense Corps defines its mission as a "God-given right to protect our lives and property."[23]

To interpret the lunacy of a fence between ourselves and one of our most important trading partners, we might consider other such barriers beginning with the Great Wall of China and including the now infamous Berlin Wall, the equally disreputable Israeli West Bank barrier, and India's 1,300-mile wall on its border with Bangladesh.[24] Political rationales for border fences focus on the need to keep barbarians out or warring factions apart. Equally important are the symbolic meanings attached to such obsessively grandiose fencing operations. Once more, Douglas's work is instructive. As she sees it, there is a correlation between obsession with boundaries and societies defined by "the fluid formlessness of their highly competitive social life" (*Purity*, 127). Douglas is referring to the Yurok Indians of Northern California whose pollution rituals were enacted on the fluid, formlessness of water and intended to make good water distinguishable from bad. Now consider our own ritual of purity as the border fence slices through a continuous topography composed of deserts, mountains, gullies, canyons, towns, and cities in an effort to separate so-called legals from illegals. If Douglas found the Yurok's obsession with boundaries as compensatory for a formless but nevertheless highly competitive social life, might we not say the same for ourselves? Do we not preach equal opportunity and democracy even while we practice rampant individualism and one-upmanship? We tell ourselves that we need the fence to keep others out—keep others from stealing our jobs and diminishing our resources. But doesn't the fence also function to keep us in, both mentally and physically? Might we not also see it as a vast national enactment of sympathetic magic against the flight of our jobs? As capitalism restructures the global economy and redistributes consumers and producers, isn't our fence a feeble attempt to transform the financial and demographic fluidity associated with global capitalism into a concrete us versus them?

I have mapped agricultural production as a series of expanding relationships that might be thought of as three photographs, shot one after the other, each at a greater remove and with a wider angle. The first photo captures the narrowest frame and focuses on a field of spinach, a fence, and a wild boar. The second photo, shot at a greater remove, shows crops extending north and south of the border, a system of buffers, and airborne GM pollen. The third photo, shot from the greatest remove, features the nation, the international border, and undocumented workers. My intent is not to suggest that undocumented immigrants are in some way analogous to wild boars and contaminated pollen, even though the photos we take— like the stories we tell ourselves—position them as contaminants. Indeed, rabid right-wingers often summon the language of pollution to condemn immigration. This ideology has worked its way into the more liberal media, including the *New York Times Magazine*, where the same issue that featured Pollan's observations on the E. coli outbreak dramatized its main story on illegal immigration with the provocative title "The Keep-Em-Out Campaign" and an ominous cover photo depicting a floodlit Border Patrol vehicle parked beside a night-darkened, two-story border fence.[25]

If we set aside the popular analogy between contamination and people deemed illegal—that is, set aside the content of the three photos—we see that what makes them homologous is their structure. Each reveals an architecture of containment that is both real and symbolic, designed to ensure purity, which is itself both real and symbolic. In all three photos, order is stated as a barrier, either a fence or a buffer. But a fence is as insufficient a solution to biological contamination as it is to the social and economic forces that shape the corporate, profit-driven system of food production that unleashes contamination (either biological or genetic) and at the same time beckons cheap labor. Still, we contemplate bigger, more technologically elaborate fencing systems like the $2.2 billion border fence and no less costly food irradiation systems.

It should be obvious that as the inquiry expanded into larger frames of reference my determination to approach the evidence as a forensic specialist fell by the wayside. In the end, structural anthropology emerges as the intellectual system best able to grasp what's at stake in a world of competing cultural signifiers. Structuralism shifts meaning into the symbolic order. Douglas's understanding of purity as a code for order gives the initial cue for how to read the E. coli outbreak symbolically. The subsequent distillation of all the variables that defined the spinach episode into the rubric of fence and boar equates with Claude Lévi-Strauss's recognition of the significance of mothers' brothers in tribal kinship systems. His insight gave him the key for reading whole systems of practice in a unified way. Structural anthropology may be criticized for banishing all the delightful oddments of daily life to the margins of interpretation. But structuralists certainly get to the haiku of meaning. Gilles Deleuze hit the nail on the head when he said of structuralism, "The real subject is the structure itself" ("Le vrais sujet est la structure même").[26] What he means is that the subject of the three photo stories is not spinach, or GM crops, or even immigration. No, the subject is order, which is achieved through containment. We are the people whose stories tell of containment—how it is threatened and how it is to be preserved.

But why? The bare bones of the structure do not reveal its organizing ethos. What is lacking in the forensic paring away of the oddments is the pregnant absence of what structuralists call "degree zero." Summarizing its various manifestations across a number of structuralist thinkers, Deleuze observes that Michel Foucault reckoned degree zero as "the place of the king" (261) in a painting by Velázquez. For Philippe Sollers, it is the "blind spot" (261) that gives rise to a particular piece of writing. And in Lévi-Strauss, it is "mana" (261), a floating signifier that doesn't itself have symbolic value but nevertheless exists throughout a structure.

What, then, is our mana, our degree zero? What for us occupies the place of the king? The answer could be no more obvious, yet is imperceptible for its unremarked omnipresence: *private property*. This is what floats throughout every story. This is our unquestioned zero sum of all meaning. Whether it be spinach in a field, life encoded in DNA, the nation itself—all are construed as private property. From this perspective, concerns over purity and contamination become secondary to the true subject, which is the structure itself.

Epilogue

To conclude his essay on the contaminated spinach, Pollan recalls that at the height of concern over E. coli he had no qualms about buying spinach at his local farmers' market. As with most people who support farmers' markets, Pollan waxes idyllic as he enumerates the virtues of buying real foods—carrots with root hairs—sold fresh from the grower in a setting where the countryside comes to the city. But how many of us live in localities where a farmers' market is an accessible, economical, year-round alternative to the supermarket? Bear in mind that residents in poor neighborhoods and inner cities often don't even have a supermarket. Some rely on convenience stores as the source for meals. While the idea of buying direct from farmers ought to imply a democratized economy, in reality farmers' markets tend to gravitate toward more affluent, professional-class suburban consumers. Nevertheless, discussions of food safety often conjure the local as a healthful alternative to more government and corporate oversight or yet another technological fix.

The problem is how to posit the local so that it doesn't smack of elitism at a time when corporate big-box retailers such as Wal-Mart have positioned themselves as purveyors to the popular classes. This is the problem that has shaped Joan Dye Gussow's lifelong advocacy of slow food and sustainable agriculture. As she puts it, "Mass-marketed prepared food thrives on, demands, a delocalized conformity."[27] To counter the corporate delocalization of food (one county and two processing plants that supply most of the nation's spinach), Gussow calls upon us to "relocalize" food production.[28] That is, we would all grow what is locally possible and eat what is locally available. What? No Chilean peaches in December? No California oranges in New England? Only potatoes and cabbage for the winter? How bleak! How imponderable!

Gussow truly does live the local. She grows most of her own food, having learned the varieties that do best in her soil, how to stretch her growing season, and how to store foods for the winter. What's more, she taught her palate to appreciate the singularity of seasonal tastes—strawberries in June, tomatoes in August. I think she wants her life and writing to provide a model for how we all might strive to live the local. But I don't think we need to take her example as a prescription. Relocation can also be a powerful metaphor, a figure for a radically different relationship to time and place. Here, I am guided by what Fredric Jameson has to say about Kim Stanley Robinson's Mars trilogy. In defining the utopian aspect of science fiction, Jameson cautions that the different social and economic strategies that Robinson has his Mars colonists explore need not be seen as prescriptive: "It's not a matter of choosing between them, but of using them to destabilize our own existence, our own social life at present."[29] This is a function of the imagination. The reader experiments with how his or her life might feel in newly defined circumstances.

By extension, relocalization can have two meanings. It can signify an actual practice that involves a real return to the local sustained by efforts to shop and produce locally. And it can also mean the relocating of ourselves in very different temporal and spatial configurations. Here, we would have to imagine a process of production and exchange that is not embedded in the preservation of private property, nor articulated in the fetishized instantaneity of a bag of spinach whose appearance on the supermarket shelf belies its 3,000-mile container shipment. Imagining relocalization destabilizes the assumed normalcy of all our borders as we begin to set aside the fear that policed, controlled, and owned spaces necessarily generate. It enables us to glimpse what Douglas had in mind when she observed, "Where there is no differentiation, there is no defilement" (*Purity*, 160).

Open systems of exchange such as those practiced by organic farmers are healthy precisely because they are immersed in the world rather than predicated on keeping the world out. The utopian logic of relocalization can also have consequences on how we envision the nation. As Alex Perrone, the mayor of Calexico, a California border town, puts it, "We should be . . . constructing bridges of good relationships with Mexico. If we don't have Mexico, we don't have Calexico."[30] We may never fully achieve a world based on the sort of open exchange with the environment that undergirds sustainable agriculture. Unlike the Mexican peasant who eats the same corn as his animals, we may never experience nondifferentiated exchange with our others. But it behooves us to begin to loosen the hold of patents and borders in order to glimpse topographies of reciprocity. Until then, contamination (both real and figural) remains the stalking horse of corporate agriculture and the corporate nation-state.

Notes

1   Eric Schlosser, "Has Politics Contaminated the Food Supply?" *New York Times*, December 11, 2006.

2   Stacy Finz and Erin Allday, "Spinach Growers Were Warned about Produce Safety," *San Francisco Chronicle*, September 19, 2006.

3   Meredith May and George Raine, "Spinach Scare Hits Salinas Hard," *San Francisco Chronicle*, September 19, 2006.

4   Associated Press, "Pattern of E. Coli Outbreaks Is Seen," *New York Times*, September 19, 2006.

5   Michael Pollan, "The Vegetable-Industrial Complex," *New York Times Magazine*, October 15, 2006, 17–20, 18.

6   Julie Schmit, "Spinach Producers Take Financial Hit," *USA Today*, September 19, 2006.

7   Daniel B. Wood, "E. Coli Cases Prompt Calls to Regulate Farm Practices," *Christian Science Monitor*, September 18, 2006.

8   Schmit, "Spinach Producers Take Financial Hit."

9   Pollan, "The Vegetable-Industrial Complex," 18.

10 Michael Pollan, "The Modern Hunter-Gatherer," *New York Times Magazine*, March 26, 2006, 38–45, 63, 66, 70.

11 Mary Douglas, *Purity and Danger: An Analysis of the Concepts of Pollution and Taboo* (Lon-

don: Routledge and Kegan Paul, 1966), 69. Hereafter cited parenthetically by page number as *Purity*.

12   This is the formula used by Vermont Natural Agricultural Products of Middlebury. A temperature of 130°F corresponds with U.S. Department of Agriculture guidelines.

13   This is included in the organic fertilization guidelines of the Northeast Organic Farming Association, www.nofa.org/index.php (accessed October 5, 2007).

14   Andrew Martin, "Free or Farmed, When Is a Fish Really Organic?" *New York Times*, November 28, 2006.

15   Amanda Gardner, "Spinach Contamination Linked to Cattle Ranch," *HealthDay News*, October 13, 2006.

16   Gar Smith, "Percy Schmeiser vs. Monsanto," *Earth Island Journal* (Autumn 2001), text available at www.thirdworldtraveler.com/Corporations/PSchmeiser_Monsanto.html (accessed December 12, 2006).

17   Mark Nichols, "Monsanto vs. Schmeiser," *MacLeans Magazine*, May 17, 1999, 17.

18   Smith, "Percy Schmeiser vs. Monsanto."

19   Alejandro E. Segarra and Jean M. Rawson, "StarLink™ Corn Controversy: Background," *CRS Report for Congress*, January 10, 2001, www.ncseonline.org/NLE/CRSreports/Agriculture/ag-101.cfm.

20   Ibid.

21   Ibid.

22   Tyche Hendricks, "Border Security or Boondoggle? A Plan for 100 Miles of Mexican Border Wall Heads for Senate—Its Future Is Not Assured," *San Francisco Chronicle*, February 26, 2006.

23   Minuteman Border Fence, www.minutemanborderfence.com (accessed December 5, 2006).

24   Hendricks, "Border Security or Boondoggle?"

25   "The Keep-Em-Out Campaign," *New York Times Magazine*, October 15, 2006.

26   Gilles Deleuze, *L'Île Déserte et Autres Textes: textes and entretiens 1953–1974*, ed. David Lapoujade (Paris: Les Éditions de Minuit, 2002), 249. Hereafter cited parenthetically by page number. Translations are my own.

27   Joan Dye Gussow, *This Organic Life* (White River Junction, VT: Chelsea Green, 2001), 160.

28   Ibid.

29   Joshua Glenn, "Back to Utopia: Can the Antidote to Today's Neoliberal Triumphalism Be Found in the Pages of Far-Out Science Fiction?" *Boston Globe*, November 20, 2005.

30   Hendricks, "Border Security or Boondoggle?"

Lynn Marie Houston

Food Safety and the Abject:
Mad Cow Disease and a Racist Rhetoric
of Contamination in the Southwest

> In the late nineteenth and early twentieth centuries,
> discourse on sexuality . . . claimed to ensure the physi-
> cal vigor and the moral cleanliness of the social body; it
> promised to eliminate defective individuals, degener-
> ate and bastardized populations. In the name of a bio-
> logical and historical urgency, it justified the racisms
> of the state, which at the time were on the horizon. It
> grounded them in "truth."
> —Michel Foucault, *The History of Sexuality: An
> Introduction*

> Capital punishment would not be maintained except
> by invoking less the enormity of the crime itself than
> the monstrosity of the criminal, his incorrigibility, and
> the safeguard of society. One had the right to kill those
> who represented a kind of biological danger to others.
> —Michel Foucault, *The History of Sexuality: An
> Introduction*

Mad cow disease, or bovine spongiform encephalopathy (BSE), developed out of a meat industry practice designed to increase production by making it easier and cheaper to fatten cattle and therefore easier and cheaper for some segments of the industry to make more money. To cut production costs, waste from the slaughtering process (parts of dead animals and what-

South Atlantic Quarterly 107:2, Spring 2008
DOI 10.1215/00382876-2007-072 © 2008 Duke University Press

ever else was on the slaughterhouse floor) was recycled back into the feed for live cattle. The motivation behind this forced cannibalism was to recuperate some of the costs of fattening up the cattle by allowing the protein and nutrients in their unsellable remains to nourish and, therefore, fatten more quickly the next herd of cattle in the feedlot. The remains that were fed to cattle, known as "rendered feed," harbored the deadly prions (found in brain and spinal cord matter) that cause scrapie in sheep, BSE in cattle, and Creutzfeldt-Jakob disease in humans.

In the contemporary U.S. meat industry, the labor involved in the various stages of production is so divided that most ranchers have nothing to do with what occurs at the feedlot stage, just as most feedlot operators have little to do with what occurs in packinghouses at the slaughter stage. The system that has developed, whereby packinghouses sell rendered feed and feedlots use it, belongs to a meat industry trend toward mass-size operations and the reduction of the industry to a few major meat companies across the country. Small family-owned ranches may not sell their cattle to feedlots (raising them on grass or hay instead), or they may send them to smaller, locally operated feedlots that are less likely to use rendered feed.[1] It grows ever more expensive to raise a head of cattle without the advantage of these practices, since legislation related to health inspection of facilities often makes it cost prohibitive to raise or sell meat products on a small scale. Thus, pressures mount on family ranches to begin to use these industrial methods (such as using rendered feed) and to increase the size of their operations, or else they risk being forced out of business and driven into bankruptcy by the competition. Small family ranches have reason to be angry with the national and international media because their businesses were even further damaged by the bad image given to the entire meat industry after the discovery of BSE, even though cattle from smaller ranches were much less likely to have been contaminated by the disease because of the differences in production practices.

The effects of BSE and globalization on the morale of those who have remained in business have begun to manifest themselves in their rhetoric of food safety and contamination. In the wake of the BSE crisis, ranchers across the United States lambasted environmentalists, liberals, television personalities, their own lobbying agencies, the government, and each other. However, at the political hot spot of the U.S.-Mexico border, certain rancher groups are using public fear and misperception of BSE as a rhetorical rationale for lashing out at immigrants who, because of their lack of resources and legal recourse, make easy targets when problems arise concerning food safety and contamination issues.

Skilled and unskilled physical labor by immigrants on ranches used to be highly valued. However, in competition with mass technology, that physical labor has been devalued. Similarly, the human-animal relationships on Southwestern ranches used to consist of humans (Anglos and Latinos) in a hierarchy over animals (cattle, other livestock, and potential predators). This relationship has been altered. As border regulations and associated xenophobic nationalism intensify, humans crossing ranchlands in the severe desert conditions of southern Arizona are considered less important than the livestock produced on the ranches. The situation is particular to contemporary ranching in the United States, in which concerns for property and livestock as commodities take priority over the lives of immigrants, which have become disposable and easily replaceable units in food production.

The distinction between the human body and the animal body is indeed eroded by BSE and its human variant Creutzfeldt-Jakob disease. These diseases suggest a radical connection between the human and the animal through the body, wherein, for the racist goal of abjection, the problem of "meat" and immigrant bodies is all one of contamination. At the same time, this connection of human and animal bodies undoes—in general and not just specifically to one racial group—the hierarchical position of the human body used to justify human dominion over animals through Western history. With dominion threatened on many levels, a small group of ranchers in Arizona and Texas has found a scapegoat in border crossers.

The actions of these rancher-vigilantes[2] came to the attention of the general public in the Southwest in 1999 and 2000 when ranchers Roger Barnett and his brothers began speaking out publicly about their practices and the situation that led them to begin patrolling their ranchland, rounding up illegal immigrants at gunpoint, and turning them in to the local division of the U.S. Customs and Border Protection Border Patrol.[3] Not long after, a right-wing, pseudo-neo-Nazi militant group based in Texas, called Ranch Rescue (whose name was changed in 2004 to Border Rescue), was formed in response to the problem, taking inspiration from the Barnett brothers' actions.[4] The group had its own Arizona chapter, but it also represented the interests of ranchers on the border in Texas and also in New Mexico.[5] Ranch Rescue members offered their services on a voluntary basis to help repair damages done by immigrants and also to work as armed security patrols to protect the homes and lands of the property owners. According to Ranch Rescue's Web site, "Drug smugglers, criminal gang members, bandits, thugs, and international terrorists cross over privately owned farm and ranch land in our border counties and they victimize the rural landowners along the way. Government has utterly ignored the victimization of these rural families."[6] Ranchers claim that their lives are being endangered, their property damaged, and their cattle killed by immigrants (or, as they call them, "criminal trespassers"), who travel over their lands while crossing the border in large numbers. They feel that Border Patrol is not doing enough to handle this problem, primarily because it is insufficiently staffed. They also feel that the U.S. government is too lax in its policies because it does not prosecute captured illegal immigrants for damages caused to the property and ranching businesses of U.S. citizens.[7] Their relationship with Border Patrol has become strained. They use rhetorical tactics to show that, as ranchers, they are better equipped than Border Patrol to handle the situation and the terrain. A February 2000 article on Ranch Rescue's Web site made fun of an agent for shooting a cow because he believed the animal was charging him, suggesting that Border Patrol agents lack a necessary knowledge base and are out of place on these border ranchlands.[8] This article also constructs the ranchers as victims at the hands of the inefficient Border Patrol staff, who contribute to business losses through accidents such as this one, and it situates the ranchers as victims of the illegal immigrants they accuse of carrying diseases onto their ranchlands.[9] Thus, they argue, they are justified in taking matters into their own hands. Ranch Rescue was proud to note on its Web site that from around 1998 to 2001 Barnett and his two brothers "personally apprehended and turned over to law enforcement over 2000 criminal trespassers."[10]

At about the same time as this situation became public through newspaper and television reports, an anonymous pamphlet began circulating the country, advertising "tours" of the ranches along the southern Arizona border near the crossing at Douglas, Arizona/Agua Prieta, Sonora. "Tourists" were encouraged to bring firearms, night-vision goggles, camouflage clothing, and other equipment to help "hunt" illegal immigrants.[11] The pamphlet's tourist rhetoric is not uncommon for ranches not involved in the affair: many smaller ranches in the Southwest have had to resort to "guest ranch" operations in order to make a living.

The racist rhetoric of Ranch Rescue was able to align itself with popular sentiment against international terrorists and the prevention of their entry into the United States. While the rancher-vigilantes used to funnel their hatred into the figure of the drug smuggler, the new pathologized, abject figure invoked to justify violence against immigrants on the border is that of the international terrorist. Besides using antiterrorist discourse and nostalgic sentiment, the rancher-vigilantes also bolster their cause using public fears associated with BSE and other diseases. While U.S. government workers were disinfecting shoes from passengers traveling from the United Kingdom and stepping up airport security, illegal immigrants, they say, were passing from ranchlands in Mexico through ranchlands in the United States on foot and were potentially carrying foot-and-mouth disease across on their shoes.

The "Media Coverage" page of the Ranch Rescue Web site once offered links to numerous articles offering justification for their fear of illegal immigrants. One of the titles read "Criminal Aliens Will Bring Foot and Mouth Disease to the USA."[12] Underneath this link to an article in the *Tucson Citizen* reads a caption placed there by Ranch Rescue: "No effective border control means no effective disease control."[13] The actual title of the article in the *Tucson Citizen* is "Foot-and-Mouth Fears Haunting Area Ranchers," a far cry from the vigilante group's rephrasing. According to the article, the risk of foot-and-mouth disease being brought into the United States on the shoes of illegal immigrants is only slight, a blatant contradiction to Ranch Rescue's claim.[14] According to the USDA officials cited in the article, Mexico has not had a case of foot-and-mouth disease since the 1950s, which would even further decrease the likelihood that immigrants who cross the border on foot might carry it.[15]

This and other means of spreading foot-and-mouth have always been possible. However, the stakes are higher now, due to the public's mistaken notion that foot-and-mouth disease is responsible for BSE and, subsequently, for Creutzfeldt-Jakob's disease. Foot-and-mouth disease is actually a viral disease that has nothing to do with BSE, but the two came to the public's attention at the same time. The Wisconsin Department of Agriculture explains the media mix-up:

> There is no connection between bovine spongiform encephalopathy (BSE) and foot-and-mouth disease. The two diseases are entirely unrelated and don't resemble one another in any way. But they ended up in the news at the same time. BSE has remained in the news periodically since the first diagnosis in 1986, but in early 2001, there was a

flurry of news stories about BSE. At about the same time, in February 2001, England reported its first case of foot-and-mouth disease since 1967. Because of this coincidence, there has been some understandable confusion.[16]

Thus, BSE offers a new opportunity for the unfounded expression of racist fears of "contamination." The nature of this alarmist rhetoric directed against immigrants is not new, but the resurgence of it by such a specialized group speaks to changing dynamics in social relations on the border influenced by larger historical trends in the meat industry and the globalization of food production.

The racially charged situation in Cochise County, Arizona, between ranchers and illegal immigrants marks a new point in the relationship between these two populations in the history of ranching. The contribution of Mexican culture to the culture of ranching is undeniable. Even the history of ranching in the United States now acknowledges the working relationship between Anglo settlers and Latinos. In the recent past, Southwestern family ranches on the border relied heavily on cheap labor from illegal immigrants or Mexican migrant workers, just as slaughterhouses and other agricultural facilities across the country still do.

Ranch Rescue effectively rewrote history so as to endow the individual ranch owners with greater meaning, downplaying the significant contributions of their ranch hands. Ranch Rescue was quick to negate the importance of Latinos in the history of ranching: "We are private Citizens who recognize that America became a prosperous nation due to the sanctity of private property acquired, owned, utilized, and held by individual Citizens and *not* by government entities or so-called 'activist' groups."[17] Not only did Ranch Rescue tap into the rhetoric of the U.S. Constitution about private property ownership, as the organization sought to justify vigilante actions by focusing on individual rights, but it did not even acknowledge the fact that work on a ranch is done by many people other than the owner. In addition, the allusion made to land held by government and activist groups refers to the difficulty that ranchers face regarding land-use rights. Much of the land in the Southwest is public land—it is controlled by government agencies such as the Bureau of Land Management and the USDA Forest Service, by state land trusts, or even by other organizations such as the Nature Conservancy. In recent years, the trend has been to deny permits to ranches for use of the land and instead to give use rights over to developers.

In other cases, environmental groups purchase land titles in order to preserve and protect lands, only allowing eco-friendly production practices.

The U.S. food industry also actively contributes to the immigration problem. A number of food companies have received national media coverage in the past few years for their practices of recruiting illegal labor from Mexico.[18] These companies make more money because they can pay illegal immigrants less money, offer them no benefits, and provide substandard working conditions. If there is any talk of unionization or of workers protesting, management simply brings in the Immigration and Naturalization Service to deport the workers (sometimes even doing so right before payday so as to keep the workers' hard-earned wages[19]). This has been standard practice in slaughterhouses for years. However, corporation management—not the rancher, and certainly not the slaughterhouse worker—is the party that receives the profit from these practices. The rancher is paid for his cattle, which are then shipped to a feedlot or slaughtering facility, and the rancher's investment in the process is done. The rancher has no incentive to become aware of what goes on at the processing stage. Thus, while one sector of the meat industry is fighting against illegal immigration (the ranchers involved with the vigilante activities), another is seeking ways in which it can bypass immigration laws to amass a body of cheap labor. The vilification of Mexicans, Mexican Americans, and other immigrants is the result in both of these situations, as well as the contamination of our food supply with diseases like BSE.

One scandal that reveals how far food companies really go in recruiting illegal immigrants for food production involves Tyson Foods. On December 20, 2001, in the *New York Times*, David Barboza reported about the indictment of Tyson Foods for a plan to smuggle illegal workers into the United States from Mexico. Tyson employees and executives had tried to arrange transportation and fake working papers for thirty-six illegal workers from Mexico. The case against Tyson states that it "engaged in the practices to cut costs, meet production goals and to maximize profits."[20] The government claims that this was a "corporate conspiracy," that "Tyson had a corporate culture that condoned such behavior," and that "Tyson sought unauthorized workers 'who would work for low wages and never complain—no matter how much they were exploited.'"[21] Only a few months before the scandal, Tyson bought Iowa Beef Packers (IBP)—a large national beef corporation—thus asserting itself as a major force in the meat industry. It became "a $20 billion company that dominates the meat counter at supermarkets and is a leading supplier to fast-food restaurants like McDonald's and Burger King."[22] In addition to Tyson's illegal immigrant scandal, the company's reputation was dealt another blow. In 1997, company executives pled guilty to charges that the company made "illegal gifts" to former agriculture secretary Mike Espy. Tyson Foods is only one example of the food industry's abuses of immigrants. Greg Denier, a spokesman for the United Food and Commercial Workers, was quoted in Barboza's article as stating quite accurately that this situation "is a cross-border trade in human flesh."[23] The conjunction here between the consumption of animal flesh and the consumption of human flesh in the form of immigrant bodies further highlights the symbolic cannibalism at work in the processes of the meat industry that has led to food safety issues impacting consumer health and national ethics. Unfortunately, Tyson was acquitted of the charges related to illegal immigrants in March 2003, but many other companies that engage in such practices await prosecution.

In 1997, Gail Eisnitz wrote about the horrific conditions of slaughterhouses and of the illegal activities that go on in them. Her book *Slaughterhouse* exposes the inhumane practices against animals and workers in meat-processing plants across the country.[24] Through investigation, interviews, and on-site observations, she uncovered the common corporate strategy of hiring illegal workers for lower wages and fewer benefits. Also, she found many instances in which slaughterhouses "owned" doctors and compensated them for misdiagnosing injuries to the company's benefit. In an environment in which few medical benefits are given as it is, even legitimate claims were thwarted and injured employees quickly fired.

A number of factors have come together at this point in history to produce the rancher vigilantism on ranchlands close to the U.S.-Mexico border. First, economic realities have caused more than 14 million acres of rangeland in the western United States to be lost in the last decade, and family ranches have had to develop new strategies to stay in business, such as raising exotic game and promoting hunting and vacation tours.[25] Second, the ranching business has inherited a sense of nationalism from the meaningfulness of the history of cowboy culture to the formation of the United States. Finally, the nature of the emergence of the BSE crisis has caused a strain on the meat industry, coupled with the awareness of the porosity of borders and the possibilities for the migration of people and diseases accompanying globalization. All of these elements have contributed to explosive tensions in the ranching community along the southern Arizona border.

Julia Kristeva's theory of abjection deals largely with issues relevant to this situation: cleanliness, contamination, and purity. Her theory describes a process of identity formation based on the rejection of an entity that was once integral to the subject's identity. Kristeva's work is useful for the perspectives it offers specifically on borders, subjectivity, and contamination, especially given this situation in which a group of ranchers is involved in the expulsion from society of those who they construct as a threat to the health of society.[26] The process of rejection involved with the abject often involves references to physical processes of waste excretion or to emotions of horror or disgust, as that which was rejected often comes back to haunt the subject, troubling the boundaries of the self. In addition to its rhetoric of contamination, Ranch Rescue employed the rhetoric of the abject by using metaphors of excrement to describe the immigrants. This is how former president and national spokesman for the group Jack Foote responded in 2000 to an e-mail message from a Mexican American who accused Foote and his organization of racism:

> You and the vast majority of your fellow dog turds are ignorant, uneducated, and desperate for a life in a decent nation because the one that you live in is nothing but a pile of dog shit, made up of millions of little dog turds like you. You stand around your entire lives, whining about how bad things are in your dog of a nation, waiting for the dog to stick its ass under our fence and shit each one of you into our back yards.[27]

Foote goes one step further than equating Mexicans to animals — he equates them to the waste produced by animals. By referring to excrement, Foote symbolizes the system of our industrial food production whereby immigrants are "chewed up" and then excreted. The real cannibalism involved in the practices leading to BSE, whereby cattle are fed the remains of dead cattle and other animals, is an outgrowth of the cannibalistic ethics of the food industry that consumes human flesh in the form of immigrant bodies. However, the racist rhetoric also implicates another issue of food safety and contamination: E. coli poisoning due to the contact of meat with fecal matter. The meat industry continues to be implicated in deaths due to E. coli outbreaks as the speed of slaughterhouse assembly lines and the conditions of labor in those facilities still allow such contact.

The work of anthropologist Mary Douglas is one of the sources for Kristeva's work on the abject.[28] Elizabeth Grosz, in her analysis of Douglas's work on the purity of boundaries, states that for Douglas dirt "is that which is not in its proper place, that which upsets or befuddles the order."[29]

Douglas's ideas in her work *Purity and Danger* and Kristeva's theory of the abject conjoin to help explain the post-BSE situation of rancher-vigilantes in the borderlands. The rancher, as cowboy, has a particularly famous relationship with dirt in the desert landscapes of the West. The Marlboro Man in the cigarette ad campaign drew on the image of the dusty cowboy to signify a renegade American spirit that appeals to consumers and increases the demand for cigarettes. In the figure of the Marlboro Man, dirt is used to signify the cowboy as outside the social order in a positive sense. Perhaps because the cowboy image is associated with "being outside the law," that is, living on the margins of abjection, the reputation of today's ranchers hinges on showing themselves less abject than others around them. After all, BSE associates ranchers with the worst kind of body limit and contamination taboo—cannibalism. By making others out to be considerably more abject than they are and then directing violence toward them, ranchers reestablish their inclusion in the social order. In this way, the crisis of BSE—prompted by a disregard of bodily boundaries in the practice of forced cannibalism and by a disregard for the separation between waste and incorporation—is symbolically made right by these ranchers who feel they are protecting the social body from "invaders" and who reestablish their status as "American heroes" in so doing.

Southwest ranchers and illegal immigrants are particularly subject to relations shaped by the abject because of their proximity to each other in the borderlands and their proximity to the lives of animals. The feminist work of Janet Price and Margaret Shildrick in reading Kristeva's theory of the abject is also relevant for elucidating the situation on the border. In their discussion of Kristeva's theory of the abject in *The Powers of Horror*, they make connections that are highly relevant for understanding the abject as it functions in the vigilante situation: "The association of the body with gross, unthinking physicality marks a further set of linkages—to black people, to working class people, to animals, and to slaves."[30] The shared history and cultural miscegenation of ranching further brings home this aspect of the abject. Anglo ranchers are sensitive to the way their everyday lives are affected by the influx of Mexican culture, both in their ranching practices and in their geographical situation in the borderlands. That which is Mexican, for the vigilantes, is that which has been rejected, but which remains present as part of the U.S. ranching identity and of the contemporary history of the Southwest. That which is Mexican is the history of American colonialism.

The connection between the theory of the abject and the situation of rancher-vigilantes in the Southwest is made more explicit by the way in which Michael Hardt and Antonio Negri, in *Empire*, talk about globalization as "contamination" and the effect it has on our experience of cross-cultural relations. They admit, "Along with the common celebrations of the unbounded flows in our new global village, one can still sense also an anxiety about increased contact and a certain nostalgia for colonialist hygiene."[31] They consider fear of contamination as "the dark side of the consciousness of globalization."[32] If, as Hardt and Negri state, "the hygienic shields of colonial boundaries" are at stake in globalization, then the rancher-vigilante problem on the U.S.-Mexico border might be the attempt at a solution by one group, when faced with the "boundless flows" of globalization, to put back in place the "shields of colonial boundaries."[33]

BSE, caused by practices of rendered feed in the U.S. and British meat industries, is not a problem from without, from "those others over there," but a problem that we should focus on from within, from a reform of practices in the U.S. meat industry (indeed, in our entire food system). Likewise, the racism evidenced by these vigilante attacks is a problem from within. The rhetoric itself says more about the undermined position of the Anglo ranchers (and their frustrated paramilitary fantasies) than it does about any security threat to the U.S. body politic. Currently, ranchers see their businesses falling apart, their lands being taken away, their family histories forgotten, their techniques surpassed by expensive technology, and, in general, their sense of themselves as models of "what America is all about" eroded. They blame the government, in part, for aiding developers and "weekend ranchers" (doctors and lawyers who own ranches for tax breaks). Now, with BSE, they are the target of consumers' suspicion for making the food supply unsafe.

All of these elements add up to a tremendous blow to the ranchers' sense of self as the modern-day ancestors of the mythical cowboy figure. Vigilantes can certainly consider themselves more important if they can say they are attacking high-profile criminals who pose threats to civilian safety rather than hungry farmers and other workers whose lives are traded against the food on our tables. So, with a heavy rhetorical sleight of hand, these immigrants and workers become vilified—in this time of renewed nationalism and concern for the safety of our national borders—as drug smugglers, disease carriers, and potential terrorists. Underlying this strategy is a response to the vilification of meat production by the media during the

BSE crisis and the dismantling of the hierarchical status of the human body in the wake of BSE, as well as a desire to reestablish a hierarchy of bodies in which the body of the white, Western male rancher assumes, once again, a position of power.

Notes

1   For instance, ranchers who run cow-calf operations (they breed cattle and sell the calves soon after they are weaned) would have no idea how the cattle are treated once they leave their ranch and would have no part in how those cattle were fed or slaughtered.

2   The ranchers in this organization object to the term *vigilante*, preferring to situate themselves as "victims."

3   One would hope that all of the captured immigrants were handed over safely.

4   Ranch Rescue's national spokesman from 2001 to 2004 was Jack Foote. The organization has, since 2004, changed its name and Web site address. It is now called Border Rescue, taking away the focus from ranching culture. Another related organization is American Border Patrol, http://americanborderpatrol.com (accessed November 29, 2007).

5   Ranch Rescue, "Media Coverage," November 7, 2001, www.ranchrescue.com/media.htm. The Ranch Rescue Web site no longer exists. See similar information on the Border Rescue Web site, www.borderrescue.com, or visit old Ranch Rescue Web pages by searching for www.ranchrescue.com on www.archive.org/web/web.php.

6   Ranch Rescue, "The Facts," November 7, 2001, www.ranchrescue.com/thefacts.htm (site now discontinued).

7   For additional information, see essays on the minutemen in "The Last Frontier: The Contemporary Configuration of the U.S.-Mexico Border," *SAQ* 105.4 (Fall 2006), http://saq.dukejournals.org/content/vol105/issue4/ (accessed October 22, 2007).

8   See also Xavier Zaragoza, "BP Agents Return Fire to Orchard's Bird 'Scare Guns,'" *Daily Dispatch* (Douglas, AZ), November 21, 2000.

9   Xavier Zaragoza, "Agent Shoots Cow While Chasing Illegals near Elfrida," *Daily Dispatch* (Douglas, AZ), February 10, 2000, cited at www.ranchrescue.com/news_articles/douglasdispatch_0002100in.PDF (site now discontinued).

10   However, the practice of rounding up illegal immigrants at gunpoint and turning them over to Border Patrol has left some ranchers frustrated at the fact that Border Patrol simply returns these "criminals" to Mexico to try again at a chance of getting across the border.

11   Geoffrey Mohan, "Arizona Ranchers Move to Limit Border Crossings," *Times Union* (Albany, NY), May 28, 2000. However, on a flyer for Ranch Rescue available on its Web site in October 2000, the organization called for "volunteers": "We are seeking volunteers from all over the USA to travel with us to Arizona with the tools to repair the broken fences and water lines and to protect the private property of Arizona ranchers against these wanton criminal trespassers. . . . The problem is in southeastern Arizona. Help us put a stop to it before it reaches our ranches and farms elsewhere in the USA." Ranch Rescue, "Flyer," October 21, 2000, www.ranchrescue.com/rr_flyer.doc (site now discontinued). See also Ignacio Ibarra, "Texans Offer to Help Curb Arizona Ranch 'Trespassers': Armed

Volunteers Recruited to Repair Entrants' Damage," *Arizona Daily Star* (Tucson), June 28, 2000; and Steve Robert Allen, "Border Crisis: Vigilante Ranchers Hunt Illegal Immigrants in Arizona," *Weekly Wire*, June 26, 2000, http://weeklywire.com/ww/06-26-00/alibi_feat3.html.

12 Susan Carroll, "Foot-and-Mouth Fears Haunting Area Ranchers," *Tucson Citizen*, May 3, 2001. See also Associated Press, "Ranchers Want Border Fence to Protect Cattle Herds," August 3, 2006, available at Minuteman National Blog, http://minutemanhq.com/b2/index.php/national/2006/08/ (accessed October 17, 2007).

13 Ranch Rescue, "Media Coverage." See also Carroll, "Foot-and-Mouth Fears."

14 Ranch Rescue, "Media Coverage."

15 See Carroll, "Foot-and-Mouth Fears."

16 Wisconsin Department of Agriculture, Trade, and Consumer Protection, "BSE and Foot-and-Mouth Disease," January 10, 2002, http://datcp.state.wi.us/ahl/agriculture/animals/disease/bse/bse-foot.html.

17 Ranch Rescue, February 3, 2001, www.ranchrescue.com/index.htm (site now discontinued).

18 PBS includes substantial information on this abuse of illegal immigrants on the Web site that supplements its television special "Modern Meat." "Modern Meat," written and directed by Doug Hamilton, *Frontline*, PBS, April 18, 2002, www.pbs.org/wgbh/pages/frontline/shows/meat/.

19 Gail Eisnitz, *Slaughterhouse: The Shocking Story of Greed, Neglect, and Inhumane Treatment inside the U.S. Meat Industry* (Amherst, NY: Prometheus Books, 1997).

20 David Barboza, "Tyson Foods Indicted in Plan to Smuggle Illegal Workers," *New York Times*, December 20, 2001.

21 "Sanctions: Tyson Acquitted," *Rural Migration News* 10.2 (April 2003), http://migration.ucdavis.edu/rmn/index.php. See also Dennis Wagner, "Migrant Deaths Lead to Prison," *Arizona Republic* (Phoenix), April 5, 2003; Ken Ellingwood, "Tyson Foods Cleared of Smuggling," *Los Angeles Times*, March 27, 2003; and Sherri Day, "Final Arguments Are Heard at Tyson Conspiracy Trial," *New York Times*, March 26, 2003.

22 Barboza, "Tyson Foods Indicted."

23 Ibid.

24 Eisnitz, *Slaughterhouse*.

25 See Ben Alexander, *The New Frontiers of Ranching: Business Diversification and Land Stewardship*, Sonoran Institute, 2000, available at http://westcanhelp.org/index.php?option=com_remository&Itemid=4&func=fileinfo&id=178 (accessed November 9, 2007).

26 Julia Kristeva describes the abject as "something rejected from which one does not part." Kristeva, *The Powers of Horror: An Essay on Abjection*, trans. Leon S. Roudiez (New York: Columbia University Press, 1982), 4. Janet Price and Margrit Shildrick explain Kristeva's concept as "both alien other who threatens the corporeal and psychic boundaries of the embodied self, and as an intrinsic, but unstable, part of the self." Price and Shildrick, "Openings on the Body: A Critical Introduction," in *Feminist Theory and the Body: A Reader*, ed. Price and Shildrick (Edinburgh: Edinburgh University Press, 1999), 1–14, 7.

27 Bob Moser, "Open Season," *Intelligence Report*, no. 109 (Spring 2003), www.splcenter.org/intel/intelreport/article.jsp?pid=50 (accessed October 19, 2007). See also "Blood on the

Border," *Intelligence Report*, no. 101 (Spring 2001), www.splcenter.org/intel/intelreport/article.jsp?pid=418 (accessed October 19, 2007).

28 Mary Douglas, *Purity and Danger: An Analysis of Concepts of Pollution and Taboo* (New York: Routledge, 1984).

29 Elizabeth Grosz, *Volatile Bodies: Toward a Corporeal Feminism* (London: Routledge, 1994), 192.

30 Price and Shildrick, "Openings on the Body," 2.

31 Michael Hardt and Antonio Negri, *Empire* (Cambridge, MA: Harvard University Press, 2001), 136.

32 Ibid.

33 Ibid.

Susan Squier

The Sky Is Falling:
Risk, Safety, and the Avian Flu

In the familiar children's story, Chicken-licken
turns the occurrence of an acorn falling on her
head into global catastrophe, spreading fear one
by one among her friends by cackling, "The sky
is falling!" Among the many species that figure
in this story—chickens and turkeys, geese and
ducks—there is also one sly fox. Though we may
be less familiar with this part of the story, it is
Fox-lox who causes the *real* trouble, not the various fowl and waterfowl, *or* the acorn. When the
birds come across him in the woods as they are
going to the king, he offers to act as their guide:
"And Fox-lox said, 'Come along with me and I will
show you the way.' But Fox-lox took them into the
fox's hole, and he and his young ones soon ate up
poor Chicken-licken, Henny-penny, Cocky-locky,
Ducky-lucky, Draky-laky, Goosey-loosey, Gander-
lander, and Turkey-lurkey, and they never saw the
king to tell him that the sky had fallen!"[1]

I take this tale as my point of engagement with
the questions of risk, safety, and the avian flu
because this far-from-expert little narrative has
access to elements of human awareness—call it
folk wisdom, if you will, of the Richard Hoggart
or Raymond Williams variety[2]—that have been
lost in the haze of agricultural and medical sci-

South Atlantic Quarterly 107:2, Spring 2008
DOI 10.1215/00382876-2007-073 © 2008 Duke University Press

entificity. This story asks us to consider what constitutes risk, where risk comes from, and who is authorized to define, manage, and respond to it, as well as what constitutes safety, where we can find it, and what bargains we make in search of it. The bare bones of the Chicken-licken story sound remarkably like current news reports about avian flu: farm fowl and water-fowl generating a panic that seems to require government intervention, while experts plan a response and Fox (which includes Fox-lox and Fox TV, as well as CNN and the like) disseminates it, thus both defining and managing the crisis.

A similar version of what constitutes both risk and safety circulates through the media and in government documents dealing with our contemporary avian flu crisis. The Centers for Disease Control and Prevention (CDC) perpetuates the discourse of risk and safety when it offers its own version of the Chicken-licken story: "Avian influenza is very contagious among birds and can make some domesticated birds, including chickens, ducks, and turkeys, very sick and kill them. . . . If H5N1 virus were to gain the capacity to spread easily from person to person, an influenza pandemic . . . could begin. . . . experts from around the world . . . are preparing for the possibility that the virus may begin to spread more easily and widely from person to person."[3] Like Chicken-licken, when faced with the risk of avian flu, U.S. citizens allow the government and the media to define the risks the nation faces—wild birds and backyard chickens rather than the dangers of the global poultry industry—and imagine that American safety lies in expert guidance. Moreover, another form of awareness is generated by the expert discourses around H5N1, the highly pathogenic avian flu, as discourses of race, economics, and nationality converge to frame the meanings of risk and safety. Here paraliterature—both the satiric popular press and the "airport paperback categories of the gothic and the romance, the popular biography, the murder mystery and the science fiction or fantasy novel"[4]—nails it, as demonstrated in an interview provided by the satiric newspaper the *Onion*: "'So, basically, the CDC doesn't have the first inkling of what to do about a potentially explosive form of flu that infects ducks and chickens,' said Fox News Science, Health, and Epidemics Commentator Marylinne Kent. 'Given the popularity of these two birds as a food source among Asians, and the fact that we have no idea how many undocumented Asians have settled illegally in our nation, the potential for danger is extremely high.'"[5] As the children's fable and satire both reveal, expert knowledge about the production of life frequently functions not to inform but to obscure. While this has been given ample demonstration in relation to contemporary biomedicine, it is also the case, as I will argue, with the converging expert discourses that construct what risk and safety mean in terms of H5N1. Risk, in this instance, is further heightened by Fox's racialized presentation. Not only is the other baldly incriminated, the other is also rendered more dangerous by the fact that the (Asian) other is the illegal source of the epidemic. The health of the nation is endangered by criminality of those who cannot be accounted for or traced.

As Ulrich Beck specifies, "*Risk may be defined as a systematic way of dealing with hazards and insecurities induced and introduced by modernization itself*"[6] (a process that of course also involves the "hazards and insecurities" of—illegal—immigration). Risk in Beck's analysis is *reflexive*, a source of ever more economic productivity as it mandates increasing expert knowledge, rationalization, and surveillance. Crucially, risk is also a source of what Beck calls unawareness (including unawareness of the life circumstances of other alien bodies), a systematic production of ignorance that operates by defining knowledge more and more narrowly as the product of scientifically mediated institutions, so that laypeople are no longer confident about the wide range of commonsense, tacit, everyday knowledge available.[7] The impact of risk may be imagined in global terms (aligning with the expert analyses of global corporations), but in reality risk has an unevenly distributed global impact. It exacerbates old inequities while producing new ones such as the devastating financial losses faced by small chicken farmers when an outbreak of avian influenza in high-density poultry farms leads to a forced cull of outdoor birds or the increased rate of assembly-line injuries suffered by poultry workers when a global dip in chicken prices leads to a speed-up on the production floor. We are promised (false) security— healthy food—in exchange for surrendering our abilities to seek out the wider range of alternative analyses and responses such as those forms of knowledge either unknown to or not sanctioned by the CDC.

Safety discourse enforces hegemonic scientific rationality, structuring what we come to think of as a state of security or freedom from hazards and insecurities; it defines the authoritative measurements of the economic and social costs of achieving such security; it authorizes expert knowledge (and in turn creates the benchmarks for such authorization); and most important, it creates a particular form of unawareness on which this whole discursive apparatus of safety relies. This "double construction of unawareness" includes both the obstruction and rejection of other forms of knowledge and the *"denial of our inability to know."*[8] To invoke Donald Rumsfeld: *We don't know what we don't know.* Because we focus on scientifically defined risks and technologically mediated solutions, we are unable to grasp aspects of experience not subject to quantification. Because we are focused on increasing the biosecurity of existing poultry production units, we do not even consider the broader social, biomedical, and cultural consequences of raising genetically similar chickens in the stressful conditions of overcrowded, confined poultry houses. "The Story of Chicken-Licken" and the *Onion* news report both reveal the systematic process of producing unawareness that plays an essential part of the reframing of risk and safety accomplished by industrial poultry production.

Part of the process of rearticulating risk is repressing from public memory the fact that low pathogen avian influenza has been around for centuries, finding its historical reservoir in the bodies of wild waterfowl and making occasional forays into flocks of chickens or turkeys, such as the eruption of H5N2 virus in Pennsylvania poultry farms in 1983.[9] There was some significant consensus that the 1918 human influenza epidemic had a porcine source. Even as early as 1919, an investigator for the U.S. Bureau of Animal Industry named J. S. Koen published an article in the *American Journal of Veterinary Medicine* arguing, "[The] similarity of the epidemic among people and the epidemic among pigs . . . [suggested] a close relation between the two conditions for the 1918 [epidemic]."[10] Since such a claim had its own economic risks to the growing pork industry, there were strong disincentives to explore the possibility of a transspecies transmission of avian flu from pigs to chickens to humans. There is, then, nothing new about avian flu. The pathogen has been with us for years—only the context has changed.

However, the entire history of the disease was reframed when a highly contagious and very lethal strain of this virus emerged in Hong Kong in 1997, gaining widespread media attention. This new variety not only killed chickens, but it made the transspecies jump to human beings, killing three-year-old Lam Hoi-Kaw in May 1997 (*Bird Flu*, 32). The Hong Kong outbreak was eradicated by a systematic slaughter of more than one million chickens, applauded in 1998 by a joint proclamation signed not only by scientist experts on the influenza virus but by the World Health Organization, acknowledging, "We may owe our very lives to their actions" (*Bird Flu*, 37). In 2004, another virulent outbreak of H5N1 avian flu spread across Southeast Asia, and the alarm generated by this outbreak triggered a media panic.

Stefan Lovgren's 2004 story in the online *National Geographic News* exemplifies this journalistic hysteria. Lovgren breathlessly reports that the virus was spreading not just from person to person but from species to species: "This year there have been 44 confirmed human cases of H5N1 flu in Thailand and Vietnam. Of these, 32 people died. There is not yet a vaccine for the disease. . . . Meanwhile the virus has undergone huge genetic changes and become even more pathogenic. It now affects not only birds, but also cats, pigs, and even tigers."[11] The *National Geographic News* article is a masterpiece of doublespeak. The author gives ample space to the alarming announcement of Shigeru Omi of the WHO that avian flu death estimates "of 2–7 million deaths were 'conservative' and that the maximum range could go as high as 50 million deaths." Then he reports wryly, almost regretfully, that despite these grim predictions, "the one thing that did not break out was mass panic." The journalist's nose for news seems to be sniffing hard, indeed, wishing for a good outbreak of public hysteria to document for his readers. He cites a comment from UCLA virologist Michael Lai, "This alarmist warning is irresponsible in using this language to rouse the public's fear," but gives Dick Thompson, a WHO official in Geneva, Switzerland, the last word: "'Are we scaring people? I don't know,' he said. 'But rather than springing on people some terrible event, it's better that they get emotionally ready for what they could face. We think a pandemic is coming. Nobody knows when. But it is good to get people prepared before it arrives.'" True to its orientalist heritage even in its title, Lovgren's piece, "Is Asian Bird Flu the Next Pandemic?" adopts the persistent racializing misnomer—the "Asian bird flu"—thus contributing to the racially inflected and pathologizing anti-immigration discourse swirling around the disease.

That highly pathogenic avian influenza could jump from an avian species to humans, so that the disease could then be spread directly from person to person the way conventional influenza does, was generally dismissed until 2005. Then, a team led by pathologist Jeffrey Taubenberger and including scientists from the CDC and New York's Mount Sinai Hospital sequenced the influenza virus contained in tissue samples of victims of the 1918 influenza that had been preserved in Alaskan permafrost.[12] In a 2005 *Nature* essay, the team announced: "Here we present sequence and phylogenetic analyses of the complete genome of the 1918 influenza virus, and propose that the 1918 virus was not a reassortant virus (like those of the 1957 and 1968 pandemics), but more likely an entirely avian-like virus that adapted to humans. These data support prior phylogenetic studies suggesting that the 1918 virus was derived from an avian source."[13] Folk wisdom had registered awareness that would remain inaccessible to science for years: "Back in 1918, schoolchildren jumped rope to a morbid little rhyme: 'I had a little bird, / Its name was Enza. / I opened the window, / And in-flu-enza'" (*Bird Flu*, 13).

Taubenberger's study, and one that followed it in *Science* in 2005, by Terrence Tumpey and others at the CDC, raised public fears not only because of the fatal conclusion but because of the methodology the researchers had used.[14] Both research groups had re-created a strain of the virus from RNA fragments preserved by the permafrost and published the full genome sequence of the virus on the GenBank database. This material was now open access, according to Jonathan Tucker of the Center for Nonproliferation Studies: "If someone wants to reconstruct the virus, says Taubenberger, 'the technology is available.'"[15]

While in 2004 former U.S. secretary of Health and Human Services Tommy Thompson described avian flu as more of a threat than bioterrorism, within a year the two threats merged, as the oversight responsibility of the National Science Advisory Board led it to define nature itself as a bioterrorist threatening the nation. The United States National Science Advisory Board for Biosecurity convened a special meeting upon publication of Taubenberger's article. While it concluded that the benefits of such research "clearly outweigh the risks," it requested that Taubenberger and his fellow researchers add a passage to the manuscript stating that the work is important for public health and was conducted safely.[16] However, as Andreas von Bubnoff observed in *Nature*: "Taubenberger admits that there can be no absolute guarantee of safety. 'We are aware that all technological advances could be misused,' he says. 'But what we are trying to understand is what happened in nature and how to prevent another pandemic. In this case, nature is the bioterrorist.'"[17] Taubenberger's recourse to the ready-to-hand rhetoric of terrorism, so constitutive of all U.S. discourse since 9/11, in response to criticism that his research methods are unsafe reveals the constructed nature of the concept of "safety," shaped as it is by multiple extrascientific factors.

Chief among these factors, of course, is the economic bottom line. In the decade of pandemic hysteria since 1997, the avian flu publishing industry has boomed. Local and national government agencies including the Food and Drug Administration, the USDA, and the CDC have issued warnings and informational pronouncements, and on May 9, 2006, ABC aired the made-for-TV movie *Fatal Contact: Bird Flu in America*.[18] The boundaries of fact and fiction blurred as this movie was the subject of analysis by the Department of Health and Human Services on a government Web site with the same title, "Bird Flu in America."[19] Clearly, avian flu also provides the opportunity for profit for businesses, the media, and even government institutions. This is amply demonstrated by one recent example: the Fifth International Bird Flu Summit held in September 2007 in Las Vegas. This conference brought "distinguished scientists, international health organizations and world leaders" together with "heads of the world's top companies to discuss how the world can survive an imminent pandemic."[20] In addition to keynote speeches by experts, there were breakout sessions exploring "Business Continuity Planning," "Emergency Management Services," "First Responders Law Enforcement/Police Department/Public Works," as well as the customary exhibition hall with its range of pharmaceutical, technological, and genomic offerings. All this was available to conference participants for the "super early bird" rate of $1,850. Well worth it, if we can judge from the New Fields conference Web page, where glowing testimonials from representatives of the United Nations, the U.S. Army, the U.S. Department of Defense, and the USDA, as well as academics, jostle with those from representatives of Dow Biocides, F. Hoffman-La Roche AG, the U.S. Department of Homeland Security, Karl Hans-Fuchs Collective Protection Engineering, and the European Influenza Surveillance Scheme.[21]

The *Chicken* in *Chicken-Licken*

However, any discussion of the "monster at our door"—as Mike Davis has dubbed it with noir irony[22]—must begin with something more prosaic and less media friendly: the transformation of chicken farming in the United States since 1900. Before the consolidation of industrial poultry farming in 1932 with the formation of the Institute of American Poultry Industries, most chickens were raised in the farmyard or the garden. In the preindustrial era, the meaning of risk in any agricultural context was straightforward: the livestock could die, leaving the farmer with no animals to sell for meat. Even in chicken farming, the risk that chickens might stop laying or might die threatened the extra income generated by the backyard flock. Safety, too, was easy to define: it referred to the chicken's state of freedom from predators, access to sufficient food and water, and the farmer's possession of adequate production and distribution avenues to generate adequate income from the chickens. Such safety depended on the individual chicken farmer's skill in managing the health and productivity of her layers and meat birds, as well as business sense—good poultry husbandry, in short. The curiously outdated term is significant: farmhouse-based chicken raising characteristic of the United States in the early to mid-twentieth century was a deeply gendered activity. Most chicken farmers were women, and the backyard flock was typically the responsibility of the farm wife or daughters, who managed the flock's illnesses with medical practices traded from farm to farm. Chickens insulated farmers against economic losses caused by crop failures or other livestock losses, providing eggs and meat for the family table as well as supplying the farm women with precious "egg money" kept separate from the main sources of farm income.[23] For farmers, sharing veterinary advice with one another was a very simple strategy of communal risk management and economic survival.

Just about the time the term *animal husbandry* entered the lexicon, around 1915 to 1920, this reliance on nonexpert or folk wisdom in chicken raising and doctoring began to change, reflecting (in part) the influence of an English-born veterinarian named Joseph Edward Salsbury.[24] "Doc" Salsbury professionalized chicken medicine, radically transforming chicken farming in the process. He provided veterinary advice and mail-order patent poultry medicines. Moreover, he sold his services as a "specialist on poultry diseases" (*API*, 63). He began offering annual poultry short courses to the general farming public. The first one, held on October 12–21, 1931, combined morning talks on specific diseases by well-known speakers with afternoon sessions covering laboratory work and clinical medicine. The no-fee courses attracted leaders in poultry farming, poultry specialists, and poultry supply dealers. By midcentury, more than 10,000 people had attended the "Dr. Salsbury poultry disease schools." "These men, to a very large degree, represented the basic school of knowledge which would help lead the commercial poultry industry into being" (*API*, 64). Certainly there might have been a woman or two who attended the short courses, but given the fact that they began as invitation-only events and expanded from that to the foundation of the poultry industry, the attendance at these short courses was overwhelmingly male. Salsbury's system for research, marketing, and educational consultation not only paved the way for the academic field of poultry science, but it also anticipated the growth of poultry raising as a profit center linking the vertically integrated poultry industry (that is, one that goes from incubation to processing) to pharmaceutical companies specializing in poultry medicine.

As Salsbury's veterinary business was growing in the early twentieth century, land grant colleges in the United States were making poultry education part of their curricula. In 1902, the University of Connecticut led the way in the establishment of poultry science departments, followed by universities in such recognized chicken farming states as New York (1907), Washington (1918), Massachusetts (1920), Indiana and Michigan (1921), and Pennsylvania and North Carolina (1924).[25] Educators and extension educators began systematizing the practices of men involved in breeding, farming, and exhibiting, like Joseph McKeen of Omro, Wisconsin, who developed the Buff Wyandotte variety; Joseph Wilson, who pioneered shipping day-old baby chicks; and Isaac K. Felch, "credited as being the first poultry judge to make his entire living from the poultry industry."[26]

Animal husbandry was starting to become a masculine field. No longer were women the primary chicken farmers, keeping their chickens healthy with home remedies. Chicken raising had been gendered female, but that era was coming to an end, as anthropologist Deborah Fink learned in her ethnographic study of an Iowa region she called "Open Country": "So completely were chickens associated with women that older Open Country people frequently categorized chicken chores as housework."[27] The extension educators of the interwar era who hoped to turn poultry raising into a scientific practice suitable for the modern male farmer faced a challenge. Fink points out, "Chickens were the classic bane of men, but this did not keep them from being the most common enterprise on pre-World War II Iowa farms."[28] Before 1940, despite the attempts to redefine poultry keeping as a masculine activity (such as the male-dominated poultry classes of Salsbury and the male orientation of emerging poultry departments), the keeping of chickens had a lingering image as a trivial, because feminized, occupation. But with the rise of agricultural extension education, chicken farming became a male activity. According to Fink: "American women's exclusion from egg and poultry production resulted from a conscious policy decision on the part of agricultural program planners. . . . Rather than encouraging and sheltering women's poultry production, the postwar extension service ceased to include women . . . unless their husbands were also participants."[29] The new academic field of poultry science linked research in basic sciences with applied research on poultry production and management, producing (predominantly male) avian scientists and managers for the growing poultry industry. As the ownership of the industry was consolidated in larger and larger corporations, class differentiation joined gender sorting, since the poultry workers for this new industry not only were frequently female, but were recruited from poor, disenfranchised migrant and immigrant populations.[30]

As the industry increasingly turned to technological innovations to manage the risks of poultry production, technologically mediated definitions of risk and safety resulted. This was certainly the case with incubation. Although it was one of the oldest technical interventions in chicken raising—a practice dating back to the ancient Egyptian practice of incubating chickens in large clay rooms heated with manure-fired ovens—the introduction of an electrically heated mass incubator in 1923, developed by Ira M. Petersime, launched a debate about the ethics and effectiveness of such practices (*API*, 26). Traditional poultry breeders argued that it was "morally wrong to hatch chicks artificially" (*API*, 27). The American Poultry Association, formed in 1873, itself joined the debate, waging a campaign that "set out methodically to tell the American farmer the quality of artificially incubated chicks was inferior, and that it would be impossible to transport them successfully" (*API*, 27). However, breeders who were selling these new "artificial chicks" countered the association by marketing their product as more scientifically advanced and thus better.

By 1916, when the American Poultry Association gave way to the new International Baby Chick Association, scientific rationality and industrial efficiency had prevailed. In March 1918, the International Baby Chick Association convinced the U.S. Post Office to allow trial shipping of baby chicks via parcel post. This trial was such a success that by the following October the new mode of distribution was permanent.[31] Chicks could now be mass incubated and delivered to customers via the U.S. mail. One of the many contemporary handbooks on poultry raising, *Making Money from Hens* (1919), characterized the result as a safer and more effective means of distinctly American chicken production:

> The development of manufacturing enterprise, coupled with our Yankee inventive genius, conceived and rapidly developed the efficient artificial incubators we know to-day, until at the present time they are far superior to the hen, in that they hatch better. . . . with incubators the time of hatching is not subject to the whims of the hen, but is absolutely under the control of the efficient poultryman.
>
> Chicks artificially hatched and reared are not subject to the parasites and disease contamination they are bound to contract to a greater or less extent when running with hens.[32]

The discourse of risk folds almost seamlessly into the discourse of safety, inflected with gender and nationalism even at this early stage in the industry's development. The risk of a poor hatch ratio is countered by the safety provided by the efficient Yankee incubator, just as the risk of exposure to parasites and disease is mitigated by keeping the artificially hatched chick indoors. Thus, closed in, under the control of the efficient "poultryman," the chick is safe from even the small degree of danger it would encounter "running with hens."[33] The rhetorical redefinition arrests in medias res the transition from backyard to industrial poultry farming: the hen-and-nest method of chicken incubation and growth is redefined as risky (unsanitary and uncontrolled) while the artificial incubator and confined growth are defined as safe. Moreover, safety becomes technologized, medicalized, racialized, and nationalized: it is conceived of as freedom from disease and parasites associated with foreign exposure, available to chicken raisers thanks to "Yankee inventive genius."

By the time of World War II, these new technologies and modes of expert knowledge had solidified into what Deborah Fitzgerald has described as the ideal of industrial agriculture, characterized by "timeliness of operations, large-scale production sites, mechanization, standardization of product, specialization, speed of throughput, routinization of the workforce, and a belief that success was based first and foremost upon a notion of 'efficiency.'"[34] Risk had been reframed, from something controlled by the individual farm wife (raising backyard chickens to manage the economic risk of farming) to something controlled by corporate risk management departments through structural innovations in poultry farming. Safety, too, had been redefined as the product of scientific rationalization and expert control, with distinctly economic overtones. Cost-benefit ratios ruled. By the 1960s, the poultry industry had adopted the conglomerate model in which one corporation has subsidiary companies that perform the various stages of poultry production in different places: hatchery, growing houses, processing houses, feed suppliers, and distributors. The companies provided the inputs (eggs, chickens, feed, medication), while the contractors supplied the housing, labor, energy, and especially the risk (whether of flock failure or price decline).[35]

With this new vertical integration, risk and safety were segmented. Risks were borne primarily by the poultry workers, both the contractors who had to provide cash and infrastructure for the poultry raising and the line workers in poultry plants, whose bodies were constantly at risk of injuries ranging from blindness to amputation. Safety became the achievement of experts in the poultry corporations who developed strategies for preventing flock failure or theft of intellectual property. These included the discovery of vitamin D, the use of electric feeders, and the application of commercial vaccines against poultry illnesses, all of which made it possible for birds to be raised inside on an unprecedented scale, thus (it was thought) keeping them safe from pathogens. As knowledge about chicken breeding was gradually redefined from public to corporate property, a corporation's genetic property could also be made safe from theft, dilution, or imitation of the breed. The poultry industry increased its economic security by hybridizing to increase egg yield or meat production, developing birds with specific qualities for designated markets.[36] So, a new three-step breeding practice produced a uniform, standardized chicken that could not be replicated by farmers but had to be purchased yearly from the breeder. As Glenn Bugos notes, "Bred directly into the hybrid chick was the means to keep them from being illegally reproduced."[37] If risk had been curtailed, so had profit—it was principally reserved for those who owned the technology rather than those who raised, tended, and slaughtered the poultry.

The risk-management strategy of increasing control over poultry as intellectual property led to innovations in both the hatchery and the scientific laboratory. A premier instance was of the Cobb Corporation, founded in 1916 by a Harvard graduate, a man originally known as New England's major breeder of Barred Plymouth Rocks. Consumers preferred the all-white birds since no dark quills were left in the skin when the poultry was processed, and Cobb responded in 1947 by hybridizing its birds (breeding its all-white hens with the white male birds produced by another corporation, Vantress) to produce a fully white bird. In 1974, just as Cobb was purchased by the Upjohn Company, its partner breeder Vantress was simultaneously purchased by Tyson Foods. Twelve years later, Tyson, the owner of the Vantress pedigree line, and Upjohn, the owner of the Cobb 500 breeding program, the systematic practice of controlled breeding to produce chickens with certain desired characteristics, merged to become the Cobb-Vantress Corporation, with corporate headquarters in Siloam Springs, Arkansas, and subsidiaries in Africa, Southeast Asia, South America, and Latin America. Apt indeed that the corporate logo of Cobb-Vantress should show a rooster whose eye is the globe.[38] No chicken, or chicken-related technology, it would seem, was beyond the Benthamite eye of Cobb-Vantress.

Once the price of chickens dropped due to a glut in the chicken market in the mid-1960s, there was little profit in selling whole birds, and chickens were increasingly designed for the competitive global market, in which the most money was to be made by adding value after processing. This technique was inaugurated by Cornell University poultry science professor Robert Baker, who laid the groundwork for chicken nuggets by inventing a deboning machine that took all of the meat off the chicken carcass and developing a variety of ways to reshape the extracted meat: into dinosaur-shaped nuggets, chicken bologna, chicken pastrami, and chicken ham.[39] The resulting interest in value adding created incentives for producers. Cobb-Vantress's most recent corporate product, the Cobb 700, was specifically designed for the South American and European markets, where "processors supplying the high meat yield, deboning and added value markets" were soon showing great interest in this new product. It was framed as a major improvement even within the Cobb-Vantress line: "Most important of all, breast meat yield of the Cobb 700 broiler had improved by a full one percent over the Cobb 500 broiler!"[40] This new bird would keep corporate profits safe, supplying postprocessors with the meat they needed to make the largest profit possible, whether they were producing precut frozen breast portions or deboned, ground, reshaped, and processed chicken products. Such "industrial" birds, designed as sequentially numbered "models," are bred, brooded, and battery-raised (that is, indoor rather than free range) in high density throughout the world.[41] In a global food industry pressured to compete with increasingly higher yields and lower costs, the U.S. (factory) model of poultry farming drives out many of the small local poultry raisers who are less insulated from the risk of price shifts and distribution difficulties.[42]

Today, the dominance of risk management strategies reaches beyond poultry corporations into the realm of avian science, as corporate laboratories work with the pharmaceutical industry in the production of engineered birds. Even seemingly pure scientific research has corporate tie-ins, though they may be obscured by the discourse of unfettered scientific progress. In 2004, the International Chicken Genome Sequencing Consortium completed sequencing the genome of *Gallus gallus*, the red jungle fowl from which all domestic chickens have descended.[43] This accomplishment, two genomics researchers explained in an article in *Nature*, would benefit "agricultural researchers attempting to breed the most productive strain by recognizing links between DNA sequences and attributes such as egg production."[44] What the authors failed to mention is the fact that *all* information obtained through processes developed with monetary support from the poultry industry is unavailable for public analysis or use. Instead, it is considered to be the industry's property.[45] Although the Dutch poultry company Hybro calls itself "your partner in breeding," the information produced by company-funded technical processes is *proprietary*—it's not available to the general researcher or chicken farmer without permission. Scientific progress is held hostage to corporate profits: no profits without science, no science that is not exclusive corporate property.

Currently, proprietary genetics has converged with big pharma and what my Mennonite butcher calls "big chicken" in the effort to generate a product that will insulate corporations from economic risk while shielding consumers from medical risk. Or so the story goes in one recent articulation of the corporate capacity to guarantee safety. On January 18, 2006, Viragen Corporation, in collaboration with the Roslin Institute, announced that it had succeeded in producing a transgenic chicken. As the company Web site described it, the Ova system turns the chicken into "a pharmaceutical bioreactor" in order to meet the growing market for "protein-based human therapeutics."[46] True to the economically productive nature of reflexive risk management, this transgenic chicken is being forecast as the answer to the needs of both the pharmaceutical and poultry industries. Because it is engineered, this new chicken could enable corporations to patent their product, rather than being forced to guard it through elaborate methods of hybridization and industrial secrecy. Moreover, it promises to replace a cheap renewable resource (the hen) for an expensive one (the factory) as the site where new drugs can be produced. Thus, the risk management strategy of poultry corporations converges with pharmaceutical companies' plans to engineer growth through creating a demand for new drugs. As one commentator observes, corporate poultry science could even use transgenics to make a profit off the avian flu, melding the goals of economic and biomedical safety: "Agribusiness companies stand to reap huge gains in the event that scientists at Cambridge University and elsewhere are able to replace the entire world chicken population with genetically-engineered chicks allegedly resistant to H5N1 virus."[47] Once again, in risk lies the opportunity for profit, whether by breeding chickens whose bodies produce valuable treatments for human illnesses or by cashing in on the bioengineering possibilities generated by avian illness.

Defining and Managing Risk

The risk of avian flu, then, is where issues of economic and epidemiological risk converge to produce a new rhetoric of safety. The major players in the global poultry industry have responded to concerns about avian flu by assuring customers that their products are safe *precisely because* they are highly engineered and scientifically surveilled. So Cobb-Vantress explains: "A cornerstone of the company's success is the adherence to strict internal bio-security and safety standards throughout all operations. Facilities are designed to accommodate the highest bio-security and safety standards to ensure consistent delivery of quality product to customers globally. Bio-security and safety know-how and experience gained internally is [*sic*] often passed onto customers as an added benefit of dealing with Cobb as a supplier of breeding stock."[48] Tyson, a major customer of Cobb-Vantress's chicken lines, takes a very narrow view of the sort of know-how to be passed on to its consumers. This is a far cry from the era when chicken raising depended on folk wisdom shared among farm women. Tyson's Web site promises "products, recipes, and peace of mind," thus effectively isolating concerns about safety to the gendered realm of cooking and consuming. In contrast, the nature of the avian flu risk is carefully delineated as foreign: "One kind of avian influenza, High Pathogenic, or Asian, H5N1, has been known to cause problems in humans. At this time, Asian H5N1 has only been found in Asia, the Middle East, and Europe, *never in the United States.*"[49]

The avian flu risk is then defined on the Tyson Web site, with stunning (if seemingly scientific) inaccuracy, to emphasize its racialized and nationalized nature. A list of the "types of avian" flu includes not only the acceptable categories of "low pathogenic" and "high pathogenic" but also a scientifically meaningless third category, "Asian H5N1 High Pathogenic": "*Currently being found in Asia and Eastern Europe, but not in the U.S. to date.* Some cases in Asia and Eastern Europe of H5N1 spreading to humans through close contact with live birds. Possibility exists of this specific strain of flu being transmitted from humans to humans, which, if it mutates, could lead to the potential 'pandemic' for which preparations are being made."[50] Defining the measures the company takes to avoid the risk of avian flu and to guarantee the safety of its corporate product, Tyson uses the same formula of Yankee ingenuity, isolation, and indoor confinement that we saw in the 1919 discussion of electrical incubation: "Tyson Foods and other U.S. chicken producers take great care to prevent chickens from being exposed to diseases. Unlike birds in Asia, which are primarily raised outdoors, commercial chickens in the U.S. are kept indoors, away from wild birds and other means of spreading diseases."[51]

The identification of risk with Southeast Asia, outdoor chicken farming, and wild birds and the identification of safety with U.S. model high-biosecurity intensive chicken farming are as misdirected as Fox-lox's "guidance" is to Chicken-licken. A low pathogen strain of avian influenza evolves into a high pathogen strain precisely because it has passed repeatedly through the great numbers of chickens held in high-density poultry houses. The sheer number of potential mutations available to a virus in such circumstances elevates the likelihood that a new strain will appear, one no longer limited to the bird-to-human infection process. This is the fear, then: that such a high pathogen strain of avian influenza *with the new capacity of direct human-to-human transmission* will emerge from the crowded, filthy conditions of the factory farm. The culprit in that case will clearly be the poultry industry, whose practices will have accelerated the movement of the virus through the avian population. Veterinarians and conservationists identify two practices common to industrial poultry production that have contributed to the seeming speed with which H5N1 has traveled from its emergence in Southeast Asia to its current outbreaks in Europe and Africa: the global shipping of day-old chicks and the practice of intensive battery-raising of young adult birds.

"The chick trade 'has made the chicken the most migratory bird in the world,'" according to Adrian Long of BirdLife International.[52] Mike Davis has laid the blame for the intensive battery-raising of young adult birds on the international poultry industry, which he argues has deliberately framed biosecurity by distinguishing between the so-called high-security, high-volume growers and the purportedly unsafe and unsanitary methods of backyard poultry growers.[53] Indeed, rather than adopting the misnomer "Asian bird flu," it might be more accurate to call this the "free trade flu," since we can attribute the increasing risk of an explosive outbreak of H5N1 to the global movement of day-old baby chicks from U.S. corporate hatcheries to contract growers overseas coupled with the exportation of U.S. methods of high-volume poultry raising. The rapid mobility of poultry has introduced a potentially new element into the international transportation of chickens: patho-politics: "When a new virus gets into a barn packed with thousands of young chickens that have been genetically selected for their plump breasts rather than their ability to survive in the wild, it leaps from bird to bird, mutating slightly each time, and sometimes morphs into a lethal strain—just as the 1918 Spanish flu was believed to become more deadly as it passed through crowded American military camps during the cold winter of 1917."[54] However, patho-politics aside, the industrial poultry industry raises issues of risk and safety even before we consider the threat of avian flu. As it is currently structured, conventional large-scale poultry production poses a risk to the physical and emotional health of human beings as well as the chickens it produces. A January 2005 report by the U.S. Government Accountability Office (GAO) documented that the young, male, and/or predominantly Hispanic workers had rates of injury "among the highest of any industry." These injuries included not only "cuts, strains, cumulative trauma caused by repetitive cutting motions," but also "injuries sustained by falls, more serious injuries, such as fractures and amputation," and illnesses caused by "exposure to chemicals, blood and fecal matter."[55] It's worth noting that even the GAO got precious little cooperation from the poultry industry in carrying out the investigation leading to this report.[56] The very characteristics of contemporary poultry farming—in which the chickens are subject to overcrowding, stress, filth, lack of sunlight, and induced immunosuppression from selective breeding and monoculture— pose a health risk for chickens and human beings. As Greger points out, "Stressful, overcrowded confinement in industrial poultry facilities facili- tates immune suppression in birds already bred with weakened immunity, offering viruses like bird flu ample opportunities for spread, amplification, and mutation" (*Bird Flu*, 214).

Despite the stress on the Western industrialized model of poultry farming for its promised "biosecurity," the global dominance of that model of poul- try farming is far from complete. While poultry growers in Thailand have exhibited stunning success in the transformation of that industry under the guidance of Dhanin Chearavanont, whose giant factory farms and contract growers have effectively marginalized the traditional method of backyard chicken farming, other Southeast Asian nations have taken a different route (*Bird Flu*, 214–15). In Laos and Cambodia, an alternative model dominates, in which many small farmers grow small numbers of unconfined chickens; the same model is followed in Africa and South America. "Despite efforts to develop intensive poultry production, family poultry (FP) are still very important in developing countries," explains E. F. Guèye. "In most devel- oping countries, the keeping of poultry by local communities has been practiced for many generations. FP keeping is a widely practiced activity.

More than 90% of rural families in most developing countries keep one or more poultry species (i.e. chickens, ducks, guinea fowls, geese, pigeons, etc.) and all ethnic groups tend to be involved in FP production."[57] These "family poultry management systems" have become increasingly significant models for so-called developing countries both because they adapt a system of chicken raising that has been working successfully for many generations and because the distinctly gendered aspects of family poultry markets (in the third world, poultry keepers still tend to be mostly women) provide valuable economic autonomy and agency to rural women.[58]

The truth, if you will, about risk, safety, and the avian flu is closer to Chicken-licken's story or the *Onion*'s satire than it is to the pronouncements of the CDC. The health risks posed by H5N1 are intersectional: interwoven with existing economic and social inequities. The major risk with avian flu is not the potential for the virus to jump from birds to humans, nor is it the risk of a pandemic, but rather it is the effects of an outbreak on those who farm, and eat, chickens. According to avian diagnostic pathologist Dr. Patricia Dunn, the greatest risk is to the *emotional* health of farmers and their families who may lose their flocks to an outbreak, thus losing their livelihood, and the potentially devastating risk to *nutritional* health if people lose their access to chicken meat and eggs, one of the few easily accessible sources of protein for people living on a subsistence level throughout the world.[59]

The bioterrorism metaphor invoked by Taubenberger to describe the avian flu is, like all metaphors, enabling as well as merely descriptive. In 2003, the Pentagon proposed a program called the Futures Markets Applied to Prediction (FutureMAP). This initiative "would have involved investors betting small amounts of money that a particular event—a terrorist attack or assassination—would happen."[60] Bad press on Capitol Hill killed this initiative, according to a CNN report: Senator Tom Daschle (D-SD) noted, "I can't believe that anybody would seriously propose that we trade in death," while Senator Barbara Boxer (D-CA) observed, "There's something very sick about it."[61] Yet no such objections seem to shadow the Iowa Health Prediction Market. Framing itself as "a step beyond disease surveillance," this initiative of the University of Iowa invites health care workers to wager donated money on the risk of an avian influenza outbreak, essentially offering them a *risk-free* investment in risk. Its Influenza Prediction Market uses the profit motive to encourage "physicians, nurses, pharmacists, clinical microbiologists and epidemiologists" to share the information that may enable the forecast of influenza activity before an outbreak actually occurs. Giving each health care worker/trader an "education grant of $100 with which to trade," the market gauges the "consensus belief" about the likelihood of an influenza outbreak. The Influenza Prediction Market Web site explains that it views the Influenza Prediction Market as a "supplement that can quickly aggregate expert opinions based on existing surveillance information. . . . The probabilities generated by this market could help policymakers and public health officials coordinate resources, facilitate vaccine production, increase stockpiles of antiviral medications, and plan for allocation of personnel and resources."[62]

Antiterrorist initiatives have also shaped another initiative aimed at increasing food safety, the National Animal Identification System (NAIS) of the USDA. This plan, a USDA pamphlet explains, was created in response to the "increasing number of animal disease outbreaks . . . reported around the globe," as well as the "*single cow* that tested positive for bovine spongiform encephalopathy (BSE) in the United States in December 2003."[63] The dizzying arrangements proposed include seven-character IDs for individual livestock producers, fifteen-character IDs for individual animals, and thirteen-character IDs for groups of animals. The NAIS received some well-deserved ridicule on the Pastured Poultry listserv, as small chicken farmers weighed the absurdity of labeling individual chickens. Yet here, too, the notion of risk and the promised goal of safety are inflected by the xenophobic and racist discourses already circulating in the "war on terror" discourse. The program proposes to "enhance foreign animal disease surveillance, control, and eradication" and thus "improve biosecurity protection of the national livestock population," by issuing "official identification for animals in interstate or international commerce."[64]

Despite the constructions of risk and safety implied by such cloak-and-dagger strategies, the real risk of the avian flu lies in its potential to compound already existing global economic and health disparities. Any real conception of safety must lie not in surveillance but in openness to modes of awareness beyond the dictates of expert science. As a Maryland poultry farmer observed, "Modern day poultry production is so highly concentrated that this disease can spread so rapidly. . . . We can't ignore this any longer" (*Bird Flu*, 356). We should take our guidance neither from Fox(-lox) nor from the (virtual) king, even though they pose as experts, and even though it may seem that the sky is falling. Instead, we should trust our own common sense, be aware of our surroundings, and look for the acorn.

Notes

1   "The Story of Chicken-Licken," in *The Waverly Juvenile Chapbooks*, no. 5, illus. by Philip Lyford (Boston: Seaver-Howland Press, 1914), 1–15. Homage to Donna Haraway's wonderful brief article "Chicken," in *Shock and Awe: War on Words*, ed. Bregjevan Eekelen et al. (Santa Cruz, CA: New Pacific Press, 2004), 23–30.

2   I am referring here to a way in which a kind of "folk wisdom" girds Hoggart's and Williams's work in, respectively, *The Uses of Literacy* and the famous essay "Culture Is Ordinary." Richard Hoggart, *The Uses of Literacy* (1957; Edison, NJ: Transaction Publishers, 1998); and Raymond Williams, "Culture Is Ordinary," in *The Raymond Williams Reader*, ed. John Higgins (1958; Oxford: Blackwell, 2001), 10–24.

3   Centers for Disease Control, "Key Facts about Avian Influenza (Bird Flu) and Avian Influenza A (H5N1) Virus," May 7, 2007, www.cdc.gov/flu/avian/gen-info/facts.htm.

4   Fredric Jameson, "Postmodern and Consumer Culture," in *The Anti-Aesthetic: Essays on Postmodern Culture*, ed. Hal Foster (London: New Press, 1983), 111–25, 112.

5   "Nation's Leading Alarmists Excited about Bird Flu," *Onion*, February 2, 2005.

6   Ulrich Beck, *Risk Society: Towards a New Modernity* (London: Sage Publications, 1992), 21.

7   Ulrich Beck, *The Brave New World of Work*, trans. Patrick Camiller (London: Polity Press, 2000).

8   Ibid., 131; emphasis mine.

9   See Michael Greger, MD, *Bird Flu: A Virus of Our Own Hatching* (New York: Lantern Books, 2006), 34; hereafter cited parenthetically by page number as *Bird Flu*. See also Mike Davis, *The Monster at Our Door: The Global Threat of Avian Flu* (New York: New Press, 2005).

10   J. S. Koen, "A Practical Method for Field Diagnosis of Swine Disease," *American Journal of Veterinary Medicine* 14 (1919): 468.

11   Stefan Lovgren, "Is Asian Bird Flu the Next Pandemic?" *National Geographic News*, December 7, 2004, http://news.nationalgeographic.com/news/2004/12/1207_041207_birdflu.html.

12   See *Bird Flu*; and Davis, *The Monster at Our Door*.

13   Jeffrey K. Taubenberger et al., "Characterization of the 1918 Influenza Virus Polymerase Genes," *Nature* 437 (October 6, 2005): 889–93, 889.

14   Terrence M. Tumpey et al., "Characterization of the Reconstructed 1918 Spanish Influenza Pandemic Virus," *Science* 310 (October 7, 2005): 77–80.

15   Andreas von Bubnoff, "The 1918 Flu Virus Is Resurrected," *Nature* 437 (October 6, 2005): 794–95, 795.

16   United States National Science Advisory Board for Biosecurity, meeting minutes, November 21, 2005, www.biosecurityboard.gov/meetings/NSABB%20November%202005%20meeting%20minutes%20-%20Final.pdf.

17   von Bubnoff, "The 1918 Flu Virus," 795.

18   *Fatal Contact: Bird Flu in America*, written by Ron McGee, directed by Richard Pearce, ABC, May 9, 2006.

19   U.S. Department of Health and Human Services, "Bird Flu in America," www.pandemicflu.gov/news/birdfluinamerica.html (accessed July 30, 2007).

20 Fifth International Bird Flu Summit, brochure, New Fields Exhibitions, www.new-fields
    .com/birdflu5/pdf/5bf_low.pdf (accessed July 17, 2007).

21 Fifth International Bird Flu Summit, New Fields Exhibitions, www.new-fields.com/
    birdflu5/index.php (accessed July 24, 2007).

22 Davis, *The Monster at Our Door.*

23 Carolyn Sachs, *Gendered Fields: Rural Women, Agriculture, and Environment* (Boulder, CO:
    Westview Press, 1996).

24 Dictionary.com, "Animal Husbandry," http://dictionary.reference.com/browse/animal
    %20husbandry (accessed July 24, 2007). See also Gordon Sawyer, *The Agribusiness Poul-
    try Industry: A History of Its Development* (New York: Exposition Press, 1971); hereafter
    cited parenthetically by page number as *API.*

25 Y. Vizzier Thaxton et al., "The Decline of Academic Poultry Science in the United States
    of America," *World's Poultry Science Journal* 59.3 (September 2003): 303–313, 305.

26 John L. Skinner, *American Poultry History 1823–1973* (Madison, WI: American Printing
    and Publishing, 1974), 38.

27 Deborah Fink, *Open Country, Iowa: Rural Women, Tradition, and Change* (Albany: State
    University of New York Press, 1987), 49. See also Sachs, *Gendered Fields.*

28 Fink, *Open Country,* 49.

29 Ibid., 135.

30 The poultry industry workforce shifted from its predominantly African American com-
    position in the 1970s to Mexican and Central American immigrants during the 1980s
    and by the turn of the next century relied so heavily on an immigrant workforce that the
    U.S. Justice Department filed a series of suits against Tyson Foods for smuggling ille-
    gal immigrants from Mexico to supply fifteen poultry-processing plants in the southern
    United States. Steve Striffler, *Chicken: The Dangerous Transformation of America's Favorite
    Food* (New Haven, CT: Yale University Press, 2005), 98.

31 C. Nisson, "Development of the Hatching Industry of the United States," press release,
    n.d., American Poultry Historical Society Personal Collection of O. August Hanke, box 1
    of 2, National Agricultural Library, Beltsville, MD.

32 Harry R. Lewis, *Making Money from Hens* (Philadelphia: J. B. Lippincott, 1919), 59–60.

33 Ibid.

34 Deborah Fitzgerald, *Every Farm a Factory* (New Haven, CT: Yale University Press,
    2003), 5.

35 Glenn Bugos, "Intellectual Property Protection in the American Chicken-Breeding
    Industry," *Business History Review* 66.1 (Spring 1992): 127–268, 146.

36 See Thaxton et al., "The Decline of Academic Poultry Science"; and William Boyd,
    "Making Meat: Science, Technology, and American Poultry Production," *Technology and
    Culture* 42.4 (October 2001): 631–64.

37 Bugos, "Intellectual Property Protection," 144.

38 Less fitting perhaps, given the arduous physical work that such industrial poultry prac-
    tices require, is the fact that Siloam is a Biblical term meaning a place where healers
    minister unto the afflicted.

39 Douglas Martin, "Robert C. Baker, 84, Is Dead; Reshaped Chicken Dinner," *New York
    Times,* March 16, 2006.

40 "Cobb 700 on Target for Low-Cost, High Meat Yield," *Cobb Focus* 2 (2002): 1.

41 Of course, the industrial model still remains one among several, alongside the family farm and the small farm. Yet, industry, government agencies such as the Peace Corps, and even NGOs such as the Heifer Project are exporting the U.S. industrial model to other parts of the world. See Sachs, *Gendered Fields.* To recap, in addition to concentration on market breeds like the Cobb 700, this model relies on contract growers, who provide the property, buildings, and risk and who are provided by the industry with the chicks, feed, and management protocols to raise them until they are sold back to the industry at a price that fluctuates with the international market.

42 Sachs, *Gendered Fields.*

43 International Chicken Genome Sequencing Consortium, "Sequence and Comparative Analysis of the Chicken Genome Provide Unique Perspectives on Vertebrate Evolution," *Nature* 432 (December 9, 2004): 695–777.

44 Jeremy Schmutz and Jane Grimwood, "Fowl Sequence," *Nature* 432 (December 9, 2004): 679–80, 679.

45 However, the story does include among the beneficiaries of the accomplishment "comparative genomicists desiring to accurately identify the functional elements of the human genome; and genome-sequence producers." Ibid., 679.

46 Significantly, Viragen's description also emphasizes the proprietary nature of the biotechnology: "Based on the creation of lines of transgenic hens which have been engineered to produce a target protein in their eggs using the LentiVector® gene delivery system licensed from Oxford BioMedica plc, this technology is being developed as an efficient and economical alternative to standard bio-manufacturing techniques, having many apparent advantages in ease of scale-up, lower costs of production and quality of product produced." "Viragen Reports Avian Transgenic Breakthrough: OVA™ System Expresses Interferon-Beta," press release, Viragen, January 18, 2006, www.viragen.com/pressreleases/2006/vipro1182006.htm.

47 William Engdahl, "Bird Flu and Chicken Factory Farms: Profit Bonanza for U.S. Agribusiness," *Scoop Independent News*, November 29, 2005, www.scoop.co.nz/stories/print.html?path=HL0511/S00351.htm.

48 Cobb-Vantress, "Research Program," www.cobb-vantress.com/AboutUs/ResearchProgram.aspx (accessed July 18, 2007).

49 Tyson Foods, "Avian Influenza Information," http://www.tyson.com/Corporate/PressRoom/AvianInfluenza.aspx (accessed July 24, 2007); bold in the original, italics here.

50 Ibid.; emphasis mine.

51 Ibid.

52 Donald G. McNeil Jr., "From the Chickens' Perspective, the Sky Really Is Falling," *New York Times*, March 28, 2006.

53 See Davis, *The Monster at Our Door*; and *Bird Flu.*

54 McNeil, "From the Chickens' Perspective."

55 Government Accountability Office, "Workplace Safety and Health: Safety in the Meat and Poultry Industry, While Improving, Could Be Further Strengthened," January 2005, 21–22, www.gao.gov/new.items/d0596.pdf (accessed July 24, 2007).

56 The GAO report suggests that the authors found industry cooperation lacking when they were compiling their report. For example, the report cites the problem of inadequate

record keeping by OSHA and alleged "underreporting in the meat and poultry industry." GAO, "Workplace Safety and Health," 43–44.

57 E. F. Guèye, "Gender Aspects in Family Poultry Management Systems in Developing Countries," *World's Poultry Science Journal* 61 (March 2005): 39–46, 39.

58 Ibid., 39.

59 Patricia Dunn, DVM, interview by author, University Park, Pennsylvania, April 5, 2006.

60 Paul Courson and Steve Turnham, "Amid Furor, Pentagon Kills Terrorism Futures Market," CNN, July 30, 2003, www.cnn.com/2003/ALLPOLITICS/07/29/terror.market/index.html.

61 Ibid.

62 Influenza Prediction Market 2007, "University of Iowa Health Prediction Markets: Avian Influenza," http://fluprediction.uiowa.edu/fluhome/Market_AvianInfluenza.html (accessed July 31, 2007).

63 USDA Animal and Plant Health Inspection Service, "The National Animal Identification System (NAIS)," July 2, 2007, www.aphis.usda.gov/lpa/pubs/Animal_ID_Brochure.pdf.

64 Ibid.

Clifton Evers

The Cronulla Race Riots:
Safety Maps on an Australian Beach

Introduction

Cronulla is a beachside suburb of Sydney, Australia. It can be a dangerous place to go surfing. Shark Island is the premier wave of the area and is revered throughout the surfing world for the intensity of its hollow rides. The waves at this surf break rise, warp, peel, and mutate over a shallow slab of rock. The men who ride the island are respected by other surfers and are considered brave and tough. The danger, relief, stoke (joy), and pride experienced in the lineup of Shark Island bond together a particular group of men — the local crew. Visiting surfers can tell who is part of this local crew by their confident body language and their knowledge of the wave. These men know how to negotiate the dangers of Shark Island. They paddle out to the waves through currents hidden below the surface of the water, which help them avoid the harm of the exploding swells. The men can tell at a glance what waves will peel evenly and allow a safe ride.

Visiting surfers tend to get caught in the impact zone (where the waves break) and wipe out. Sometimes the newcomers' inexperience puts others in danger. Local surfers get angry if they have to save them or maneuver around them

South Atlantic Quarterly 107:2, Spring 2008
DOI 10.1215/00382876-2007-074 © 2008 Duke University Press

because it increases the possibility of being hit by the curling lip of the wave and being pushed onto the rocks just meters away. A pecking order is set up and strictly policed to prevent this scenario, particularly when crowds mean greater competition for waves.

Hierarchies at surf spots are increasingly being challenged as surfing becomes more popular.[1] Easy-to-ride surfboards are changing the playing field, enabling novices to access and compete for waves with longtime locals. But the rules of surfing are fluid and complex. They change to suit the amount of time a surfer has spent at a surf spot and how well they surf. Newcomers become confused. This means they regularly transgress rules and upset the local surfers who expect order at their break. When newcomers catch a wave before they are given permission, they will be sent to shore or assaulted to let them know not to do it again.[2] By claiming the responsibility of safety for themselves and others, local surfers have priority with waves and a sense of entitlement.

As researchers Ryan Barclay and Peter West have suggested, "Nobody owns the beach; it is a space shared by those who turn up."[3] But many of the local surfers would disagree. They regularly extend their policing and knowledge of safety from the water to the sand. In surfing culture this process of dominating a territory and imposing its cultural laws on others is known as *localism*. Surf media researcher Paul Scott explains that localism operates from a paranoia that surf spots are under siege from "outsiders."[4] Localism works at a micro level, similar to the way nationalism does at a macro, in that it creates an us-versus-them situation in which "the them is never as good or as right as we are."[5] Surfers have a long tradition of spray-painting "Locals Only" on footpaths and rock walls to let people know that particular beaches and pieces of turf are "theirs." Cronulla has a long history of localism because its surfing culture runs deep.

This essay looks at how localism has produced a particular hegemonic, masculine sense of safety, shaped and practiced at Cronulla, and how it was challenged and influenced by a conflict known as the Cronulla race riots. Through an analysis of this event, I show how safety works in an everyday context as a complex embodied, social, and spatial practice I call a *safety map*. By this I mean a personal, embodied construct used to assess possible dangers or threats and employed by individuals to "make their way in public."[6] A safety map draws on wider discourses of gender, ethnicity, culture, age, and sexuality, as well as on the experiences a person has accumulated over his or her life.

People soak these discourses and experiences into their skin. French sociologist Pierre Bourdieu calls our embodied history our habitus.[7] Bourdieu was concerned with how individuals are corporeally informed by social positions and expectations. Our bodies continually speak of their pasts in everyday actions—gestures, manners, and small ways of being and inhabiting social space. The set of rules inscribed on these spaces is what Bourdieu calls the field.[8] Time spent in a field develops our habitus; a body can learn to wear arbitrary rules like a glove. The rules are largely unstated because we have incorporated them. Our bodies seem to know when they are at ease in a situation, and conversely, they also tell us loudly when we are not.

People's habitus inform their safety maps. They develop particular ideas about safety—what is safe and what is not. Eventually, they develop a script for safety much in the same way that a dancer learns steps, acquiring a memory of how to arrange behavior, values, and tastes as part of their safety maps. But these components intermingle and shift as people hang out, so safety maps involve "an ever-changing, personalized, yet shared matrix of attributes and relations" (*Spectacle*, 84) that helps us to assess and negotiate the dangers and threats of our environment at any given time.

As I move through a description of the personal level of safety, I explain how larger Australian national myths, icons, and discourses played a role in people's safety maps during the conflict. Reading the sense of safety at Cronulla through the complex assemblage of these different scales of safety enables us to account for how conflict arose on the beach. It also allows us to consider how safety maps work as a site within which larger community, national, and international issues are played out.

When viewed through the lens of safety maps, the Cronulla race riots can be read as a complex interaction of discourses, bodies, space, and sociopolitical institutions. I take this a step further by employing this complexity as a methodological point of departure. By this I mean that the event cannot be reduced to a single cause or trajectory. This essay argues for thinking safety as a lived, embodied activity and for considering what goes into constituting safety as people negotiate it.

Cronulla

On December 11, 2005, there was not much swell. Shark Island lay dormant. Some of the local surfers in the pub joined about 5,000 people gathered at Cronulla Beach protesting against the reportedly offensive, unacceptable, and ultimately "un-Australian" behavior of "gangs" of young Australian men of Lebanese descent.[9] Descriptions of these men sexually harassing local women, intimidating other beachgoers, and being boisterous (such as littering, driving recklessly, and playing loud music) had spread by word of mouth and through print and broadcast media.[10] These concerns tapped into discourses that have framed men of Middle Eastern descent as a "dangerous other" from whom Australia must be protected.[11] This is particularly the case in light of September 11, Iraq, the London bombings, and the Bali bombings.[12] Many of the Lebanese Australian men who go to Cronulla are Christian. But this does not seem to matter. As Sara Ahmed observes, within the current international political context, *Muslim* is often conflated through metonymic slippages with *Middle Eastern*, *terrorist*, and *illegal immigrant*.[13]

The demonstration escalated into a riot, which was surprising to many. However, fighting "outsiders" for turf is not unusual. From the 1950s to 1970s, fights occurred between surfers, bikers, and rockers over the use of Cronulla Beach. Those turf wars were class based.[14] Over the decades, Cronulla has become increasingly middle class. This is very different for a suburb that used to be full of working-class battlers. However, increasing gentrification of beach suburbs in Sydney has seen these people pushed inland or turned into "aspirationals"—people with working-class backgrounds and economic prosperity that aspire to be part of the middle class. Rather than class, in December 2005 ethnic and cultural differences became the dominant markers of who the outsiders were. Cronulla is considered an Anglo-Celtic, Christian heartland.[15] To understand its changing demographics, the residents' attitudes toward outsiders, and why the beach is considered hallowed turf, it is necessary to consider how Australia's beach history informs Cronulla today.

Robert Drewe, renowned Australian literary figure, in his introduction to *The Picador Book of the Beach*, refers to Australians as "the world's great beachgoers," describing their relation to the beach as "a lifelong love affair."[16] Keith Moore explains that during the 1960s Australians enjoyed a booming economy and material success. This success included a benevolent government, family holidays, and high rates of employment and home ownership. People embraced the leisure time of going to the beach as emblematic of their success. Politicians and the popular media promoted beach culture and the middle-class values it symbolized as constitutive of Australian life.[17] This middle class was largely of northern European and

British descent. By 2005, the Australian beach had been constructed as a place of racial purity for decades.[18]

Cultural critic Meaghan Morris claims that the Australian beach has come to be representative of nationalism.[19] The beach is where people celebrate Australia Day, a holiday marking British settlement.[20] Australia's relationship with the beach means that it is the "stage upon which our national dramas, big and small, are played out."[21] The current government entrenches the nationalism of the beach by creating a climate of fear, mistrust, and tension over threats to Australia's coastal borders. It is interesting to note that during the 2001 federal election the incumbent Australian government's approval rating was positively correlated to the increase of its claims to protect Australia's national safety from "floods of 'illegal immigrants.'"[22] Suvendrini Perera explains that in recent years the "Australian beach and shoreline have been refigured as the frontline against the incursion of a new threat in the form of refugees and asylum seekers . . . [and] reimagined as the homeland in the context of the war on terror."[23] This refiguring of the beach and shoreline as borders is evident in an everyday way. With the increasing multiculturalism of Australia, many ethnicities other than Anglo-Celtic middle-class Australians have enjoyed going to Cronulla Beach. A train line and road connect Cronulla directly with an area of Sydney known as the Western Suburbs. The area is made up of a large immigrant and working-class population, particularly those not of Anglo-Celtic descent. While the area is framed as the Western Suburbs, it is the demographic heart of Sydney. It is a part of the city where unemployment is high and socioeconomic disadvantage is marked.[24] The low cost of and accessibility to Cronulla Beach mean that during summer people from this part of Sydney join the crowd. They have favored a small area at South Cronulla, while Anglo-Australian locals dominate the rest. Cronulla Beach has been demarcated according to different types of bodies, both classed and ethnic. But some in contemporary migrant communities now refuse their "place" in society. When the Lebanese Australian men moved beyond the turf allotted to them in December 2005, the reaction was ugly.

The day of the riots began with barbecues and beer in the sun on the beach—well within the tradition of Australian celebrations. Australian flags were waved about, draped over people's shoulders, hung from balconies, or temporarily tattooed onto people's bodies with water-based stickers.[25] There had been a recent rise in patriotism at Cronulla and the wearing of the Australian flag to demonstrate it.[26] By the afternoon many families went home as large groups of men began to get drunk. Slogans appeared, painted on T-shirts or naked torsos: "We crew here, you flew here," "Love Nulla fuck Allah," "Wog-free zone," "Lebs go home," and "Osama don't surf."[27] White pride organizations became increasingly visible by the early afternoon, and people started screaming to "get Lebs off the beach." Angry people yelled into megaphones and whipped up the crowd, which soon began to attack anyone of "Middle Eastern appearance." Innocent beach-goers were set upon by the crowd, who threw food and bottles and beat them over the head while chanting "kill the Leb." The crowd also assaulted anyone assisting the victims, including police officers and ambulance crews.[28]

Criminologist Scott Poynting identifies the primary cause of the riots as the demonization by the government and the media of Middle Eastern people as the Arab/Muslim other of contemporary Australia. In Poynting's analysis, the Cronulla riots are the result of a coalition between the Aus-tralian government (both federal and state) and Australia's "largely supine and domesticated media."[29] He cites media research, in which he himself was involved, that identified media vilification as the cause of anti-Arab and anti-Muslim racial violence, and he concludes that the Cronulla riots offer a "clear-cut causality" ("What Caused," 86) between racial vilification in the media and racial violence.

It cannot be denied that, as Poynting argues, "racism was a major causal factor of the riot" ("What Caused," 89). Nor is it in question that sections of Australia's media and government, through tirades against "Muslims," "Arabs," and "Middle Eastern" people (these are often conflated), in part provided "permission to hate" ("What Caused," 88). But I do question the primacy given to the media and government as the sociopolitical actors that reinvoke a top-down political analysis of safety in which citizens feature as pawns on a political chessboard. To presume that the people gathered at Cronulla were simply duped by the media, which in turn is "largely supine" to government interest, risks eliding what was at stake in the Cronulla riots for the participants. From my perspective at stake were the very different modes of feeling safe, as well as what or who ensures it.

Localism

The authority of providing safety in Cronulla and local safety maps is con-stituted by localism. Through the specific experiences of the local surfers, I will now demonstrate how this process works. As mentioned, localism is the process of dominating a territory and policing its cultural laws. As a convention, it consists of unwritten rules, rituals, and codes of conduct that are shared by members. From an early age, surfers learn their primary habitus based on a particular language, physical ability, clothing, looks, rules, ethnicity, and the like. But like the surf break of Shark Island, this field is complex and fluid. Inexperienced beachgoers can become confused and transgress beach rules, often unintentionally, because these practices are unfamiliar, and locals can get frustrated at what appears to be a breakdown in order. If this happens, the local crew would stand to lose certain privileges: priority for waves, shady areas, picnic benches, and car parks.[30] But they may also have their sense of safety put into jeopardy.

The local surfers get to move about freely. Their bodies are relaxed as they negotiate safety and expectations at the beach without thinking. They know that cloudy dusks and cold water mean big sharks are more prominent. The surfers also know that turbulent sandy-colored water signals a rip. If caught in a rip, a surfer will let it carry him or her out to sea and deposit him or her beyond the breakers. Then the surfer will paddle back to the beach through calmer water. The local surfers complain about how newcomers try to swim against the rip, tire, and have to be saved.

Central to local surfers' knowledge of safety at the beach is the recognition of someone else's turf. They will mark off territory and colonize patches of sand by spreading their towels and surfboards out. If newcomers move too close, they will begin talking in a loud and offensive manner to intimidate the transgressors. Borders can be acoustic. Given that the codes of conduct are unwritten, such forms of intimidation are necessary to communicate them. Locals will get defensive or aggressive if anyone threatens their turf, or sense of ease—safety. The threat may be real or perceived, such as when they see a friend being made to feel unsafe. Personal safety is a perception as well as a bodily experience. Individuals can recognize "their own vulnerability in the victimization of others with similar identities or lifestyles" (*Spectacle*, 85).

During October 2005, police were called to Cronulla three times to break up altercations between groups of reportedly "Arab" youths and young male surfers. The youths of Middle Eastern descent had tried to move into spaces where the surfers hung out. The last straw it seems was the reported bashing of three North Cronulla volunteer lifesavers by Middle Eastern–appearing youths. The lifesavers had supposedly told the youths to swim between the red and yellow flags, and the youths refused. These flags are put up by lifesavers to indicate where it is safe to swim—locals know this but newcomers may not. The media claimed that the refusal by the Lebanese Australian youths to obey the rules of safety was a challenge to the lifesavers' authority and led to the fight.[31] This event was a trigger for the riots in December.[32]

Lifesavers and Australian Masculinity

Some read the attack on the lifesavers as an attack on Australian masculinity and Australianness itself. Barclay and West argue, "To attack lifesavers was to commit a very provocative act which was likely to cause an angry reaction."[33] It goes without saying for these authors that "lifesavers get respect from the Australian community."[34] This intuitive argument needs to be read against the history of the lifesaver if we are to understand its symbolic import for the Cronulla riots.

Historian Kay Saunders reads the iconic figure of the lifesaver dialectically in relation to World War I and in particular to Australia's massive defeat at Gallipoli.[35] During World War I, forces from Australia, New Zealand, and Great Britain suffered a massive defeat on the Gallipoli peninsula in Turkey. While the battle was fought on a peninsula, in the popular historical imagination in Australia it has been imagined as a fight for a beach. This imagination was evident in a text message circulated prior to the Cronulla riots: "Who said Gallipoli wouldn't happen again! . . . Rock up 2 Cronulla this Sunday were [*sic*] u can witness Aussies beatin Turks on the beach."[36]

The popular imagination has also turned the Aussie Digger (soldier) into a martyr. The returned soldiers from Gallipoli were a sorry sight, with many maimed and psychologically scarred. Others were left begging on the streets. The national emasculation and defeat at Gallipoli in World War I saw the values traditionally associated with the Aussie Digger reinvested in the lifesaver. Through the lifesaver, humanitarianism, mateship, able-bodiedness, racial purity, heroic sacrifice, and public service/duty continued from the rhetoric of war to public safety. As historian Richard White observes, the lifesaver became a figure in whom "Australians could . . . identify nationhood with an ideal type of manhood."[37] Ian Moffit expresses this imaginary when he describes the surf lifesaver: "Vic Rushby, surf club captain, was my first Australian Hero: tall and grey as a digger monument, straight as steel, iced saltwater in his veins . . . strong as granite: austere, inviolate . . . like a Viking in the surfboat."[38] According to Perera, the central nature of the Anglo-Australian body in this guardianship compounds "the effect of exclusionary violence and xenophobia" on the already "racially contested white site of the Australian beach" ("Race, Terror," par. 41).

What the Australian media had construed as a blatant attack on an Aussie icon was actually missing an important detail: the lifesavers had provoked the Lebanese Australian youths by taunting them with "Lebs can't swim."[39] Added to this convenient public amnesia was the fact that the lifesavers were not actually on duty or in uniform at the time. It would have been impossible to tell that they were lifesavers. To consider this would have devalued the symbolic value of the conflict that the media were ready to exploit ("What Caused").

In the week prior to Cronulla and during the riots, the attacks on the Australian lifesavers were conflated with a white masculinity under threat. This semiotic recoding was performed by the Australian media, particularly shock jock Allan Jones. The result was that Lebanese Australians, men in particular, were epitomized as anti-Australian, which is further evidenced in the use of *un-Australian* in the popular media to describe them or their behaviors.[40] When the local surfers joined other Anglo-Australian local men in the riots, they were effectively letting everyone know that they were still "real" men like the Diggers, at the top of the pecking order, and proud of the "Australian way of life."

Fuelled by alcohol, xenophobia, masculine pride, nationalism, and the mateship that localism fosters, locals participated in the violent reclaiming of turf and ideals. "Taking back our shire" or "claiming back the beach" circulated in the SMS text messages, on talkback radio, and during the event.[41] One Cronulla resident, Coral, claimed, "This place has changed in the past 30 years and now the young ones are taking it back."[42] "Taking it back" meant taking it back from the Lebanese Australians and making it feel safe again for the locals. A way of providing safety was employed that did not exempt violence.

In surfing culture, violence is a common tool used to teach safety and to deal with perceived danger. The local men use violence to ensure their climate of safety and to provide safety for others, because it is how they formed their personal safety maps. Many young male surfers in Cronulla grow up in a space where violence and masculinity go hand in hand. Violence is used to shape what they see and how they know certain things, including what is safe and what is not. To belong as a "local boy," a young man has to "pay his dues." He will be mocked, abused, and beaten up.

The argument goes that when you are a grommet (young surfer) you get bumped around and learn that safety depends on the others in the group and behaving like they do. It can reach the point where violence feels like a normal way to settle conflicts and to provide for one's safety and for the safety of those around you.

Local men who use violence to provide safety do so collaboratively. They gang up on those who transgress the rules or threaten a group member's safety. This is because localism fosters a process of masculine bonding. The homosocial surf sessions, afternoons at the pub, fights, and so on constitute a collaborative experience for the group of men.[43] The mateship formed through shared experiences means that the men are expected to stick up for each other to chase off outsiders—people their mates claim need to be taught a lesson.

Those in need of a lesson this time were the Lebanese Australian men. Their taste for particular cars, sports, food, and ways of dressing were read not simply as different but as an obstinate refusal to toe the line. Even their bodily posture was read for its cultural coding: how they stand, walk, and sit were interpreted as arrogant, rather than subservient, as the locals thought they should be. This confident body posture and belief in their own cultural ways of doing things transgressed the "normal" safety maps established by local surfers. For example, the Lebanese Australian men had very different ideas about where it was safe to play football (soccer) on the beach. These men (or indeed anyone believed to be Middle Eastern) were having to negotiate other people's unwritten rules. What constitutes safety for locals can seem strange and frightening to newcomers. There were also accounts of racist remarks and intimidation by groups of local men.[44] People interpret such oppressive gestures and words as a threat to their safety in light of what they could lead to.

The men of Middle Eastern descent refused to acknowledge a sense of inferiority and having their safety maps encoded for them. Through acts of masculine bravado, some of them exploited their difference to confirm their status as the "dangerous other." They intimidated and threatened locals passing through a car park they had colonized, sometimes using racist taunts. As cultural anthropologist Ghassan Hage writes, "The division of people as good and bad relies on a common racist conception of racism as always white . . . [however], everybody can be racist. White people of a European background do not have a monopoly on racist beliefs and attitudes; it is a feature of all cultures."[45] In effect, the Lebanese Australians marked out some turf where they would have the authority to provide safety. They used intimidation because they had limited alternative economic and cultural resources to draw on. Like the surfers, these men were willing to back each other up to establish their claims. Social marginalization has seen these men bond closely. Mateship is not the preserve of Anglo-Australians. According to Randa Kattan, the executive director of the Arab Council of Australia, there is an old Arabic saying: "Me and my brother against my cousin, me and my cousin against the world."[46]

Over several evenings after the riots, young Middle Eastern–appearing men drove into Cronulla and the surrounding suburbs in what has become known as "the revenge attacks." These men attacked anyone appearing to be Anglo-Australian with knives, baseball bats, or bare hands, leaving some unconscious and others with knives still stuck in their bodies. They slashed tires, broke windscreens, smashed shops, and beat up anyone who got in their way. The attacks made those who usually feel safe (i.e., Anglo-Australians) feel unsafe in their own backyards, and the attacks were revenge for making them and their families feel unsafe at Cronulla.

Rene Girard refers to such violent retaliation as "mimetic rivalry."[47] This is a concept that stresses the mimetic, imitative, or reciprocity of violent acts in situations of conflict. Girard observes that in a blood feud, the initial violence is preceded by another violent act that uses the former as its justification, which in turn becomes justification for another violent act. In this way, "mimesis becomes a chain reaction of vengeance, in which human beings are constrained by the monotonous repetition . . . Vengeance turns them into doubles."[48]

What is clear from this discussion of the rivalry between different groups of men is that masculinity is sometimes built on actions in which safety and violence are not mutually exclusive. In fact, they can work to support each other. The men involved in the Cronulla riots and revenge attacks related their masculinity to an ability to fight for a piece of turf where they would feel safe and would have the authority to provide safety for those around them. This relationship between masculinity and the ability to provide safety was evident when men involved in the violence claimed that they wanted to get revenge for harassment of their women. In this logic, women were once again returned to the position of property, a part of the turf to be defended.

"Protecting" the Safety of Women

Feeding into the local men's concern for "their" women's safety was anti-Muslim and anti-Arab sentiment stemming from a series of gang rapes in western Sydney by some Arabic-speaking men. Some urban myths claim violent and rapist attitudes are endemic to Lebanese, Arab, and Muslim cultures.[49] While these attacks had nothing to do with Cronulla, "abusive, hostile and violent acts" are often interpreted "within a continuum of [possible] interconnected dangers" (*Spectacle*, 85). Stories circulated about the safety of women. One Cronulla man recounted a story on a news program: "They [Lebanese Australian men] were playing soccer I think. And they kicked the ball at some girls and started harassing the girls."[50] Some women at Cronulla felt intimidated: "I can't go to the beach, normally, and wear what I'd usually wear. Because when I do I feel as though I'm getting targeted. Like people saying to me, like, just names and stuff, that I'm being called for wearing a bikini in my own shire. Like, I've grown up here and I'm a local at the beach. And I just don't think I should feel like that."[51] The concerns about the safety of local women were believed to be real. Taking part in the riots was a way for local men to counter this perceived threat and provide safety. They did it in the most familiar way—with violence.

While there were complaints about sexual harassment and the safety of local women at Cronulla, there was little concern displayed for women from non-Anglo-Australian backgrounds. During the Cronulla riots, one young woman was identified as a Muslim because she was wearing a headscarf, and she had to take shelter in a shop as a mob outside chanted, "Aussie Aussie Aussie."[52] Muslim women were abused, and many were spat on. Another woman who had earlier been targeted on the beach had her headscarf removed by the crowd, which was carried off like some sort of war trophy. It is because of this behavior that the Lebanese Australian men drew on the same trope of providing safety for women when explaining their violent retaliation: "We had to respond. . . . Your mum, your sisters and all that, they're going to be scared to walk in the street. Because there's no-one to protect them."[53]

There was little, if any, reflection by the men who committed the violence on their overarching behaviors and attitudes toward women, which regularly include objectification, misogyny, sexism, and sexual harassment by many different groups of men at Cronulla.[54] Even though picking up a woman or leering at her may seem minor to some men, "Many women interpret a 'minor' or 'everyday' form of unwanted sexualized attention or aggression within the context of other, more serious possibilities" (*Spectacle*, 84). After the Cronulla riots and revenge attacks, many people took stock of their own safety maps, and some moved to adjust them. Often people will barely register the performance of their safety map until a threat or danger draws attention to it. Personal safety maps carry many attitudes, discourses, ideologies, and the like that remain hidden until our safety maps are disturbed.

After the Cronulla riots, there were some reports of women who decided not to wear a veil because they felt that they were endangering themselves. But it was not just women of Middle Eastern descent who had to develop new safety maps. One male journalist wrote: "But now, being Lebanese has changed. . . . A night out involves planning, preparation and strategy. My friends, cousins and I have to consider location, numbers, male-female ratio and grooming."[55] Personal safety maps provide techniques for maximizing personal safety in one's daily life. These daily practices of a safety map are designed to minimize risk and involve a process of self-regulation.[56]

In contrast, the locals' safety maps at Cronulla remain intact. While some locals say they disliked the use of violence during the riots, it has had the effect of keeping in order what could have otherwise frayed. There does not have to be a lot of violence—a little is enough to engender the pain, shame, guilt, humiliation, and ridicule that communicate what is allowed and what is not and to determine who will feel safe and who will not. Many residents feel safe again, but it is at the expense of others. Through the riots, local men had sought to reestablish safety by trying to intimidate people of Middle Eastern descent, whom they had found threatening and dangerous. Ultimately, the only solution to the xenophobia of those involved in the riots was to reestablish Anglo-Australian male dominance. In this perverted logic of safety, however, the perpetrators did nothing more than establish a new sense of fear and perpetuate the belief that differing cultural values are irreconcilable.

Conclusion

The Cronulla riots were enabled by the tension between different safety maps held by different groups. There was no overarching sense of safety: safety for one group meant a threat to another. These maps gave the groups of men a sense of safety by defining a cultural order as well as affording them a sense of belonging through certain practices of masculinity. Prior to the Cronulla riots, these differing senses of safety provoked the groups into multiple minor conflicts, digging a deeper trench between the two groups. But on that hot summer day those minor conflicts were transformed into a turf war.

What is clear is that the Australian beach was already invested with Australian national myths and littered with national icons, and these became tied up in the safety maps as people lived them. The escalation in the interethnic conflict was due in part to the media's handling of the attack on the lifesavers in October 2005. The media drew on a series of national myths and icons already established in the Australian discursive terrain. For Cronulla locals, the attack on the lifesavers was figured as the last straw, a catalyst for a reaction to something that had been going on for some time. The figure of the vulnerable lifesaver offered locals a symbol for the threat they had felt to their safety. One thing that arises from this enquiry is that the media did play a significant role, but it was not a unilinear causality. We need to pay heed to how the media discourses link or hook into the complex and existing tensions and safety maps.

Both federal and state governments billed the Cronulla riots as an issue of law and order: in short, public safety. Australian Prime Minister John Howard distinguished between the racists at Cronulla and "real" Australians. While he agreed that attacking people on the basis of race was unacceptable, he refused "to put a general tag of racism on the Australian community" because "it's a term that's flung around carelessly."[57] Instead, in a media release Howard framed Cronulla as an issue of law and public order.[58] Howard's rhetoric of safety left in place a politics of fear based on protecting the Australian people from a "flood of illegal immigrants" and a "war on terror."[59]

Following information that both sides were planning revenge attacks, the New South Wales government responded by increasing police powers to allow searches of cars and mobile phones of anyone entering major Sydney beaches. Alcohol bans were implemented, blockades were set up, and cars were searched for weapons. Even mobile phones were checked at the blockades, and some were confiscated by police as evidence. Large numbers of police on horseback, in dune buggies, and in cars patrolled the beaches for the next month. From the government's perspective, what had been transgressed was public safety, and talk of "racism" merely muddied the waters too much. Such an approach gave the state an easy response—to increase police powers, thus fortifying institutional control of public safety.

There is clearly a need to reestablish public safety, because what was missing from the beach was an overarching shared sense of safety. It was precisely the lack of safety felt by both sides that led to the use of violence as a means to reestablish that safety. Ironically, for both sides, such violence has merely increased the general sense of insecurity through revenge attacks. But if establishing a larger communal safety map is to work, it cannot proceed only from state institutions. The increase of police powers has the significant potential of adding to, rather than reducing, the problem insofar as it can lead to overpolicing and oversurveillance of ethnic minorities, through, for example, "profiling, enumeration and classification" ("Race, Terror," par. 61).

The Cronulla riots were connected to the sense of insecurity and frustration that young Australians, Anglo or not, are currently feeling—a sense of unsafety that goes unnoted in academic, media, or governmental political debates. To continue the finger-pointing is to continue to fail to listen to a deeper set of social, political, and cultural problems that are besetting Australia at this time. Such problems are often seen as an incoherent conflation of international struggles (globalization, transnational terrorism), national problems (deregulation of industries, multiculturalism), and personal problems (increasing sense of insecurity, loss of job safety, instability of sexual/gender identity, confusing romantic relationships). Ironically, the blame game among media, government, and academics has ultimately reproduced the initial failure to listen to youth and their problems, which provoked the unsettling of safety maps in the first place.

Notes

This essay is the culmination of working alongside my colleague Gilbert Caluya. I would like to thank him for his insights, discussions, and arguments. His contribution was invaluable. I would also like to thank Lawrence Schehr and Grant Farred for their support and patience.

1   For many years surfing was seen as "antiestablishment" and full of antisocial behavior such as drug taking. However, increased commercialization of surfing and the proliferation of "surfing schools" have led to the increased popularity of surfing.

2   To avoid violent confrontations, local surfers claim that if you give respect, you will get it. But that is not really true. The respect is one way because it is the local way, and hierarchy is considered the authentic or authoritative way to do things. Other ways of doing things will be tolerated, but they will not put an outsider on equal footing with the locals. This tolerance relies on the outsider being subservient to local rules and privilege. Political philosopher Preston King observes: "There is something intolerable about the concept of 'tolerance.' If one concedes or promotes a power to tolerate, one equally concedes a power

not to tolerate." The locals' version of respect sets them up as legislators and guardians of their own laws and has perpetuated a very narrow sense of how things can be done. King, *Toleration* (London: Frank Cass, 1994), 6.

3 Ryan Barclay and Peter West, "Racism or Patriotism? An Eyewitness Account of the Cronulla Demonstration of 11 December 2005," *People and Place* 14.1 (2006): 70.

4 Paul Scott, "We Shall Fight on the Seas and the Oceans . . . We Shall: Commodification, Localism, and Violence," *M/C Journal* 6.1 (February 2003), http://journal.media-culture .org.au/0302/05-weshallfight.php (accessed December 1, 2006).

5 Gunter Swoboda, "Tribal Pissings," in *Surf Rage: A Surfer's Guide to Turning Negatives into Positives*, ed. Nat Young (Angourie, Austr.: Nymbodia Press, 2000), 74–84.

6 Gail Mason, *The Spectacle of Violence: Homophobia, Gender, and Knowledge* (New York: Routledge, 2002), 84. Hereafter cited parenthetically by page number as *Spectacle*.

7 Pierre Bourdieu, *Distinction: A Social Critique on the Judgement of Taste* (Cambridge, MA: Harvard University Press, 1984).

8 Ibid.

9 These groups of men were referred to as "gangs" by locals, the media, and politicians, even though they were mostly simple friendship groups. The same people and institutions racialized these groups to confirm their status as "dangerous." Ethnic profiling and criminalizing of groups of nonwhite men is common in the Australian media. See Scott Poynting et al., *Bin Laden in the Suburbs: Criminalizing the Arab Other* (Sydney: Institute of Criminology, 2004).

10 Damien Murphy, "Thugs Ruled the Streets, and the Mob Sang Waltzing Matilda," *Sydney Morning Herald*, December 12, 2005. See also Neil McMahon, "A Lesson in Beach Etiquette, Shire-Style," *Sydney Morning Herald*, December 10–11, 2005.

11 Australia's ethnic categorization is different from that in the United States and the United Kingdom. To understand more fully, one would need to go into comparative labor history. Suffice it to say that during the era of the White Australia policy the category "white" was reserved for those with "Anglo heritage," mainly English, Irish, and Scottish, but those from Eastern Europe and the Middle East were not considered white. It was only after World War II that Australia's immigration policy extended the category of white to include Eastern Europeans, mainly to increase Australia's population to protect against the "Yellow Peril" from the north. On the level of racial categories, however, Eastern Europeans became "white" to Australians in opposition to the "yellow" Asians, but not as white as those of English, Irish, and Scottish descent. This difference between Eastern Europeans and Anglo-Australians was maintained by the term *wogs*, which was originally reserved for those of Mediterranean heritage. During this period, Asians were the main ethnic other. Consequently, Lebanese immigrants, some of whom were Muslim, were put into the category of "wogs" based on appearance in opposition to Asians. Obviously, the current media furor around Muslim terrorists has served to reconfigure these ethnic categorizations. Those who appear to be Lebanese, Muslim, or Middle Eastern are now conflated with each other and are seen in opposition to white, Anglo-Australian Christians.

12 Six women from Cronulla were killed in the 2002 Bali bombings, and the riots took place at the site where there is a memorial for them. Various members of Jemaah Islamiyah, a violent Islamist group, were convicted in relation to the bombings.

13 Sarah Ahmed, *The Cultural Politics of Emotion* (Edinburgh: Edinburgh University Press, 2004), 75–76.

14 Douglas Booth explains that the rockers and bikers represented working-class youth solidarity against the middle-class sensibilities of the surfers. The rockers were resentful of the affluence and individualism favored by the surfers. Booth, *Australian Beach Culture: The History of Sun, Sand, and Surf* (London: Frank Cass, 2001).

15 James Forrest and Kevin Dunn, "Racism and Intolerance in Eastern Australia: A Geographic Perspective," *Australian Geographer* 37.2 (2006): 167–86.

16 Robert Drewe, introduction, *The Picador Book of the Beach*, ed. Drewe (Sydney: Picador, 1993), 6.

17 Keith Moore, "The Beach, Young Australians, and the Challenge to Egalitarianism in the 1960's" (paper presented at the "Social Change in the 21st Century" conference, Centre for Social Change Research, Queensland University of Technology, Brisbane, October 27, 2006).

18 One of the most celebrated images that captures this racial vision of the beach is Charles Meere's 1940 painting *Australian Beach Pattern*. Begun at the end of Australia's 1938 sesquicentennial celebration of the founding of Australia as a British colony, the painting depicts a "clutter of well-toned, super-race bodies" reflecting the ideals of fitness and physical beauty playing on the beach. The Museum of Modern Art in Heide, *The Beach* (Bulleen, VIC: The Museum of Modern Art in Heide, 1994), 32. For a discussion of the Australian beach and eugenics, see Grant Rodwell, "The Sense of Victorious Struggle: The Eugenic Dynamic in Australian Popular Surf-Culture, 1900–50," *Journal of Australian Studies* 62 (1999): 56–63.

19 Meaghan Morris, "On the Beach," in *Cultural Studies*, ed. Lawrence Grossberg et al. (New York: Routledge, 1992), 450–78.

20 While many Australians celebrate Australia Day, the holiday offends Indigenous Australians, who express sadness at the fact that Australia Day implicitly commemorates their colonization.

21 Juliana Engberg, "Flotsam and Jetsam," *The Beach*, 19–26.

22 What has come to be known as the *Tampa* crisis happened on August 26, 2001. In a traditional act of maritime responsibility, the captain of the Norwegian tanker MV *Tampa* took aboard his ship 438 people from a sinking boat. The group of (mostly Afghan) people were refugees. The Australian government refused to allow the asylum seekers to land on Australian territory. The MV *Tampa* was boarded and taken over by forty-nine fully armed members of Australia's armed forces. This event occurred prior to an election, and the incumbent Australian government's approval rating rose steadily because it claimed to be stopping the flow of "illegal immigrants." The Australian government struck a deal with the Pacific island nations of Nauru and New Zealand, which agreed to house the *Tampa*'s asylum seekers.

23 Suvendrini Perera, "Race, Terror, Sydney, December 2005," *Borderlands* 5.1 (May 2006), www.borderlandsejournal.adelaide.edu.au/vol5no1_2006/perera_raceterror.htm (accessed December 12, 2006). Hereafter cited parenthetically as "Race, Terror."

24 Katherine Betts and Ernest Healy, "Lebanese Muslims in Australia and Social Disadvantage," *People and Place* 14.1 (2006): 24–41.

25 After the event in Cronulla, many young men from the area permanently tattooed the

Southern Cross, the Australian flag, and the zip code of Cronulla (2230) on their bodies. Alice Brennan, JJJ Radio, Australian Broadcasting Corporation, April 27, 2006.

26 Karen Kissane, "Latest Outfit Flags Trend in Patriotism," *Age* (Melbourne), January 26, 2006.

27 *Nulla* is an abbreviated slang term for *Cronulla* and is used regularly by locals. *Wog* is a slang term in Australian English and was originally a racist slur or insult toward Australians of Mediterranean ancestry. It came into popular use in the 1950s when immigration from this part of the world was high. More recently, the term has been used to refer to people from the Middle East. See note 11.

28 "Cronulla Mob Attacks Beachgoers," ABC Online News, December 11, 2005, www.abc .net.au/news/newsitems/200512/s1528544.htm. Murphy, "Thugs Ruled the Streets."

29 Scott Poynting, "What Caused the Cronulla Riot?" *Race and Class* 48.1 (2006): 89. Hereafter cited parenthetically by page number as "What Caused."

30 Clifton Evers, "Men Who Surf," *Cultural Studies Review* 10.1 (2004): 27–41.

31 One of the local youths, a nineteen-year-old, was pushed against a metal fence spike that punctured the skin above his eyes. The other two, one of whom was fifteen years old, suffered bad facial bruising.

32 Caroline Overington and Drew Warne-Smith, "Countdown to Conflict," *Australian* (Sydney), December 17, 2005.

33 Barclay and West, "Racism or Patriotism?" 81.

34 Ibid., 77.

35 Kay Saunders, "The Lifesaver as National Icon," in *Australian Legend and Its Discontent*, ed. Richard Nile (St. Lucia: University of Queensland Press, 2000), 221–33.

36 Sean Hayes and Steven Kearney, "Call to Arms Transmitted by Text," *Sydney Morning Herald*, December 13, 2005.

37 Richard White, *Inventing Australia: Images and Identity, 1688–1980* (Sydney: Allen and Unwin, 1981), 155.

38 Ian Moffit, "March Past of an Image," *Walkabout* 39 (1973): 50.

39 Jock Collins, "Ethnic Gangs, Ethnic Youth, and the Cronulla Beach Riots" (paper presented at the "National Symposium Responding to Cronulla: Rethinking Multiculturalism" conference, Multi-Faith Centre, Griffith University, Nathan, February 21, 2006).

40 Kenneth Nguyen, "Jones Incited Cronulla Violence on Air," *Sydney Morning Herald*, April 11, 2007; and David Marr, "One-Way Radio Plays by Its Own Rules," *Sydney Morning Herald*, December 13, 2005.

41 Jonathan Pearlman, "Text Messages, Emails Continue to Stir Poison," *Sydney Morning Herald*, December 14, 2005; and Gerard Goggin, "SMS Riot: Transmitting Race on a Sydney Beach, December 2005," *M/C Journal* 9.1 (2006), http://journal.media-culture .org.au/0603/01-goggin.php (accessed December 1, 2006).

42 "War of Words," *Sydney Morning Herald*, December 12, 2005.

43 Gender theorist Eve Kosofsky Sedgwick explains that *homosociality* is a term for the way heterosexual men will show physical affection and emotional intimacy for one another, while rejecting homosexual desire. In a homosocial setting, the male body is protected from homoeroticism by a plethora of rules about how and where to look. Sedgwick argues that women are used as objects of exchange to allay any anxiety about male-male bonding and to prevent any blurring of homosociality with homoerotica. Sedgwick, *Between Men:*

English Literature and Male Homosocial Desire (New York: Columbia University Press, 1985).

44 Lebanese Australian men had their masculinity challenged when lifesavers and surfers mocked them while they played football, calling the sport "unmanly." Anglo-Australian men privilege full-contact football codes such as rugby.

45 Ghassan Hage, "Racism Is Not Simply Black and White," *Online Opinion: Australia's E-Journal of Social and Political Debate* (2006), www.onlineopinion.com.au/view.asp?article=4577 (accessed June 20, 2006).

46 Randa Kattan, "Kid Gloves Syndrome," *Australian* (Sydney), January 28, 2006.

47 René Girard, *Things Hidden Since the Foundation of the World*, trans. Stephen Bann and Michael Metteer (London: Athlone Press, 1978).

48 Ibid., 12.

49 Jock Collins, "Ethnic Crime and Cultural Diversity: Perceptions and Experiences of Gangs, Crime, and Community Safety in Multicultural Sydney," *International Journal of Diversity in Organisations, Communities, and Nations* 3A (2003): 1–25.

50 "Scott," interviewed by Liz Jackson, "Riot and Revenge," *Four Corners*, Australian Broadcasting Commission, March 13, 2006.

51 Jackson, "Riot and Revenge."

52 Murphy, "Thugs Ruled the Streets."

53 Jackson, "Riot and Revenge."

54 The relationship between local men and women in the surfing culture of Cronulla is documented in *Puberty Blues* (dir. Bruce Beresford, 1981). The film takes place in 1974 and exposes the hidden realities of gendered relations at the Australian beach and in the surfing subculture. Underage sex, harassment, and gang rape were evident, as were the severe restrictions on women's freedoms, such as not being allowed to surf. While women now surf, little else has changed.

55 Roland Haddad, "Treat Us Like Dogs and We'll Bite Back," *Sydney Morning Herald*, December 13, 2005.

56 Since the riots in December, many families from non-Anglo-Australian backgrounds have been too scared to return to Cronulla Beach. Instead they favor Brighton-le-Sands, a neighboring beach that might as well be on another planet. Brighton is not a surf beach and is far more racially and ethnically diverse than Cronulla. Sharon Verghis, "Welcome to Cronulla—Unless You'd Fit in Better at Brighton," *Sydney Morning Herald*, December 13, 2005.

57 John Kerin and Nick Leys, "We're Not a Bunch of Racists, PM Says," *Australian* (Sydney), December 13, 2005.

58 John Howard, "The Mob Violence Does Not Mean We Are a Racist Nation," *Australian* (Sydney), December 13, 2005.

59 See "Race, Terror"; and Nick McKenzie et al., "Win Hearts and Minds in Terrorism Fight: Nixon," *Sydney Morning Herald*, August 25, 2007.

Lawrence R. Schehr

"Mine Shaft Gap":
Vigipirate and the Subject of Terror

> Mr. President, we must not allow a mine shaft gap!
> —General "Buck" Turgidson, *Dr. Strangelove*

The safety and security system known as Plan Vigipirate has been in place in France in one form or another since 1978. Established to deal with various threats from terrorists and splinter groups, the plan was activated a number of times in the 1990s. After the attacks on U.S. soil on September 11, 2001, the plan was refined and has essentially been active since then, with levels of security or heightened awareness changing according to perceived or real threats or actual attacks like the bombings in Madrid (2004) and London (2005). In the form promulgated in October 2001, as a reaction to the events the month before, Vigipirate's catchy slogan, "Unusual procedures for exceptional circumstances" ("A circonstances exceptionnelles, procédures inhabituelles") was used to mark the temporary nature of the phenomenon, as if the war on terror, as it is inappropriately named on this side of the Atlantic, were going to end anytime in the near future.[1] This slogan seems to have disappeared from the current form of the plan on the official Web site of the French prime minister.[2]

South Atlantic Quarterly 107:2, Spring 2008
DOI 10.1215/00382876-2007-075 © 2008 Duke University Press

What happens when exceptional circumstances become habitual circumstances, that is to say, when we are constantly in a state of alert, when there is no possibility of not being alert to a possible terrorist threat? How is the subject addressed as a subject during a constant state of siege? In the plan of Vigipirate as it is now used, there are four states of alert: yellow, orange, red, and scarlet. But unless the plan is abandoned, there is never a neutral, unguarded moment in which the individual subject cannot be vigilant. The lowest state of alert is yellow, during which the role of the government is to "accentuate vigilance, faced with real but still uncertain risks" ("Plan"). But this obviously means that the government must accentuate that vigilance not only through local agencies but also through the agency of each citizen of France. It is not enough for local agencies and institutions to be aware of possible threats if the citizens go around blithely unaware of what might happen. So even if there were a lower state of alert—there is not—the subject not only must always be vigilant, but must always increase his or her vigilance. The reinvented subject must spiral into the stages of Vigipirate, whether or not he or she wants to.

At the orange level, the government's role is to "warn of/foresee the risk of a terrorist action considered to be plausible" ("Plan"). This occurs "even at the cost of moderate constraints and perturbations in normal activities." In the red stage, the government must "take the necessary measures to warn of/foresee the confirmed risk of one or several serious attacks" ("Plan"). At this level, the cost is not to "normal activities" but to "social and economic activity." Finally, at the scarlet level, the government is supposed to "warn of/foresee the risk of major attacks, be they simultaneous or not" ("Plan"). In such an event, the government can resort to "particularly constraining measures" ("Plan"). So as soon as the subjects are implicated by the Vigipirate plan, which seeks to protect them from terrorism, they are bound to a system that steadfastly costs them part of their absolute liberty.

While it is certainly comforting to know that the government as Big Brother is always looking out for the safety of its citizens, there must also be the recognition that the subjects so constructed by the vigilant post-9/11 Benthamite eye of the government can never again let down their guard. Indeed, each vigilant subject literally and figuratively invoked by the plan gives way to the simulacrum of a subject, a virtual placeholder of subjectivity in the French war on terror. Whereas the Cartesian subject was in fact an exception—the French exception, we might say—the vigilant postmodern French subject is anything but that. Risk is always present and always real, be it simultaneous, displaced, or virtual; the subject is haunted by the possibility of terror. The time is out of joint in that the feared risk always precedes any real one, and the subject is displaced into an elsewhere that is anything but the ex-stasis of ecstasy.

Plan Vigipirate was first created in 1978 during a wave of terrorist attacks in Europe and was eventually approved by Prime Minister Pierre Mauroy in 1981.[3] Deployed in 1991, it has since gone through three modifications. While levels of alert were raised after the Madrid bombings in 2004 (first to orange and then to red) and again after the London bombings in 2005 (when they were raised directly to red), it is difficult to imagine, at least in the near future, that France will ever not be in some phase of the plan. Some things, of course, make infinite common sense: identification checks to board planes or the Eurostar, no unattended luggage, and the like. Some things, however, are harder to fathom, especially in a society that is argu-ably less gullible and more suspicious than that of the United States. What sense is there, a train conductor asked me in June 2005, of having to have a visible luggage tag on your valise when "everyone knows" that this is just an invitation for robbers to go to your house and steal things? Skepticism of authority, long a mark of the "French exception," plays out against a state-sponsored discourse of security and safety.

What indeed does everyone know? Well, if France has not yet gotten to the fourth and final stage of Vigipirate, beyond red alert to scarlet, the citi-zens know that the possibility of apocalyptic violence is always there. The nation is now always addressed as vigilant, virtual subjects in a posthuman France in which the citizens are no longer able, indeed, no longer allowed, and no longer free to be the independent subjects authorized by the Revolu-tion (July 14, 1789) and the fulfillment of the promises of the Revolution in the Declaration of the Rights of Man and of the Citizen (August 26, 1789). The first words of Article I state a citizen's rights succinctly: "Men are born and remain free with equal rights."[4] If the Reign of Terror, under Robes-pierre, abrogated those rights for some, matters were rectified, and with a few exceptions such as Vichy, the German occupation, and the events of May 1968, there has been steadfast observation of these rights.

However, the new Reign of Terror may now be not a direct eighteenth-century construction of a guillotine for public executions, but a reign because of terror—perceived, invented, or real—a terror that is the raison d'être of the ways in which the government, the state, and individuals must proceed. Indeed, a letter from the prime minister reads, "It is clear that it is difficult to return to the simple level of alert after that date [September 11, 2001], for the threat of an attack remains possible in the country [*sur le territoire*]. Doing that would mean 'lowering one's guard' in the eyes of public opinion relative to terrorists. However, there are periods that are calmer than others."[5] It should be noted that the prime minister says *difficult* when he means *impossible*. There is no turning back. September 11, 2001, marks us always and forever, and no prelapsarian simplicity will ever appear again. It is not that the Europeans were innocent or naive, as many Americans were, before the attacks. It is rather that there is no possibility of pretending, even for a moment, that Europe is not in a state of alert. It will, always, it seems, be in a state of alert from now—or, then, 9/11—on.

The last statement from the prime minister seems at first to be what the French call a *lapalissade* or "une vérité de la Palisse," which could best be translated as a truism that states the obvious.[6] But the prime minister's remark is anything but that; it is really an inversion of the current account of the truth, for it is clear that there are moments that are *less* calm than others, but there are indeed no calm moments. The subject can never see himself or herself in a state of calm, for the government or the state has usurped that privilege of the free subject, who is now always subject to a terrorist threat. That threat of an attack is always immanent, even in the yellow stage of alert. For in the yellow stage, one must be more vigilant. But more vigilant than what or whom? More vigilant than at earlier times when terrorist attacks were perceived as being local phenomena and not part of a more generalized strategy. In the yellow stage, there are real but undefined or imprecise risks. The average citizen in France, who cannot know what those threats or risks may be, should go about daily life with a minimum of interruptions to normal activity, yet he or she should be prepared to go to stage orange or red within the matter of a few days or sooner, even. Normal indeed.

Let us analyze the language and the rhetoric here. According to the prime minister's office, the plan is made "to protect the French" at home; additionally, there is the "protection of French citizens abroad" ("Questions"). This bizarre reappropriation of the idea of citizenship as theorized by Sade in "Français, encore un effort si vous voulez être républicains" ("Frenchmen, another effort if you want to be republican") and as actualized by the Declaration of the Rights of Man is a preposterous amalgamation of proximity and differentiation that is as impossible as it is ludicrous.[7] Are the modes put into place supposed to protect the French but not other

European Union citizens living in France, not to mention non-EU citizens, tourists, transients, or illegal aliens? In a France without borders, there is no way to distinguish between citizens of France and citizens of the rest of the EU, who are free to travel on EU passports through all the member countries. Are these same actions meant to protect French tourists in Bali or diplomats on a mission in Latin America or Asia?

The distinctions are part of a rhetoric that seeks to instill a feeling of safety in the "citizens of the republic," when, by all accounts, any realized terrorist attack makes no distinction regarding nationality among its victims. It is even more fatuous to believe that French citizens abroad can be protected at a distance by the forces marshaled according to the regulations of Vigipirate. Azouz Begag, the French minister for equal opportunities, traveled to the United States in the fall of 2005 on a diplomatic passport. A Frenchman of North African descent (a *beur*), Begag was stopped by U.S. authorities in the Atlanta airport and was questioned by them for fifteen minutes.[8] If Vigipirate could not protect a minister of the government from the clutches of the terrorist in chief—that is, the current resident of La Maison Blanche—whom could it protect? Or are some French ministers more protected by virtue of who they are than others?

I have indicated Begag's ethnic background for a reason. Vigipirate protects the French—if it protects anyone at all—provided they are, or would appear to be, white French people of French descent, called either *franco-français* or *Français de souche*. *French* here could serve as a metonymy for *Western European*. Everyone else is already considered to be suspect, as they are perceived as other. In states of heightened awareness, according to the rules of Vigipirate, one can observe seemingly racial differential treatment in many public arenas in France, as was visible during the riots of 2005 throughout France. But it is visible in less violent times as well: a walk through Châtelet–Les Halles, the big central station of the Paris regional rail lines (RER), often is testimony to this. The (white) writer of this essay "passes" for French and can walk freely through the station, while young men (and, to a lesser extent, women) of color are frequently stopped by the police and asked to show proper documentation. So that minimum disturbance in stage yellow is doubly or triply false. The *Français de souche* may be minimally disturbed from the routines of normal life, only if that normal life is no longer defined by republican, universal values. The *Français de souche* must now be somewhat xenophobic to protect his or her normalcy, protected bizarrely, therefore, by paranoia and schizophrenia. Second, anyone who is not *Français de souche* is never addressed by the system of Vigipirate, even as a subject under stage yellow, but is always already minimally orange in the eyes of the other. The stranger (*xenos, hostis*) is always one level beyond: red when the French are orange, scarlet when they are red, and the impossible other of mine shafts and meltdowns should France ever go scarlet.

People of color are assimilated to the terrorists by the system of heightened security. It is a simple, indeed simplistic, logic grounded in racism and ignorance: since terrorists are other, and specifically an "Arab" other, all those who look like potential terrorists need to be treated as such. Born and raised in France, they are no less French in the eyes of the law than a French citizen who can trace his genealogy back to a Burgundian village during the time of Charlemagne. This racialized logic means as well that the French citizen who is not *Français de souche* is never fully protected by the implications of Vigipirate. He or she is never fully addressed as a subject "against" terror but is implicated as a subject "for" terror—the terrorist as such. He or she, therefore, is never addressed by the rhetoric of safety that Vigipirate seeks to instill in all citizens of France. So even at the level of rhetoric, Vigipirate divides French citizens and alienates the rights of some of them in favor of protecting the rights of those who at least look as if they are French citizens.

This schizoid re-deterritorialization of the subjects addressed by Vigipirate shows us that the system does not and cannot work as it thinks it does because it is always in two or more states of alert. There is no single universal code; there is always more than minimal disturbance to normalcy. Somewhere, someone is always scarlet, someone for whom tomorrow is not another day, but precisely, tomorrow is today: the future is not, the failsafe mechanism has gone off, and in the virtual world that is our future, Slim Pickens's character Major "King" Kong is already riding the nuclear bomb that unleashes violence. It is the apocalypse now.[9] The French are no longer subjects as such but are rather virtual subjects in a field of surveillance cameras, protagonists in the daily film being shot of what were once French lives. Real safety has been replaced by a virtual rhetoric of safety; terror has become a cinematic spectacle that impinges rudely on the real. The apocalyptic meltdown of nuclear war, for example, may have been deferred indefinitely. At the same time, a sense of global war—the so-called war against terror—rather than having been staved off by actions of international organizations, has been hastened. This is not the first time this has happened: World War I, the "war to end all wars," was swiftly followed by an even more terrible second war, some seeds for which were found in the punitive peace treaty. But with the end of the cold war, many thought that the possibility for global conflict was endlessly delayed. It was not.

But there is no need to be so dramatic, because tomorrow does have a name today: it is what the prime minister, in his letter about Vigipirate, calls the "permanent position of security" ("Questions"). This seems entirely logical: someone must posit hypotheses in the war room; someone must make risk analyses. Indeed, that someone is named in the letter: "We know that the terrorist threat, at various levels, will be present for years to come. We have thus kept the idea of a permanent position of security, which must be that of everyone in a position of responsibility and that constantly aims at raising the level of security of the activities of the nation" ("Questions"). The terrorist menace—insidious to be sure, for it has been produced within the West by the West—is a feature that will not be present just for years to come but forever. To raise the level constantly: the sky's the limit, and there are colors beyond scarlet as yet undreamt. To quote Hamlet, "There are more things in heaven and earth . . . than are dreamt of in your philosophy."[10] More things, more colors, more states of siege, more schizophrenic versions of terror.

Again the rhetoric is as deceptive as it is potentially threatening to the freedoms guaranteed by the Declaration of the Rights of Man. The rhetoric instills a permanent us-versus-them mentality at the heart of the ongoing activities of France as France. The French nation precedes its citizens, some of whom may be included in the project of heightened security and others who may not be. But beyond that, the future direction of the activities of the country is not simply determined by a guarantee of freedom seconded by a discourse of protection against enemies. It is determined first and foremost by a security against terrorists' actions and then, and only then, by an ongoing commitment to the activities and rights of the nation as a whole and its citizens in particular.

Yet it is not so simple when all is said and done, because the discourse of the prime minister barely hides a different agenda. So this is not simply a pragmatic, realistic, or deontological analysis or mechanism for protecting the French, but rather it is a somewhat cynically deployed mechanism for protecting neoliberalism: "Thus, if one takes into account the risk of terrorism and ill will, upstream from the technical definition of investment programs, for example, one will get at this level, just as one does for the prevention of industrial accidents, better results for a better price" ("Questions"). Again, terrorism, which lies upstream from even a definition of what is done by capitalists (or the state), is closer to the source than the manifestations of contemporary late capitalist society. Terrorism and ill will have inserted themselves in a kind of travel back in time, an analeptic movement that is a fulfillment of Jacques Derrida's idea that the West is the breeding ground or the guarantee for terrorists' activities, in addition to being, in a bizarre twist, the idea that capitalism (or neoliberalism) is not the source of its own evils, but is the good, just, and benign activity of goodwill. The evils of capitalism are not inherent in it; they retrospectively insert themselves and, in so doing, serve as a scapegoat that disables capitalism's culpability for its own negative and harmful sides.

Still, the remarks of the prime minister are telling because they relate safety and terrorism to the prime figure of neoliberalism, capital itself. What price safety? one might very well ask. For safety against terror has its costs in this permanent war against the permanent threat of terror. In this instance, Stanley Kubrick had it wrong. In Kubrick's *Dr. Strangelove*, General "Buck" Turgidson says to President Merkin Muffley, "But it is necessary now to make a choice, to choose between two admittedly regrettable, but nevertheless 'distinguishable,' postwar environments: one where you got twenty million people killed, and the other where you got a hundred and fifty million people killed."[11] What the French neoliberal model is cynically saying is that we have to choose between a model of safety that costs 20 billion euros and one that costs 150 billion euros. We all know which one will be chosen. Paradoxically, then, to bankrupt the state over the cause of terror, no matter how much the slogan is brandished, is, in a strange way, to let terror win.

Indeed, it is easily argued that the plan is not really designed to protect the French but to change them into good, neoliberal subjects, different from the way they have been socially constructed since the French Revolution. Again, as the prime minister's letter says: "It is also this 'culture of security' that the plan aims to develop in France. It concerns each of us" ("Questions"). The interests of the individual or common goals shared by individuals are subsumed under the "us" in an oppositional mentality that not only folds each individual into that collective "us" but also values "us" over either the individual or some value that is perhaps not part of the collective identity. The collective defines what is and what is not a valid characteristic or quality in all of its citizens, to the detriment of what the state may believe to be irrelevant to the constitution of citizenship. In this way the culture of safety and security finds a home within the culture of freedom and in direct contradiction to it. We are restrained by this culture and kept from moving about. To be French means being less free than before and even more so if, say, you're a *beur*—government minister or not. It means accepting the "no" of authority—in the suburbs during the fall of 2005, of course, but in all daily undertakings.

I shall insert a personal story, for it is clear that the phenomenon I am discussing here finds parallels in many Western societies. In the spring of 2006, I needed to meet with a colleague from another department who is Moroccan by birth. He and I communicate in French. He could not meet with me on campus the next day because he was flying out to give a conference talk. As I was doing the same, we agreed to have the meeting at the airport. When I got there, I ran into another French speaker I knew, who joined the conversation after the meeting, and out of the blue, a fourth French speaker overheard us and entered the conversation. Needless to say, we were being stared at by many other travelers. Had this not happened numerous times before on the way to or returning from conferences, I would not have given it any thought, but the frequency of the penetrating stares leads me to believe that to some minds I might possibly be a terrorist: my colleagues and I have been made other simply by a linguistic difference from the "us." If I "pass" in France, I find myself "passing" less in certain situations in my own country.

However, it goes far beyond that. The subject addressed by these discourses or even the subject stared at is not only subjected to this new law determined by the other, but he or she is not allowed to know the letter of the law; indeed, ignorance is the only excuse. Again, we read the following in the prime minister's letter: "For reasons that will be easily understood, the plan is classified as secret for defense purposes: the complete list of measures cannot be made public. What can be said is that there is a graduation of measures corresponding to the graduation of the threat taken into account by the plan: a group of measures adapted to treating the threat corresponds to each level of the alert" ("Questions"). Now on the surface, of course, there is nothing to quibble with here. One would not expect the government to show its hand as to the exact procedures to be used during an attack or even an elevated state of alert. Giving away all the protective measures would be as naive and wrongheaded as someone named Scooter Libby revealing the identity of an undercover agent. But at a deeper level, the government marshals reason for its own ends in a disconnect of a gulli-bility gap. The reasons are never stated, so we cannot understand if the plan is reasonable or not. How can we know if the measures taken are part of a rational approach to a real threat or if they are nothing more than a measure of political control?

Terrorism becomes a chronic condition, the collective malady of the twenty-first century, something with which all of us are infected, from which we probably will not die, yet from which we will never recover. As I have indicated, for Derrida, this is an autoimmune situation: terrorism comes from within the collective of the West. For Derrida, the origin of terror is within the freedoms offered by democracy itself; hence, terror, whether nurtured at home or in some remote training camp, can find its target only in a relatively free, democratic society. Yet this is part and parcel of the democracy, a price to pay for the luxuries of freedom. Here, however, the government has sidestepped the issue, and every French citizen is ill with some sort of chronic, incurable disease. Perhaps, with this combina-tion therapy offered by the government to its *franco-français* population, white people, upstanding citizens that they are, will not die of AIDS or ter-rorist threats (at least not too many), but they will never be healthy again either. Terror will be extinguished only when there is no more Western democracy to nurture it. Terror is a kind of permanent death-in-process.

The disorder and guerilla nature of terrorist threats seem to be easily trimmed to fit the plan, so that the architects or peacekeepers can analyze the nature of the threat and determine which category of alert the nation should be put on. It little matters that the disorder is inscribed in the event, while it is seemingly controlled through language. For example, in a yellow alert, which is now the baseline, "surveillance measures" [les consignes de surveillance] will be reinforced in public forums along with actions "to carry out patrols, to prepare [legal] constraints, to verify the availability of safety measures and behavior during a crisis" ("Questions"). But to what end? Under what circumstances? We cannot be told the nature of the means of control, yet it determines our existence. Subjects must therefore be in a position of ignorance relative to their own existence in this postmodern world. They are the subjects of constant surveillance, but they are never allowed to look back. Jeremy Bentham's panopticon is in the here and now, and Michel Foucault's concept of the prison in which the aims are "to watch and to punish" [surveiller et punir][12] is home for society as a whole.

Now, as much as that constant imprisonment seems ubiquitous, it does in fact get worse, for the orange state of alert requires "even more stringent surveillance measures," along with "monitoring people and luggage in train stations and airports" ("Questions"). There is a double problem here. On the one hand, if the surveillance techniques at stage yellow are indeed surveillance techniques, they already have to be working ubiquitously. There cannot be surveillance without surveillance. So the more demanding measures, while seemingly a good thing if conditions necessitate them, are already in place. On the other hand, monitoring of people and luggage already happens all the time in airports anyway, as well as on the Eurostar (to protect *franco-français* people traveling to and from the United Kingdom, among other advantages). So like it or not, we are pretty much always already in stage orange. What I alluded to earlier as the absence of a stage below yellow now seems a quaint notion, for there seems to be little below orange.

The prime minister's letter skips a description of stage red, jumping straight to scarlet, which happens "when the threat of an attack is confirmed and perhaps in part [is] already occurring" ("Questions"). What happened to all that vigilance and surveillance? What results were there to the nicely trimmed groupings that determined what stage we would fall under? For the plan is designed to include its failure to sift, mediate, separate, or determine. The plan is always at stage scarlet, whether it is actually there or not. Scarlet "corresponds to a mobilization of all means available to the State and includes particularly constraining measures" ("Questions"). Prison tactics? State of siege? Police state? Perhaps. Yet, we are specularly already there. For if we are always already in the prison of the Benthamite or Foucauldian panopticon, we are always under real and virtual surveillance in that prison. What more constraining a position could there be for the postmodern subject of terror?

Again, I am not talking about the individual, walking around on a daily basis, stopping at red lights, and going ahead on green. It is not that kind of constraint (which we all accept) that interests me here, but rather the constraint on the subject. The subject is always marked by the constraints of scarlet specularity, always fixed by the eye of the other, always diminished in his or her subjectivity by the gaze of Big Brother. Yet, the disease is even more insidious than we thought at first, for it multiplies before our very eyes: "One must be protected against the risks of multiple attacks, a technique used henceforth by terrorist groups" ("Questions"). They can form groups with like-minded goals; it is the collective "us" who are no longer permitted to do so, for we must let ourselves be guided by the consequences of their goals. The insidious disease spreads and multiplies, and terrorism itself evolves into the superinfection of epidemic proportions. Terrorists are no fools, the government is telling us; they are smart enough to evolve with the times. As Derrida says: "One day, people will say: 'September 11,' those were the ('good') old days of the last war. Things were still gigantic: visible and enormous."[13]

Indeed, in the meantime, the French, as subjects, virtual, real, and variously vulnerable, can sit and wait for the "detection and prevention of NRBC [nuclear, radiological, biological, and chemical] risks, etc." ("Questions"). Faced with all that, we can just sit back and be calm. Faced with that "etc.," which has the stunning effect of a permanent and endless copulative, we can just sit back and wait. In the meantime, enjoy living under "Vichypirate." It might not last very much longer. However, if those were the "good old days," what could possibly lie ahead?

Notes

1 Plan Vigipirate, http://perso.orange.fr/mrap_siege/octobre_2001/PLAN%20VIGIPIRATE .htm (accessed December 13, 2006; site now discontinued). On the legal and historical background of Vigipirate, see Stéphanie Dagron, "Country Report on France," in Christian Walter et al., eds., *Terrorism as a Challenge for National and International Law: Security versus Liberty?* (Berlin: Springer, 2004), 267–86.

2 Web site of the French prime minister, "Le Plan Vigipirate," archive, August 18, 2004, www.premier-ministre.gouv.fr/information/fiches_52/plan_vigipirate_50932.html (accessed December 13, 2006). Hereafter cited parenthetically as "Plan." All English translations by author.

3 I should point out that even then terrorist attacks were not new to Western Europe, as there had been attacks by the Irish Republican Army and Basque separatist groups, among others.

4 Conseil Constitutionnel, "Déclaration des Droits de l'homme et du citoyen du 26 août 1789," www.conseil-constitutionnel.fr/textes/d1789.htm (accessed December 13, 2006).

5 Préfecture de la région Auvergne, Préfecture du Puy-de-Dôme, "Vigipirate en quelques questions," www.auvergne.pref.gouv.fr/pdf/vigipirate_questions_reponses.pdf (accessed October 15, 2007). Hereafter cited parenthetically as "Questions." All translations are mine. Some of this text was taken from a fall 2001 letter from the prime minister to the nation addressing various aspects of Vigipirate.

6 Named for the Seigneur de la Palice (or la Palisse), a *lapalissade* is a truism of masterfully silly proportions. The standard French saying is, "Fifteen minutes before his death, Monsieur de la Palice was still alive."

7 "Français, encore un effort" is a long discourse that is part of *Philosophy in the Bedroom*. Sade breaks the dialogues of the novel to offer a long monologue by one of the characters,

the Knight, who speaks for Sade. The polemic encourages the French to push in various directions in order to become citizens of a republic. See D. A. F. Sade, *Philosophie dans le boudoir*, in *Œuvres complètes du Marquis de Sade*, vol. 3 (Paris: Pauvert, 1986), 490–536.

8 Embassy of France in the United States, daily press briefing, October 21, 2005, www.ambafrance-us.org/news/briefing/us211005.asp (accessed October 18, 2007).

9 These references to three well-known American films—*Gone with the Wind* (dir. Victor Fleming, 1939), *Dr. Strangelove* (dir. Stanley Kubrick, 1964), and *Apocalypse Now* (dir. Francis Ford Coppola, 1979), not coincidentally all war pictures—emphasize the schizoid re-deterritorialization that has epic, cinematic, and virtual qualities.

10 William Shakespeare, *Hamlet*, act 1, scene 5, lines 187–88.

11 *Dr. Strangelove*.

12 Michel Foucault, *Surveiller et punir: Naissance de la prison* (Paris: Gallimard, 1975).

13 Jacques Derrida, "Autoimmunités, suicides réels et symboliques," in Jacques Derrida and Jürgen Habermas, *Le "concept" du 11 septembre: Dialogues à New York (octobre–décembre 2001) avec Giovanna Borradori* (Paris: Galilée, 2004), 154. See also Giovanna Borradori, *Philosophy in a Time of Terror: Dialogues with Jürgen Habermas and Jacques Derrida* (Chicago: University of Chicago Press, 2004).

Notes on Contributors

DAVID F. BELL is a professor of French at Duke University, where he is also senior associate dean of the Graduate School. He writes on literature and technology and has recently published a book on speed in France in the first half of the nineteenth century, *Real Time: Accelerating Narrative from Balzac to Zola* (University of Illinois Press, 2004).

MEGAN BROWN is an assistant professor of English at Drake University. She recently completed a manuscript on the concept of corporate culture and has written articles about popular management books and workplace health policies.

CLIFTON EVERS surfs at Cronulla. He is a senior research associate at the Centre for Social Research in Journalism and Communication at the University of New South Wales. His research is on critical masculinities and sporting cultures. Clifton is currently writing a book that analyses surf culture and masculinity.

DARA E. GOLDMAN is an associate professor of Spanish at the University of Illinois at Urbana-Champaign. She is the author of *Out of Bounds: Islands and the Demarcation of Identity in the Hispanic Caribbean* (Bucknell University Press, 2007) and is currently completing a manuscript on contemporary Latina lesbian narratives.

ROBERT HARVEY is professor and chair of comparative literature at Stony Brook University and a directeur de programme at the Collège International de Philosophie. His book in progress, *Witnessness*, is about untranslatability, the imagination, and responsibility.

LYNN MARIE HOUSTON is an assistant professor in the English Department at California State University, Chico. She is the author of *Food Culture in the Caribbean* (Greenwood Press, 2005) and numerous articles on food culture. Her article "Food Safety and the Abject: Mad Cow Disease and a Racist Rhetoric of Contamination in the Southwest" is a chapter from her dissertation, "The Mad Cow Nexus: Biopower and the Stakes/Steaks of Personhood in Global, Industrial Food Production."

JAMES MANDRELL is an associate professor of Hispanic studies at Brandeis University, where he also chairs the Women's and Gender Studies Program. He is currently completing a study of gender and national tradition in the discourse on food in nineteenth-century Spain.

ELSPETH PROBYN is a professor of gender and cultural studies at the University of Sydney. She is the author of several books, including *Blush: Faces of Shame* (University of Minnesota Press, 2005), and is currently working on a book about taste.

LAWRENCE R. SCHEHR is a professor of French at the University of Illinois. He is the author of several books, including, most recently, *Gay French Modernism* (University of Illinois Press, 2004) and *Figures of Alterity: French Realism and Its Others* (Stanford University Press, 2003). He writes on nineteenth- and twentieth-century French literature and culture, cultural studies, and queer theory.

SUSAN SQUIER is Brill Professor of Women's Studies, English, and STS at the Pennsylvania State University. Her most recent books are *Liminal Lives: Imagining the Human at the Frontiers of Biomedicine* (Duke University Press, 2004) and the edited collection *Communities of the Air: Radio Century, Radio Culture* (Duke University Press, 2003). She is currently writing a book on chickens in science and culture.

DAVID THOMSON is in the Centre for Comparative Literature at the University of Toronto. Portions of his current book project, *View from a Kettle*, have appeared in *The Trumpeter* and *Stride*.

GREGORY TOMSO is an assistant professor of English at the University of West Florida. He is the author of "Bug Chasing, Barebacking, and the Risks of Care," in the journal *Literature and Medicine*, and of "Risky Subjects: Public Health, Personal Narrative, and the Politics of Qualitative Research," forthcoming in the journal *Sexualities*.

SUSAN WILLIS is an associate professor in the Literature Program and English Department at Duke University. She is currently heading a collective project on Las Vegas along the lines established in her previous collective effort, *Inside the Mouse: Work and Play at Disney World* (Duke University Press, 1991).

TOPIA

CANADIAN JOURNAL OF CULTURAL STUDIES

Published by:
Wilfrid Laurier University Press
in partnership with
Cape Breton University Press

Subscription address:
E-mail: press@press.wlu.ca
Wilfrid Laurier University Press
75 University Avenue West
Waterloo, Ontario
Canada N2L 3C5
Telephone: (519) 884-0710 Ext. # 6124
Fax: (519) 725-1399

Editorial address:
TOPIA
E-mail: topia@yorku.ca
Graduate Programme in
Communication & Culture
TEL Centre, Rm 3017, 88 The Pond Road
York University, 4700 Keele Street
Toronto, Ontario M3J 1P3
Telephone: (416) 736-2100 Ext. # 22238

Editor: Jody Berland
Annual Subscription Rates:
Institutional $80 Individual $40 Student $25
(Orders outside Canada remit payment in U.S. dollars)
ISSN 1206-0143

yorku.ca/topia